THE
EDGE

THE
EDGE

50 TIPS FROM BRANDS THAT LEAD

ALLEN P. ADAMSON
Foreword by **STEVE FORBES**

palgrave
macmillan

First published in 2013 by PALGRAVE MACMILLAN® in the United
States—a division of St. Martin's Press LLC, 175 Fifth Avenue, New York,
NY 10010.

Where this book is distributed in the UK, Europe and the rest of the world,
this is by Palgrave Macmillan, a division of Macmillan Publishers Limited,
registered in England, company number 785998, of Houndmills, Basing-
stoke, Hampshire RG21 6XS.

Palgrave Macmillan is the global academic imprint of the above companies
and has companies and representatives throughout the world.

Palgrave® and Macmillan® are registered trademarks in the United States,
the United Kingdom, Europe and other countries.

ISBN 978-0-230-34224-8

All photographs are courtesy of Landor Associates and are reprinted with
permission.

Library of Congress Cataloging-in-Publication Data

Adamson, Allen P.
   The edge : fifty tips from brands that lead / Allen P. Adamson.
      p.   cm.
   Includes index.
   ISBN 978-0-230-34224-8 (alk. paper)
   1. Product management. 2. Branding (Marketing) I. Title.
HF5415.15.A33   2013
658.8′27—dc23
                                                              2012037532

A catalogue record of the book is available from the British Library.

Design by Landor Associates

First edition: January 2013

10 9 8 7 6 5 4 3 2 1

Printed in the United States of America.

CONTENTS

ACKNOWLEDGMENTS

When you take on a book-writing project as broad in scope as this one, there are many people to thank, be it for their intellectual contributions, their perspective on a given topic, or their time and effort in helping get the manuscript to the finish line. There are also, of course, the people to whom you return home every night. This said, I would like to start by thanking my family: my wife Maddie, my son Josh, and my daughter Elissa. They are not only my personal cheerleading squad, but much more. They continue to help me see the world with fresh eyes, which, as you'll read in this book, is critical to being successful in the brand-building business. Whether it's being a kid with my kids at the Apple store, our vacations to The Wizarding World of Harry Potter and the world beyond, the monthly runs to Target, or watching the Disney channel together, my family has widened the lens through which I view the marketplace and consumers of all ages. (To my wife, who keeps reminding me that there's more to life than brands and branding, a special tip of the hat.)

Moving on, I would like to thank my colleagues at Landor for not only giving me the freedom and flexibility to take on this endeavor, but for providing an amazing palette of learning opportunities. At Landor, I continue to have the privilege of working with some of the best and brightest in the industry, inclusive of a wonderfully diverse group of genuinely gratifying clients. Every day brings with it the chance to learn a new category, a new product, a new technology, or a new way of looking at a competitive situation. The challenges never cease, and never cease to amaze me, satisfying my curiosity and keeping me at the top of my game. It is through this book that I have had the pleasure of sharing the expertise and many of the exceptional lessons I've learned from both colleagues and clients about building and managing successful brands.

Also deserving of sincere acknowledgment is the extensive Landor team that assisted me in getting the book from initial concept to final execution. Given their "day jobs," no simple task. To Leonie Derry, thank you for keeping the myriad administrative details in check and saving me from total chaos. To Andrew McDonald, a special thank you for supervising key project activities and ensuring all deadlines were met. To Philip VanDusen, much appreciation for your meticulous design oversight. And to the team listed below that worked thoughtfully on research, fact checking, marketing, publicity, and proofreading, much gratitude for your efforts.

NEW YORK OFFICE:

Jessica Crandall	Ashley Rosenbluth
Craig Dobie	Cameron Searcy
Rietje Gieskes	Jasmine Tanasy
Sunny Hong	Cassandra Yeager
Kelley Kugler	Candy Washington
Mindy Romero	Jo Wheeler

CINCINNATI OFFICE:

Natalie Brown	Tracey Lanz
Cameron Butler	Kris Linkugel
Grant Collinsworth	Veda Nagpurkar
Will Henry	Chad Shackelford

Last, but not least, as with my first two books, I'd like to thank my writing partner Betsy Karp. Without her perspective, proficiency, commitment, and diligence, *The Edge* would not have gotten off the launchpad.

FOREWORD

I was born into a brand and quite an iconic one at that. My grandfather, B. C. Forbes, a penniless immigrant who became a financial columnist for the Hearst newspapers, founded *Forbes* magazine in 1917 and was Editor-in-Chief and CEO until he died in 1954. My father, Malcolm, and his brother, Bruce, took over. I took the helm in 1990 after my father's death. As Chairman and Editor-in-Chief of Forbes Media, I see every day that the management of the business and the stewardship of the brand are intimately tied together.

Most successful businesses have long understood what makes for a compelling brand. It's an asset that must be carefully stoked and protected. Every such brand has a history, and what comes through clearly is that what made it strong yesterday may not be the same as what is required to make it strong today. This idea is more true than ever before. Marketplaces are changing not by degrees but exponentially. The Forbes brand is no different from any other in its need to assess its meaning to consumers and its employees: A strong business must ensure that its brand is relevant and highly credible.

That's why I approached Allen Adamson and his team at Landor. We at *Forbes* knew that Landor is a leader in the world of branding experts and could give us surefooted guidance. What's more, Allen has been a contributing writer at Forbes.com for more than three years with almost 100 articles that speak to the issues of brands in a mercurial market. Clearly he and his colleagues had the broad perspective we needed. Many of the stories in this book are taken from the articles he wrote for Forbes.com. I felt that an account of how Landor took the history and heritage of Forbes and came up with a brand strategy for the future would be a perfect way to convey the challenges that all first-rate brands must confront and win. When he asked me to write the foreword for this book, I readily agreed.

Forbes Media has changed dramatically in recent years thanks to the web. We have become a technology company with apps and websites. We have gone international in a major way with local editions with local partners in more than 20 countries, including India, China, Mexico, Brazil, and Russia. Our websites—principally Forbes.com—now reach more than 30 million business decision makers each month. We are producing a growing number of conferences and special events. Moreover, our traditional competitive category has changed dramatically. Like every brand in the business journalism category, we now share a crowded platform with an ever-widening field of new websites and numerous online content creators. The way we go about our business is being fundamentally transformed. Most of our editorial content for Forbes.com comes from hundreds of contracted contributors; we create a virtual magazine online every day. The interaction among editors, contributors, marketers, readers, and visitors is expanding at warp speed.

To help hold our edge, we decided to examine our brand strategy with fresh eyes, which is why we approached Landor.

The Landor team grasped immediately the unique challenges inherent in reshaping a heritage brand to give it widespread appeal in a modern market. We would, of course, preserve the spirit of B. C. Forbes and my father, Malcolm, while revitalizing our identity.

The process led us to examine carefully what we do now and how we do it. That is, how do we remain an essential tool for our current audience? For a younger generation, entrepreneurship and free enterprise have taken on an expanded meaning. Thus, we could expand as never before our purview to include topics like philanthropy. This wasn't seen as a stretch but was part of our natural ability to get to the essence of what makes people successful.

The folks at Landor spent a lot of time with us. They interviewed people at Forbes from all departments and on every level. They sat in on some of our internal meetings, and they went back into our archives to get to the heart of our culture and to devise a strategy that would link our past and our present. It is difficult to take something that is as precious as your brand, especially when it is your family name, and ask someone else to examine it and suggest ways to preserve its core and have it inspire in a rapidly changing world. It takes confidence and trust.

What we discovered together is that our revitalized brand was hiding in plain sight. It was in our DNA. The roots of our brand go back to 1917 when B. C. Forbes launched Forbes with a simple idea that success is about "doers and doings." It was when we and Landor pondered our original subhead for Forbes 1917—"Devoted to Doers and Doings"—that everything clicked to produce that "aha" moment. We looked at things that we already had and brought them to life in a new way.

At the heart of the modern Forbes brand are people who are "doing" great things—entrepreneurs, innovators, inventors, investors, and philanthropists.

To reinvigorate this idea and make it relevant to a new generation of people here at Forbes as well as our readers, website visitors, and our marketing partners, we decided to express it as the question: "What are you doing?"

We did this for a number of reasons. First of all, it draws attention to the fact that what drives Forbes is not theory, but action. We have never been focused on theoretical notions, but on the people who go out into the world with their ideas and make them real. These people make a difference across a broad range of disciplines. It could be anyone from Harvard professor Clayton Christenson, who works with companies to infuse what he calls "disruptive innovation" to their businesses; to Jay-Z, the iconoclastic rapper, record producer, and entrepreneur; to Sara Blakely, the founder of Spanx and the youngest woman to join the world's list of billionaires. These people are harnessing their skills and their ingenuity, along with the new tools of business, to build companies and jobs.

"What are you doing?" is also a rallying cry, a call to action to our internal audience, the people who make Forbes Media "happen." Everyone talks about having an impact. We want to be part of making this happen.

All this is why Landor is so successful: It makes the painstaking effort to grasp the unique needs of a client. Our work with them was a real-time example of how great brands get built and how great brands stay ahead—and keep the edge. It is with great pleasure that I share this story and know you will find insight, wit, and wisdom in all the stories you are about to read.

—Steve Forbes

THE
EDGE

INTRODUCTION

Like many people in the marketing business, I enjoy spending my Sunday evenings with Don Draper and the other folks who work at the Sterling Cooper Draper Pryce agency. In other words, I watch *Mad Men,* the AMC blockbuster drama about life inside the boardrooms and bedrooms of Madison Avenue in the 1960s. I enjoy seeing the realistic and gritty depiction of life in the heyday of the advertising industry, from the IBM Selectric typewriters to the fashions, the hairdos, and, of course, the often politically incorrect behavior of the show's characters. It was a frenzied but fascinating time, and it's captured pretty authentically, which is what makes the show so appealing. It was at the very end of this era that I myself got into the industry, and, while it had become somewhat more politically correct by then, it was still fascinating and often frenzied. And it was a lot of fun (yes, it still is).

As if by coincidence, the day I sat down to write the introduction to this book, that evening's episode of *Mad Men* was going to be followed by the launch of a new program called *The Pitch,* after the process by which advertising agencies "pitch," or compete, for new business from clients. (Whether the show will still be on the air when this book is released a few months or so from now is anyone's guess.) In any event, it was smart programming strategy on the part of the show's producers to preview it right after *Mad Men,* given that it was the audience they wanted to reach. And given my desire to be in on anything having to do with my work-a-day world, I didn't pick up my remote control to change the channel after the *Mad Men* credits rolled, but stayed seated to see whether *The Pitch* would prove as realistic and absorbing as the preceding show.

I don't make my living as a professional critic of television shows, but from my vantage point as a marketing guy, I'll tell you that *The Pitch* was a well-produced, at times realistic, but generally superficial look at our business. Call it *Mad Men* meets *The Apprentice* meets *The Office.* There were two teams of talented people, one of which was going to get hired to do the advertising for, in this case, a new addition to the Subway breakfast menu, and one that was going to get, you know, fired. The drama of the show was built on the very genuine tension any agency feels in its bid to win a pitch. In the most poignant segments, this was brought to life through the voice-overs of individual team members as they talked about what it really feels like to work in advertising and what goes into convincing clients that you understand their brand better and will do a better job of selling it than any other agency.

According to the creator of *The Pitch,* the show is meant to portray what happens—what *really* happens—during the tense, pressure-filled days when those responsible for selling a product or service must come up with a great advertisement that will convince millions of people that they can't live without one brand or another. Now, I've been in lots of pitches. And I will tell you that making television commercials can be a lot of fun. But the reality of the situation, one that is not made clear in this "reality" television show, is that convincing consumers to fall in love with a particular type of soap, bread, automobile, bank, or Subway sandwich does not happen as the result of even the most provocative or amusing advertisement or promotion. It does not happen as a result of a supercharged week of meetings and brainstorming sessions. And most important of all (something even Don Draper knew), a pitch isn't where the process of building consumer loyalty to a brand—building the brand itself—starts.

While the excitement and drama of a pitch is real, the excitement and drama of building a brand actually begins much earlier. It begins with trying to sort out what you want your brand to stand for in the minds of consumers. What is it that makes your brand's product or service different in a way that the people you want to reach care about? It's only after you've done this, after you've clarified and codified the idea, that you can communicate the story. The advertising is only one piece of how this story gets told. And it comes at the end of the brand-building journey—not the beginning. Although it is a minor inaccuracy in terms of television fare, *The Pitch* reinforced the false notion that all you need to sell a brand is a great advertising campaign.

Most strong brands do have great advertising, but it's the advertising along with all the other experiences and expressions of the brand that give them the edge. The stories in this book are about the reality of brands and branding. They are not academic theories or jargon-filled concepts. They are real-time accounts of what goes into the making—or breaking—of a brand and are meant to point out what gives leading brands, well, the leading edge. That said, they are also accompanied by tips, easily digested bites of insight, that any brand, no matter what size or category, can use to gain its own leading edge. In this book, you'll find 50 examples of what some of the best companies know to be true about building brands. Each chapter is dedicated to one of the key principles smart brands abide by to keep their edge, and each includes particular stories that illustrate these principles in play. Unlike other books on the topic, this one takes into consideration the world we live in: a world of tweets and texts and information that is here today and gone, not tomorrow, but in a double click. The stories are short, get right to the point, and, like all great brands, are meant to express—from one expression to the next—the unified experience that is branding. Before you jump in, however, it's important to spend just a few minutes on some context setting. A bit of preamble will help put these stories in the proper perspective.

BRAND AND BRANDING AREN'T THE SAME

As I mentioned earlier, there is a big difference between the meanings of the words "brand" and "branding," but it bears repeating. Quite simply, a brand is what its name represents to people. It's the picture or feeling that pops into someone's head when a particular product or service, organization or celebrity, is mentioned. Branding is the process by which this picture or feeling gets into someone's head. It's everything that communicates, either tangibly or emotionally, what the brand stands for. Branding includes everything from the advertising and the logo, to the packaging and what's inside, to the manner in which customers are treated, to the product placement in television shows and movies. It's the retail environment, the Facebook page, the tweets and blogs and review sites, as well as the social responsibility initiatives and tie-ins with other brands or causes. Anything that signals something about the brand is branding. Anything that contributes to what a brand means to a consumer is branding. Companies whose brands have the edge know this and know exactly what kind of branding best expresses their meaning and where and how to spend their branding dollars. The bottom line is that companies whose brands have the edge know how critical it is to use branding initiatives to get people to think about their brands in just the way they want them to. They know, too, that all of their branding initiatives must work together in harmony to create a cohesive experience.

The tips and stories in this book cross many categories of brands and explore many aspects of branding. Some of them have to do with what has remained the same in the industry from decade to decade, but a good number of them have to do with what has made marketing and brand building so much more challenging over the past decade—the shifts that have changed the way companies must think about their brands and their branding. You don't need to be a social scientist, a rocket scientist, or someone involved in the art and science of branding to know that things seem to be changing faster than ever before. I remember hearing Thomas Friedman, author and *New York Times* political pundit, say that if you look under the letter "F" in the index of his book *The World Is Flat,* published in 2005, you won't find any notation for Facebook. It hadn't been invented yet, let alone become part of our culture, or a publicly traded company, for that matter. Young people don't have land lines (that's a phone attached to the wall, FYI), they don't know what it means to do research for a term paper without Google, two-year-olds learn to read on e-books, tweets are more than just noises made by birds, the word Pinterest doesn't have a typo, and Amazon is no longer simply a river in Brazil.

Now, of course, change isn't anything new relative to the way brands and branding have evolved over the years. And smart companies have always done what's required to adapt their way of thinking and operating to reflect these changes. But, given the rapid-fire movement in technology, the amazing pro-liferation of products and services, and the evolving effects of the "flattening world," companies have had to deal with changes of a more seismic nature, and they've had to move more quickly. There have been significant movements that have had an even stronger influence on the industry than the invention of radio and television. Perhaps the best way to talk about these changes and their impact on brands and branding is to go backward before I go forward.

BEING DIFFERENT IN A WAY PEOPLE CARE ABOUT IS A KEY TO SUCCESS, BUT IT'S JUST THE CONVERSATION STARTER

Early in my career I spent some time at the advertising firm Benton and Bowles, and I had the distinct pleasure of having Procter & Gamble, specifically, the Dawn dishwashing liquid team, as a client. (I say "pleasure" because P&G is masterful at building and marketing brands.) In any event, it was after much research and analysis that P&G identified a consumer insight relative to washing dishes—greasy dishes are the worst offenders. Dawn was the product it developed that could literally get rid of grease in dishwater. Needless to say, the idea on which the brand was based was that "Dawn takes grease out of your way." As the result of the branding that followed, all driven by this simple yet meaningful notion (to those who pull sink detail, anyway), the product went from being the newest choice on the shelf to a category leader in a few short years. This branding, from the way the product performed to the advertising and promotions, was based on "what" this brand did. Okay, hold this thought for just a minute.

In 1984, a pre-med freshman at the University of Texas came up with a unique idea for the way technology, especially PCs, should be designed, manufactured, and sold. Michael Dell left school and started a company founded on the simple and relevantly different idea that a personal computer should be just that—it should fit your personal needs. His brand of PC, unlike all the others, would be built to a user's specifications. By focusing on delivering literal out-of-the-box technology solutions rather than being just another off-the-shelf PC provider, Dell became a successful brand as the result of "how" it went to market. Custom solutions are at the core of everything Dell does. While PCs are a commodity category, "how" Dell does what it does—how it goes to market—is how it sets its brand apart in a way that people care about.

The starting point for all great brands has always been the ability to identify a point of difference that is meaningful to people. The industry term is "relevant differentiation." Brands with an edge have it and have always had it. It used to be that a brand could gain an edge in the market by establishing a point of difference based on "what" it did or "how" it did what it did. Whatever this was couldn't be marginally different. It had to be truly different, and it had to be genuinely meaningful to people, by allowing them to get the dishes done faster and more easily so they could spend more time with their families, or by giving them computers specifically configured to meet their needs. There is no brand that has become successful, or that remains successful, that hasn't started out by identifying something relevantly different on which it could set itself apart from its competition and, more important, in the minds of consumers.

Even my colleague Don Draper had this principle of brand building down pat. I remember an early episode of *Mad Men* in which he's presenting a television ad campaign to his clients from Kodak for the company's Carousel slide projector, using the actual product to cast poignant pictures of his own life, his wife and children, as a backdrop to his emotionally moving voice-over. "Technology is a glittering lure," he tells the rapt audience sitting at his conference table, "but there is the rare occasion when the public can be engaged on a level beyond flash."

People form "a deeper bond" with a product, he says. "Nostalgia. It's delicate but potent. . . . It's a twinge in your heart, far more powerful than memory alone. . . . It's a time machine. It goes backwards and forwards. And it takes us to a place where we ache to go again. It's not called 'The Wheel.' It's called 'The Carousel.' It lets us travel the way a child travels. Around and around and back home again to a place where we know we are loved."

Kodak had developed a wonderful way to catalog and share family pictures, something people had never seen before and something that even Don felt was not just useful, but personally meaningful. What made Don's "pitch" to his clients all the more powerful was that he didn't focus on the facts and figures of the machine, how many slides it held, that it had a timer, or that you could move the slides backward and forward. Rather, he laddered up to a more emotional attribute to communicate what made it relevantly different. The Kodak Carousel was a family "time machine" that let you capture, keep, and share memories forever.

Now, as much as I appreciated this scene for all its dramatic reasons—it's beautifully scripted and shot, and it captures Don's own nostalgia for a life he's allowing to let slip away—it points up one of the key changes that makes brand building more of a challenge today: Where once you had one slide projector, or maybe two, and a relatively short list of automobile companies, cereal brands, soaps, insurance companies, etc., today the market is flooded with stuff. It's harder than ever before to identify something relevantly different on which to stake a brand claim, and especially if it's based on a "what" or a "how." These days, what makes one product different from another can be measured by degree, not exponentially. We've all walked down supermarket aisles dumbstruck by the number of choices and brand extensions. There's organic and lite and gluten-free. There's detergent with fabric softeners and detergent that smells like a spring meadow, a spring rainfall, or like nothing at all for those with allergies. And forget about the technology sector. It's not just the perceptual overload, but the fact that the gap between the time one new gadget and the next hits the market is shrinking as fast as the size of the gadgets themselves. Smartphone apps are fast replacing web-based apps as the resource of choice. Kids are leading indicators of which modes of communication to use. A better mousetrap is a better mousetrap until it isn't. And even if you ladder up to a more emotional level to find a way to help your brand stand out, à la Don Draper, it's still a tough sell. As for asking consumers what they want as a way of finding something to set your brand apart, they can't tell you—until after it's on the shelves. Consumer hindsight with regard to what's missing from their lives is 20/20.

YOU'VE GOT TO HAVE ENERGY

This change, in and of itself, is an enormous challenge for marketers: the ability to identify something people have never seen before and that they'll care about. But there's a collateral dynamic that is becoming instrumental in gaining an edge, and the colloquial term for it is "buzz." Companies are fast coming to the realization that as the world becomes more connected, as word of mouth and, well, buzz become a natural part of every day, it's not enough to come up with something unique that people find meaningful. The idea also has to have *energy.* It has to be imbued with a sense of momentum, be active, and feel super-charged. Consumers today want their brands to be "happening" brands. It's almost like every brand has become a "badge brand," evidence of what a person thinks or believes in. For a brand, just being relevantly different isn't sufficient in today's marketplace. People want brands that are going somewhere.

AND YOU'VE GOT TO HAVE PERSONALITY

As if this weren't enough, in ad-speak, wait, there's more. While "what" a brand does or "how" it does it still needs to surpass the competition if the brand wants to win fans, this has become table stakes. Of course a brand must be tastier, easier to use, bigger, smaller, or whatever is required as the cost of entry into the category. Move on. Consumers have become very interested in a brand's personality—who it is and why it's motivated to do what it does. I'm not talking about the brand's voice (so old school) or a plastic card printed with a stream of generic adjectives, as in, "We're the friendly, accessible, honest, and reliable brand." Much as people are becoming like brands—you pick an avatar for how you meet people on Xbox, or you develop a Facebook identity— successful brands are becoming like people. Why? Two reasons. First, it's a transparent world. Consumers have the ability to see through the product to the company behind it. Digital technology has made it easy, if not natural, to compare and contrast, and we are all expanding our criteria beyond the tangible. At the same time, consumers have become accustomed to "friending" whole organizations and institutions. They are fans of everything from human beings to websites, and they not only have conversations with brands, they expect them to be available 24/7. (Isn't that what friends are for?) Consumers are forming relationships with brands, and, as in any relationship, they want to feel comfortable before opening their hearts or their pocketbooks.

The second reason a brand needs to establish a personality that transcends the tangible nature of its products or services is that consumers, especially those in the younger generations, want the companies they keep to share their beliefs and values, be it with regard to the environment, social issues, or simply the way they treat their employees. More and more people want to do business with brands that are not only different in a way they care about, but that make a genuine difference in the world. They want brands that are driven by an ideal—a *purpose*—beyond making money. They expect companies to put their skills and resources to work for the common good, and they're willing to reward those that do. To be seen as authentic, and to be believable, the way a company expresses its "who" and "why" must be seen as a natural extension of its corporate culture. The story you tell versus the real story will be found out pretty quickly.

Although the process of establishing a brand persona is not quite as cut-and-dried as getting to the "what" or the "how" (it's sort of like psychoanalysis, actually), once done, it gives a brand significant advantages. To begin with, consumers foster deeper bonds with brands they feel they know personally versus brands that are built on factors of a more tangible or practical nature (and isn't loyalty the holy grail?). As in any human relationship, connections are formed as the result of having something in common. More than this, a brand with a credible persona is given greater license to evolve and change its product lines, or the way it brings them to market. As in, if I have respect for your inherent beliefs and values, I'll trust your decisions to do something in a different way.

For example, when Jeff Bezos created Amazon.com in 1994, he had in mind to offer up the quintessential shopping medium for books and music, the purpose being to let people browse and explore to their hearts' content. He knew that the "who" of the brand had to come across as friendly and accessible—and it does. And he wanted the "why" to be self-evident—to give people freedom of choice, which it does. Since both the "who" and the "why" of the brand's identity are clear, consumers have given the brand permission to move into selling more than books, which it most definitely does. Amazon.com has grown to be the quintessential shopping medium for everything from books to barbecues to Barbie dolls.

On the flip side, when a brand develops a relationship with its customers due, in good part, to its persona, consumers are likely to forgive and forget more easily. Coca-Cola is a prime example. The hands-down global leader in the beverage industry, whose purpose has forever been to inspire moments of happiness and refreshment, didn't exactly inspire happiness among its most loyal fans when, in 1985, it took a risk and announced that it was going to change the formula for the most popular soft drink in its line-up: Coca-Cola. "New Coke" was the first formula change in the company's then 99-year history. The company's intention was honest and based on solid business analysis. It wanted to reinvigorate the brand. For those too young to remember, it didn't take long for the company to abandon its efforts (79 days, to be exact, and there wasn't even any Internet back then) and go back to the original formula, referred to as Coca-Cola

Classic. That the brand remains among the most valued brands on the planet is testament to the fact that the company was permitted to use its "get out of jail free" card because of the deep relationship the brand had built with consumers worldwide—not based on just the taste of its products, but because of what it meant on a deeper, more personal level.

SIMPLE IS SIMPLY MORE VITAL

So, to recap, companies whose brands have an edge have established something to stand for that's different and that matters to people. Whatever this is—the core idea—has energy. More than that, these brands have personality! Not just based on what they do, or how they do it, but on who they are, and why. Brands with an edge have gotten to where they are as a result of something else. They have been able to capture the essence of what they stand for in a simple, sticky set of words, or a phrase, that evokes imagery beyond the phrase itself. More often than not, this is referred to as a Brand Driver because it's meant to drive everything associated with the brand. Boiling down what you stand for forces you to make the phrase or statement something that will inspire and motivate those charged with bringing it to life in a way that will connect with the consumers you want to impact. A Brand Driver must be something that people can grasp intuitively, without any guidelines or explanations. Consider Zappos, the online store for shoes and more that is driven by the desire to deliver happiness through "wow" service; or IBM, whose gazillion employees are driven to help build a smarter planet; or FedEx, which was founded on the idea of delivering peace of mind; or Virgin Atlantic Airways, built on the simple notion of bringing "good times" back to the skies.

Establishing a successful Brand Driver is sort of like winning the brand equivalent of a game of Telephone. You want your idea to travel and stay intact from one person to the next. That's because you'll be playing this game of brand Telephone with the hundreds, if not thousands, of people inside your company, as well as the many who work with your brand outside the organization's walls—the ad agencies, the product manufacturers, the folks who work in the call centers worldwide. If you can't preserve the clarity and coherence of the brand's driving idea with the groups inside your organization and out, it will have dire consequences for your branding—for your ability to send focused and consistent signals about what your brand stands for. Successful branding occurs when your brand idea is simple and clear and sticky enough to stand up to a game of Telephone without any slips between one messenger and the next.

14

While this principle of brand building has not changed, the number of messengers involved has. There are simply more ways to reach and interact with consumers, and more people who have responsibility for the branding experiences, than ever before. While once you may have had 10 or 20 points of touch, today you have double that number, what with pop-up stores, virtual malls, taxi toppers, athletic stadium walls, and all the tweets and blogs and digital whatnot. Companies used to deal with two or three agencies, now they deal with 10 or 12. It used to be a challenge just to get the packaging designers to align with what the promotions department was doing. Today it's exponentially challenging. When you're dealing with all of these branding constituencies, from the product developers to the customer care and user interface folks, all of a sudden you have a much larger orchestra that must execute the branding in concert. It puts huge pressure on a company to do it right and to get it right from one brand experience to the next. As I said, consumers can see all, and they have the power to share all that they see. An experience that's off-brand won't be a secret for long. If your brand idea isn't focused and concise and sticky, your branding will come across like a game of Telephone run amok.

Companies with an edge have gotten what their brands stand for down pat, and they ensure that everyone associated with the brand, across every department, every agency, in every outsourced role, in every country in which the company operates, has the brand's meaning down pat as well. Anyone with any responsibility for the branding must be able to grasp, instinctively, how to bring it to life in the appropriate way. People who are tasked with delivering on the brand's promise must feel a genuine sense of ownership for its expression in the marketplace. And while I know it sounds like a cliché, the fact is that it's empowering for those in an organization to know what it means to "be the brand," whether it's the way to answer a customer's phone call, write a technical manual, design a package, hire people who work in the store, or actually work in the store. It's gratifying to be able to do your job in a way that reflects well on both you and the company for which you work.

THE EDGE // *Introduction*

A BRAND IS AS A BRAND DOES . . .

And this brings me to another branding dynamic that has evolved over the past few years. While it has always been true, it has never been more apparent, literally, that a brand is as a brand does. In a transparent, skeptical, show-me-the-beef marketplace, if a brand doesn't live its promise day after day, nothing else will matter. Companies with an edge know that every point of touch with a customer is an opportunity to deliver on the brand promise. Or, as a former chairman of SAS put it, "Our company has a chance to make the brand—or break the brand—100 times during every flight." One of the best ways for a brand to tell its story is through its actions. Another of the best ways is to have its *customers* tell the story.

There is no doubt that smart brands understand the contagious nature of today's marketplace and leverage it well. They know that if some aspect of their brand or branding is worth sharing, for any reason, it will be shared, whether it's an exemplary customer service experience or an incredibly brilliant advertisement. While not new, the power of word of mouth has become a far greater branding force as the result of digital communication. Even with the prevalence of sophisticated tools and strategies designed to measure customer satisfaction, the most accurate measurement of whether a customer is happy or not can be answered with one question: "Would you recommend this product or service to a friend?" This has been proven by companies who espouse what are known as "net promoter scores," a metric devised by Fred Reichheld, a Harvard professor. In his studies, he found that net promoter scores—which measure the difference between the percentage of "promoters," those who give high responses to the question, and "detractors," those who give lower scores—align closely with a company's revenue growth. Whether used in a formal manner by a company or not, the fact is that more people than ever before are putting their own reputations at stake to recommend any and every type of brand, be it a movie, a book, a restaurant, or a dog groomer. And, likewise, more companies have sprung up to harness the power of consumer advocacy, from OpenTable to Angie's List. While some companies see the transparent, talkative marketplace as a threat, those with an edge recognize it as the ever more positive dynamic it is. They don't just look at data. They know what to do with it. What smart organization wouldn't want feedback to enable it to serve its customers better? And what smart organization wouldn't want some of its branding done for free, compliments of happy customers?

And that brings me to the last point in this context-setting preamble: brands with an edge know where they can play and win. The increase in venues in which to spend marketing dollars means that companies have to assess their options carefully. Over the last few years, those in the business of marketing brands have been besieged by an onslaught of shiny new objects. Every time something new comes along, every company thinks it has to have it in its branding arsenal, whether it makes sense strategically or not. When the Internet became ubiquitous, every company needed a website. Then they all needed Facebook pages, Twitter accounts, they just had to be LinkedIn, develop an iPad app, or become connected to Yelp. As branding channels have expanded, they have, at the same time, fragmented the audience and raised a slew of new questions about the best way to get a message across. Don Draper (yes, him again) had the advantage of being able to create a mini-movie, a 60-second television spot that spoke to at least 60 percent of the consumers he wanted to reach at once. Today, knowing where to play has become much more difficult. Brands with an edge know how to pick their battles. They know which of their branding initiatives will have the greatest impact. They know how to tell their story, and they know where to tell it so that all the pieces are woven together.

So there's my "pitch." What you need to know before you read about what brands with an edge know about branding in this evolving marketplace. Each chapter will deal with one of the topics just discussed, starting with just a bit more detail and then jumping into the stories that will bring the topic to life.

CHAPTER ONE

To Have an Edge, a Brand Has to Be Different, Relevant—and Have *Energy*

Kevin Plank knows how to build a brand, and he knows how brands get built. No, these thoughts are not redundant. They each, in their own way, have something to do with what it takes to gain an edge in the marketplace. Let me explain.

For those who may not be into sports, or even sporting goods, Kevin Plank is the founder and president of Under Armour, a company he launched in 1995 when he was a walk-on special-teams football player for the University of Maryland. Tired of constantly having to change during the course of a game when the T-shirt he wore under his jersey would become heavy and sweat-soaked, he noticed that his compression shorts stayed cool and dry—they were made of a polyester blend that wicked away moisture. Like many brand entrepreneurs, he had an "aha!" moment. Or, as Jerry Seinfeld might put it, "Ever wonder why no one's ever developed a T-shirt using the same moisture-wicking fabric out of which the shorts are made?" Working in his grandmother's basement, Plank set out to see if he could come up with a shirt that would remain drier and lighter and perform well under the most extreme conditions. After a year of fabric sourcing and product testing, he created just what he was looking for—times three: a shirt, a new category of sporting apparel called performance apparel, and a brand that would rocket in revenue from $17,000 in 1996 to more than $1 billion today. Under Armour now holds nearly 3 percent of the sports apparel market in the United States, holds a significant place in the global market, and sells everything from shirts (of course) and shorts to cleats, to underwear and outerwear, to gloves and shoes. Its clothing is worn by teams at more than 100 universities, and by professional players of football, baseball, basketball, golf, rugby, ice hockey, and even mixed martial arts, and its products have been proudly placed in movies, including *Any Given Sunday,* and television shows, including *Friday Night Lights.* The Under Armour logo, an interlocking "U" and "A," is fast becoming as recognizable as the Nike swoosh.

Plank launched a new sportswear brand that is now among the category's fastest-growing sectors. He did it by identifying something different that people, specifically athletes, really cared about. He saw the opportunity to fill a gap in the sportswear market to which no other company, not even Nike or Reebok, had laid claim. And he did it with products that don't just promise to be relevantly different but *are* different—they perform like champs. More than this, Plank is determined not to become a one-hit wonder. His product development teams are focused on coming up with new fabrics, applications, and designs that will keep the brand in the center of its field. Athletes of both the professional and weekend variety swear by this brand of gear, and they're fierce advocates. Under Armour's trademarked rallying cry "Protect This House" can not only be heard at athletic events worldwide, it's the heart of the brand's bold idea.

Kevin Plank built a brand on a relevantly different idea. And from a procedural point of view, he understood that this is how great brands get built. Unlike the premise pitched by *The Pitch,* and assumed by many folks, building a brand does not start with awareness—a great advertising campaign or promotion that alerts consumers to the fact that you're out there. In terms of building a brand, this is backward. To achieve success in brand building, the first thing you need to do is identify a differentiated meaning for your brand and determine if it really matters to anyone. Is there a large enough audience of people who will care? It's only after you do this that you can think about generating awareness. Consumers need a way to make a distinction between one brand and another. This is how they form preferences and make choices.

One of the most respected proprietary tools in the industry proves this point. Named BrandAsset Valuator (BAV), it was created by Y&R, an agency that is part of the same communications family as Landor, the company for which I work. BAV is an incredible diagnostic tool for figuring out how your brand is performing relative to all other brands in the market—not just the brands in your category. More important, however, is that, unlike many other brand valuation tools that attempt to place a current dollar value on the brand, BAV indicates what you must do to keep your brand strong. BAV can gauge the current health of your brand, project its future health, and indicate prescriptive actions. Why is this important? Ask Kevin Plank or the leaders of any other brands with an edge. Odd as it may sound, Wall Street doesn't just care about the value of your brand today. It cares about whether you can increase its value tomorrow.

The key challenge for brands has always been the ability to increase their dominance. BAV is a great indicator of whether this will happen and how this will happen, and the way it works is actually pretty simple. It's based on the interrelationship of what started out as four criteria, but as the result of how the marketplace has changed over the past few years, now includes a fifth.

- Differentiation—what makes your brand unique
- Relevance—how meaningful this difference is to the people who matter
- Esteem—how well regarded your brand is in the marketplace
- Knowledge—how well consumers know and understand your brand
- Energy—how dynamic the brand is, reflective of its ability to adapt and evolve

Brands generally get built one dimension at a time, with differentiation being the first, most critical step, and relevance an obvious second. A healthy brand has high levels of both difference and relevance. It's unique in a way that's meaningful to lots of people. Target is a perfect example, as are Dove, Clorox, and Gatorade. A strong niche brand has a high degree of differentiation and is relevant to a smaller group of people. This might be a brand like lululemon athletica, which with almost no advertising has cultivated a devoted group of yoga enthusiasts, or a luxury brand, such as Rolex, whose devotees are likely to have deep pockets and an appreciation of fine timepieces. If a brand stays relevant but starts to lose what made it different, it will become a commodity. Wall Street begins to worry. If it loses what made it relevant, same story. All healthy brands have a greater degree of differentiation than relevance, which gives them room to expand both their offerings and their audience.

Esteem and knowledge, the second pair of criteria, make up a brand's stature. If a brand has a higher level of esteem than knowledge, it means that while not a whole lot of people know about the brand, those who do really love it. Bang & Olufsen, for instance, is a Danish company well known for its finely crafted audio products, television sets, and telephones. People have heard a lot about the company, and, based on its solid reputation, they'd like to know more. Too much knowledge and not enough esteem? Well, ask the Kardashian sisters.

In the case of leadership brands, those with an edge, all four of these criteria must be strong. But the experts on the BAV team, those who study brands, have come to the realization that for a brand to be healthy and stay healthy, it's got to have something else. It's got to have energy. Shaped by the accelerated pace of the marketplace and by consumer change, it's become evident that the difference between the success and failure of a brand is due in part to its ability to generate buzz, mojo, momentum—call it what you will. Energy is like a steroid for all other brand valuation criteria. If a brand has energy, it means that people are talking about it. It helps draw attention to what makes the brand relevantly different and helps build knowledge about the brand. Metaphorically, it helps the brand achieve lift-off velocity. It encourages brand loyalty and makes the brand more valuable. Consumers want a brand that's going somewhere.

Now lest you think that energy is the stronghold criterion for just the latest and newest and funkiest brands like Facebook or Instagram or Red Bull, consider this: IBM, Disney, GE, Ford, and even the venerable Procter & Gamble are all brands that keep their edge because, in addition to being at the top of the charts on the four original criteria for brand health, they've got energy. These companies constantly keep their brands invigorated and sparked with innovation; as a result, they remain global leaders. As one of my colleagues said to me, "A brand is not a place, it's a direction." In this chapter, you'll read stories about brands who know that the only directions are "up" and "ahead." They all started their journeys, and achieved an edge, by establishing something that was different and meaningful to the people they wanted to reach. And they've all recognized that, in this fast-moving, fast-talking, contagious world, it takes more than this to keep the edge.

TOP TIPS: ESTABLISH A RELEVANTLY DIFFERENT IDEA THAT HAS ENERGY

The stories in this chapter are about brands that have achieved an edge by establishing something that is different and meaningful to the people they want to reach. These brands *keep* their edge by ensuring that the ideas on which they are based remain different and relevant; they have the energy required to propel the brand forward. More than this, these ideas are brought to life consistently and brilliantly wherever and however consumers experience the brand. While simple in concept, as many things are, "passing go" is a bit more complicated. Here are a few tips to guide your own thinking on the matter:

- A different feature is not a different idea (not to mention the fact that features can be easily copied or become obsolete overnight).
- Relevance is relative. There is no long-term value in a brand if people can't use it to make their lives better in some significant way.
- You won't find a relevantly different idea on which to build your brand by staring at a computer screen. Get out from behind your desk and talk to people. Walk the supermarket aisles, go to the food courts in shopping malls, and listen to folks in coffee shops (in Cedar Rapids and Fresno, not just New York City.) Get your hands dirty.
- In your search for a brand idea, wonder why. The most innovative brand ideas have come from people who refused to accept "it is what it is" for an answer.
- Frame your idea as a compelling story. The power of a great story cannot be underestimated as a way to engage people.
- Your story must be simple and focused. You need to be able to pitch it before the elevator doors open.
- Your story must be sticky. People have to able to hear it once, remember it, and pass it along, intact.
- Make sure you deliver on your brand idea consistently and brilliantly, not just on your best day, but every day. A brand is a promise. Keep it.

P&G'S TIDE AND MR. CLEAN FIND NEW WAYS
TO SCRUB THE COMPETITION

Remember when airlines served breakfast? In coach? It was during those days, way back when, that I was a regular on a 6:15 a.m. flight to Cincinnati to visit my clients at Procter & Gamble as an ad guy on the Dawn dishwashing liquid account. I thought about this period in my early professional life while watching an interesting documentary that aired on CNBC titled "Behind the Counter: The Untold Story of Franchising." I wasn't surprised to see that while many things in the world of business have changed, some haven't, key among them Procter & Gamble's reputation as a master marketer and builder of great brands. Most pertinent to the topic of this chapter, as made clear in the documentary, is P&G's ability to look at a category, even a category as mundane as dry cleaning or car washing, and figure out how to make the experience different and better in a way people care about. The company's jump into dry-cleaning and car-wash franchises confirmed for me that P&G is still as good as it gets when it comes to unlocking consumer insights and delivering something both innovative and relevant. They're champs at asking the question, "Ever wonder why?" about a situation and doing something about it.

Here's what I mean. Think of all the dry-cleaning places you've frequented in your life. Unless you've encountered a really great proprietor—someone who will replace buttons you didn't even know were missing—they all probably register in your mind as pretty much the same: dingy and small and smelling of chemicals. P&G, with its typical due diligence, looked at the same-old-same-old dry-cleaning experience and asked, "Wonder why, with all our fabric-care ex-pertise, we couldn't go into this line of work and improve it in a way that makes people's lives a bit better?" Well, in typical P&G fashion, it stopped wondering and figured out how to make it happen.

In 2008 it launched what has become a quickly expanding Tide Dry Cleaners franchise business. Wonder why these P&G retail venues have caught on so well? For the same reason other P&G products catch on. The folks at Tide Dry Cleaners don't just get clothes clean and pressed—the obvious cost of entry—they've been able to put in place all the advantages of Tide's well-respected

research and development, which ensures the most up-to-date color guarding, stain release, and fabric restoration. More than this, at Tide Dry Cleaners, as is true of all P&G brands, there is a purpose that transcends the obvious benefits. With its commitment to improving people's lives beyond just giving them clean and well-pressed clothing, Tide Dry Cleaners uses environmentally friendly solvents and GreenEarth processing, among other planet-safe cleaning products and services. As one franchisee said in the documentary, "No start-ups go to the levels that P&G has to understand the consumer, the industry, and the operations. As a result, we don't just clean it, we make it better." At newly launched Tide Dry Cleaners franchises, owners not only benefit from the instantly recognizable and trusted Tide name, built on more than 60 years of fabric-care experience; they benefit from P&G's expertise at identifying new ways of looking at things people have been doing the same old way for years and giving them an innovative and socially responsible spin.

The same is true of P&G's Mr. Clean Car Wash franchises. While there's generally not much difference between one car wash and another, and hasn't been for years, with the possible exception of green versus non-green cleaning agents, P&G, with its "wonder why" perspective, took a long, hard look at the category and discovered ways to make the experience more effective, more efficient, and even more fun. While the owners of these enterprises, again, benefit from the P&G name Mr. Clean, an iconic brand since 1958, they also reap the benefits of P&G's copious research into what consumers expect from a car-wash experience, down to the towel drying and the mats on the newly vacuumed floors.

More important than the actual details I took away from working on any one particular P&G brand, back in the days when I traveled to Cincinnati, it was the overall thinking process that P&G follows when establishing and growing a brand that was, and remains, so impressive to me. The ability to look at something and ask, "Wonder why?" is a key to the company's success. The ability to look at a category that's been the same for 20 years and see something that others haven't is what keeps its brands fresh and their names top of mind. Taking Tide to the cleaners and driving Mr. Clean into hot water are just par for P&G's winning course of brand building.

MARKETERS CAN LEARN FROM RIO'S GOLD-MEDAL OLYMPIC VICTORY (BRANDING VICTORY, THAT IS)

The Olympic Games are about competition. Not just among the incredible athletes, but among the incredibly (ridiculously?) diverse group of brand names hoping to reap the rewards of "official sponsorship." There is, however, one more competition relative to the Olympics that's a must-watch for anyone interested in the game of brand building. And that is the bid to host the games. As in any other industry category, the metric for success in this branding effort is very much the same: find a simple and compelling story that helps set your brand apart from all the others. I happen to think that the folks who were in charge of the Olympics branding strategy in Rio de Janeiro did a phenomenal job differentiating Rio's promise from the other cities in contention and then clearly establishing its relevance to the International Olympic Committee (IOC). (And, having worked on the bid made by New York City, I can personally

appreciate the effort.) In other words, the "Brand Rio" team followed a couple of the basic rules of smart brand management and gained an edge as a result.

There is almost no brand category that isn't awash in choices. Whether cars or cosmetics, beverages or baby carriages, there's simply a lot of stuff out there, and most of it is pretty similar. The competition for consumer attention is fierce, and it can no longer be won on table stakes. The only way a generally good brand can ever hope to become the absolute best brand is to find something to stand for that's completely different in a way that people care about and are jazzed about. In an ever-expanding global marketplace, this is getting harder and harder, even when the brand in question is a city. And even when the brand cities in question are as diverse in culture and geography as were the contenders for the 2016 branding Olympiad: Baku, Chicago, Doha, Madrid, Prague, and Tokyo.

> *The competition for consumer attention is fierce, and it can no longer be won on table stakes.*

When these cities vying for the attention of the IOC began their brand strategizing, each had to identify something about itself that would distinguish it in a meaningful way in the eyes of the judges. Taking a look at the video portion of the various presentations, it was easy to see that each potential host city had the table stakes down pat. They were all good options. With visions of happy, friendly people and vistas of evocative cityscapes, with voice-overs touting the financial wherewithal and political clout to get things done, and with an outpouring of respect for the athletes, each city had the basics covered.

Having said this, only one bidding city was able to promise something none of the others could promise. It was an idea that had great meaning to the audience of judges looking to showcase the Olympics brand and one that, by the way, the judges felt the world could get jazzed about. Rio had it all, above all the others. Aside from the above-mentioned table stakes, in addition to its glorious beaches and gloriously sexy bathing suits, and its world-famous carnival and world-renowned HIV/AIDS program, the Rio brand team's differentiating factor was Brazil's growing international influence and leadership among emerging nations. The brand team communicated skillfully that, under its current president, it had become one of the hottest countries on the world market and that its current economic boom had placed it among the world's wealthiest nations. Core to its brand promise was the fact that Brazil was the only one of these nations never to have hosted the Olympics and that, if chosen, it would also be the first country in South America to enjoy the privilege of having the world's athletes as its guests. No amount of branding acumen, no matter how brilliant the execution, offered the IOC judges what Rio gave them. Rio's promise was different and relevant and resonated with an energy that the judges knew would make it a draw for Olympic fans and "official sponsors."

As wonderful as the other venues' bid presentations were, Rio's team came up with a distinctive idea on which to sell the city, and they communicated it with style and self-confidence. Not only would hosting the games help strengthen Brazil's emerging economy, it would build on the country's burgeoning spirit of national pride and cooperation.

Vying to be a host city for the Olympic Games is very big business and a very intense branding challenge, and it's only going to get increasingly difficult. As the world gets "flatter," as country sites become commoditized in terms of being able to support Olympic infrastructure, as cultures start to meld together in terms of smiling, happy people, great nightlife—even glorious beaches and sexy bathing suits—the task of identifying something that truly sets one country apart from another is going to be a tough sell to the IOC. Most recently, the South Korean city of Pyeongchang was awarded the 2018 Winter Olympics after it sold the IOC on the idea of "New Horizons" by emphasizing its strategic position in Asia and its access to a fast-growing youth market, making it a vibrant environment in which to showcase the Olympic Games. Whether its branding team took a page out of Rio's brand book is beside the question. They knew, as do all smart brands, that to win, to gain the edge, it takes difference, relevance, and the knowledge that your brand is where it's at.

HOW SMARTYPIG TAUGHT AMERICANS TO SAVE—AGAIN

Are you old enough to remember when your mother had a Christmas Club account at the local bank or S&H green stamp booklets stuffed into the kitchen junk drawer waiting to be redeemed for pots, pans, or clock radios? I am, and, given that I'm an old (enough) branding professional, I also know how hard it is to breathe fresh life into a moribund market segment. While many entrepreneurs look to invent something altogether original that meets the formula for brand success—to be both different and relevant—some ask the best question a seeker of a new brand idea can ask: "Ever wonder why?" as in, "Ever wonder why we can't bring the old savings club plans into the new, digital marketplace?" The founders of SmartyPig asked, and they—and their customers—are literally reaping the benefits.

SmartyPig (which, by the way, is a nifty name, similar in its quirky but intuitive quality to Google and Instagram) is basically the ultimate online piggybank. Launched in 2008 and still going strong, it allows you to save with a specific goal in mind within a specific time frame, and it makes it worth your while by giving you a competitive interest rate on your savings, not to mention added incentives like cash back or significant discounts from major brand names in retail, travel, technology, and entertainment companies. Whether it's for baby furniture, a car, a vacation, a set of luggage, a home remodel, or a new spring wardrobe, SmartyPig, with its easy, informative website, allows you to set up your account, automatically transfer funds, track your progress, and, without wear and tear to your credit score or credit cards, enjoy the rewards of your fiscal conscientiousness. Pure and simple, it's a new and meaningful take on the old Christmas Club, green stamp category. It makes saving money a tangible and achievable thing to do, about as relevant as an idea can be at this economic moment in time.

Also interesting to me is the fact that the SmartyPig brand makes heroes of its many brand partners. Best Buy, Macy's, Amazon, Neiman Marcus, iTunes, Hyatt, and Babies "R" Us are just a few of the many companies that have signed on to enjoy the collateral goodwill that comes from helping consumers become more financially responsible. More than this, because it is the first "social" bank, users

specific
. Even if your
reach that
en you get

have the option of sharing their saving goals with friends and family, allowing anyone to contribute to the account—a genuine brand advantage for gift-givers and giftees alike. This extra support from others is also, in my opinion, a great way to help keep the account holder motivated to keep the savings goals. (And in this day and age, saving is a goal we should all keep.) That all accounts are FDIC-insured makes the whole SmartyPig value equation even stronger.

That SmartyPig has used its "smarts" in social media to sustain its business without paying for advertising is another of the brand idea's strengths. It is very much in line with the word-of-mouth world we inhabit. The company is able to rely on its satisfied users to promote the brand through social media channels. For example, every time one of its account holders reaches a savings goal, SmartyPig prompts them to share the achievement on their Twitter or Facebook accounts.

As I said, coming up with an entirely new brand idea is hard. Turning an old idea on its head and figuring out how to make it meaningful to a new generation of consumers may be harder still. The founders of the SmartyPig brand have done just that. They've made saving for a rainy day fun and rewarding, not to mention as fresh and appealing as its cheerful pink mascot.

PEPSI HAS TO CONSTANTLY KEEP ITS EDGE TO KEEP UP WITH COCA-COLA

Come on, guys. Let's make it a fair fight. No, I'm not referring to the ongoing efforts at tax reform or the battle of the network morning-show news hosts. Rather, I'm referring to the Pepsi versus Coca-Cola challenge and, more specifically, Pepsi's continuous efforts to win the "cola wars."

Reflecting on this purely from a branding point of view (my beverage tastes run more to sparkling water), I can tell you that the pursuit of brand dominance will always be more difficult for Pepsi. Why? Way back when, Coca-Cola launched its brand on a simple idea: refreshment and happiness. A Coke and a smile, as it were. This positioning was very smart as it can never go out of style. It's a simple story, always fresh and relevant, that can be easily executed as long as the company's branding communicates refreshment and happiness. How hard is that? Pepsi, in contrast, launched its brand on the notion of choice, and, more specifically, the choice for people who don't hew to conventional tastes. As a result, the company must always have its pulse on what's new and edgy. It must be in continuous reinvention mode to keep up with what's hot and cool. This presents a very tricky marketing state of affairs and is somewhat similar to what fashion, entertainment, and beauty industries experience in their initiatives. Here's what I mean.

Several years ago I had a fascinating conversation with Antonio Belloni, who is the group managing director at LVMH, the folks who bring us luxury brands, including Louis Vuitton, Givenchy, Dior, and Dom Pérignon. In the course of our talk, he gave me an interesting analogy relative to branding in an industry in which you always have to be a trendsetter. "Think about a surfer balancing on a wave," he told me. "This surfer has to be responsive to several things at once: the height of the wave, the speed of the wave, the wind, and even the currents running beneath him. He has to be responsive to all these forces simultaneously. He needs to make dozens of very quick, almost intuitive adjustments to keep his balance. His ability to react to minute changes determines success, or lack of success."

In other words, and apropos of Pepsi, when your brand has staked its claim on being the choice for non-traditionalists, it must take care not to get too far

ahead of the "wave," resulting in a wipe-out, and it must ensure that it doesn't get too far behind the wave, letting the perfect moment pass it by. It has to keep many factors carefully balanced at once. Not only does Pepsi have to stay on top of current trends, things that interest its audience, it must bring its story to life in ways that appeal to those for whom the "real thing" doesn't. In terms of its last holiday campaign in which a very hip Santa Claus eschews the offer of a Coke in favor of a Pepsi while vacationing at a Club Med–type resort with a hot Mrs. Claus, I'd say Pepsi hit the mark on two levels. First, the work is clever, a bit mischievous, and it pokes fun at its staid rival with wit and self-assurance. Second, it plays up its competitive edge by demonstrating that when Santa's not working, when he's given a personal choice, Santa will opt for a Pepsi. The campaign is totally on-brand for the company—but only for the moment, mind you. And therein is the brand's ongoing challenge. When you're on top of the wave and having a glorious ride, all's right with the world. Obviously, the key to Pepsi's continued success is its ability to stay on top of the prevailing conditions and catch all subsequent waves just as perfectly. Gnarly, dude.

STARBUCKS WAKES UP AND SMELLS THE COFFEE—
AND BUZZES BACK UP THE LEADER BOARD

I find it very interesting that the more consumers use digital technology, the better their sense of smell becomes. I don't mean this in the literal sense, of course, although I imagine someone somewhere is inventing computer aroma-ware. What I mean is that because digital technology is making it possible for people to learn more and share more than ever before, the consumer nose for authenticity has become increasingly sensitive. Woe to the brand that doesn't deliver the real deal as promised. And any company that doesn't appreciate this had better wake up and smell the coffee, which is exactly why Starbucks took steps to strengthen its customer relationships a couple of years back when it recognized how far it had strayed from its original purpose of providing people with a genuine neighborhood coffeehouse experience. That the company is now the third largest restaurant chain in the world is testament to the fact that those in charge (including the chairman, president, and chief executive officer, Howard Schultz, who reclaimed the helm in 2008 after leaving for a time) saw exactly what was required to recapture and recultivate the true essence of the Starbucks character, from the aroma of fresh-roasted coffee beans to the cheery nature of the folks behind the counter. For many of us, Starbucks is what we talk about when we talk about coffee.

I recently had the pleasure of talking to Starbucks' chief marketing officer, Annie Young-Scrivner, who joined the company in September 2009 after serving as chief marketing officer and vice president of sales for Quaker, a division of PepsiCo. She started with the company, not coincidentally, in the midst of its major brand relaunch and the myriad preparations for its fortieth anniversary, in-cluding a remake of the iconic Starbucks logo and the introduction of a number of new products. While we talked about the company in general, the primary focus of our discussion was the critical role authenticity plays in today's market-place. Here is but a taste of our conversation.

   ALLEN ADAMSON: It has never been more apparent that "a brand is as a brand does." A company's actions define it more than anything else.

How does the idea of what we used to call "inside-out" branding play in your world?

ANNIE YOUNG-SCRIVNER: We really think a lot about who we are at our core. We are coffee. We are innovation. Howard saw an amazing opportunity to change how coffee is consumed in the United States and around the world. So much of who we are is how our customers experience us. We serve 60 million customers every week across 55 countries, which means that we have an opportunity 60 million times a week to make the Starbucks experience perfect for them.

AA: Meaning that the authentic Starbucks brand is about the moment of connection. It's not just about how you roast the coffee, but how you work with your employees—your partners—to ensure that the espresso is made perfectly and handed over with a smile.

AYS: We truly believe that when we deliver an amazing experience, we can have a positive impact on someone's day and that they, in turn, can pass on the positive momentum, starting a ripple effect that can potentially start a movement. So much of what we believe in is the humanity of our brand. It's the relationships we build with our customers, the communities we operate in, and, of course, our partners.

AA: It makes sense then that social media are such an integral part of your brand's success story.

AYS: We are taking the emotional connection we've created inside our stores and expanding it beyond our stores. Leveraging social and digital media consistent with our brand promise, we feel privileged that over 22 million Facebook fans in the United States, over 30 million fans globally, and over 1.5 million Twitter followers have invited us into their daily lives to participate in a dialog. We continue to stay focused on the authenticity of our communication, ensuring that we are talking with our customers and not at them.

AA: You must get a ton of ideas from your customers about what you're doing, or how you could do things differently.

AYS: Not just our customers, but our partners, too. We have a site called "My Starbucks Idea," where we've received over 150,000 ideas for products and services. We review these ideas, let them percolate, so to speak, and align them with trends we're seeing around the globe to determine which to launch. For example, when it became clear that people were looking for a bite of something in the afternoon, we launched Starbucks Petites, delicious treats that would give our customers a mid-day lift. We also use the site to get new flavor ideas. Our Mocha Coconut Frappuccino was a request from My Starbucks Idea to bring a popular item back nationwide.

AA: One of the secrets to any brand's success is keeping the experience fresh and different, but still keeping it familiar and relevant.

AYS: It's a fine balance between new innovation and returning favorites. Innovation is part of our heritage; we plan to continue that tradition. We look at our stores around the world for best practices to see what might work elsewhere. You can't get too comfortable. You have to leverage all your strengths and opportunities to give your brand the edge to stay ahead of the competition. Balancing innovation are the returning seasonal favorites that our customers crave. Our holiday food and beverages are great examples.

AA: You're relatively new to the organization. Did anything surprise you coming in?

AYS: Prior to working for Starbucks, I was already a super-fan. My surprise was how deeply our partners love this company and the brand— everyone is a super-fan! It's a privilege to work for a company where the customers are so engaged. Customers feel personal about us; this is my store, or this is my chair. Personalization is an intrinsic part of our brand. It's the little things, like, "Allen, your coffee is ready." We use the world's best ingredients, and we make your coffee and latte just the way you want it. We're all about the experience of a local coffeehouse. We have a product people want to buy and partners who understand their role in bringing the brand experience to life in an authentic way. The not-so-secret recipe for success is to cultivate this authenticity and give our customers what they're looking for and to enrich the communities where we do business.

THOMAS FRIEDMAN ON WHAT'S REQUIRED TO
REBUILD A ONCE-STRONG BRAND

As I reviewed the list of speakers at one of the many marketing conferences
I attend, it was obvious why Thomas Friedman, Pulitzer Prize–winning author
and columnist for the *New York Times,* was on the agenda. In his newest
book, *That Used to Be Us,* written with Michael Mandelbaum, director of the
Foreign Policy Program at Johns Hopkins University, the authors assert that
the United States no longer leads the world in its ability to innovate and to
efficiently create new things and ideas. Reading this fascinating book, it struck
me that many of the principles the authors advocate about rebuilding "Brand
USA" could be applied to any company looking to revitalize a brand that has
lost its once-powerful edge.

Among the key "rebranding" principles outlined in the book is that the quotation "90 percent of success in life is just showing up" lost its relevancy ages ago. Building a strong brand takes more than just getting the basics right. As the authors assert, "Average is over." For a brand to grow and thrive, it's necessary to "think like an immigrant." Go the extra mile. Act with greater ambition and determination. Friedman and Mandelbaum make clear that, much as in the days before mass marketing when artisans would put their initials on the products they created to distinguish or "brand" them, companies today must ask themselves: is our product something that is distinctive enough, that we feel proud enough about, to put our name on it?

In a marketplace that has become exponentially competitive, in which keeping up is just barely the cost of entry, the future belongs to the institutions (the countries) with the ability to not just think big thoughts, but act on these ideas creatively and deftly and with the enthusiastic engagement of people at all levels. Friedman and Mandelbaum's well-reasoned contention that in an absolutely global, interconnected economy something "extra" is demanded is a principle any and every brand should live by to gain—or regain—its edge. Given that I had interviewed Mr. Friedman for my book *BrandSimple* and appreciated his thoughts on the intersection of business, politics, culture, and world events, I thought it would be interesting to have a follow-up discussion relative to his new book and his thinking about rebuilding brands in this new era. Here is just a bit of our fascinating conversation.

ALLEN ADAMSON: Albeit much larger in scope, it seems that some of the principles that pertain to regaining a leadership position for "Brand USA" are similar in nature to rebooting any brand or institution these days. What is your take on this?

THOMAS FRIEDMAN: One of the points in my book is that things have really changed out there. The world has gone from connected to hyperconnected. The whole global curve has risen. That's because your boss, everyone's boss, has greater access to cheaper, more highly productive labor; cheaper, more highly productive automation or software; cheaper and more highly productive operations; and cheaper, more highly productive genius. This means that in every company, in any category, every worker is going to be asked not to just do their job, but to reinvent or reengineer how their jobs can be done.

AA: This obviously means that there is a much higher premium on creativity in all areas of an organization. You can't simply rely on management to be order-givers. People in all areas, on all levels of the organization, must be genuinely engaged and inspired enough by what they're doing and, more so, empowered to act. They've also got to understand what purpose their brand—my expression—serves for consumers.

TF: Absolutely. In fact, management must not just look to, but count on, the people on the front lines, employees in the field who are closer to the customer, to the newest technology, and to market dynamics, to help them determine where there are gaps, or product openings. You, as a boss, can't possibly know what's happening on the shop floor, so to speak.

AA: In your book you refer to this dynamic as "Carlson's Law," which speaks to the role of management, whether CMO, CFO, or CEO in our hyper-connected, fast-moving workplace. Tell me more about this.

TF: Curtis Carlson is the CEO of SRI International, a company in Silicon Valley that advises many corporations and government agencies on how to unleash innovation in a world driven by globalization and constantly evolving information technology. Carlson's Law—our term, not his—is that things that come from the top down are slow and dumb, and things that come from the bottom up are smart, but chaotic. The role, actually the challenge, for management is to find the right level of top-down and bottom-up—which is the sweet spot for innovative solutions. And the sweet spot is moving down because it's the people who deal with the customers day in and day out who know exactly what's happening out there.

AA: So, one of the central messages in your book, whether it's directed at the government or at an audience of marketers, is that you need people at all levels who are inventors, who are creative, and you need people at the top who edit all the stuff that's coming at them and can identify a great idea when it's presented to them. It's no longer enough to move the line. You've got to be willing and able to reinvent the line.

TF: Right. You can't just look at the past to determine in which direction you must head, but rather ask what world you're living in now. Every day, the best companies ask, "How do we thrive in this world?" This is not just a matter of focusing on what questions consumers are looking to have solved but, more critically, discerning what customers want or need before they even ask. If you wait for customers to tell you what they want, you'll never be a leader. To succeed in this environment, you need people, creative people, who come up to you and say, "We must, and can, do our work in a new way."

THE IPAD SELLS ITSELF: MOST BRANDS DON'T

To branding veterans, including myself, there was a headline written in 1958 by super-adman David Ogilvy that represents one of the best ever created. "At 60 miles an hour the loudest noise in this new Rolls-Royce comes from the electric clock." This bit of advertising history came to mind recently when I read an article in the *New York Times* about a contest being hosted by OgilvyOne, a direct descendant of the famed marketer, to find the "best salesperson in the world." However, it's not a Rolls-Royce that contestants must convince consumers to buy, but an ordinary red brick.

News of this contest by the consummate ad firm hit the business pages and blogs just as reports about Apple's latest innovation, the iPad, hit the front pages and every other media channel. As a branding veteran, I couldn't help but note how these individual stories characterized two fundamentally different starting points for achieving the same ultimate marketing objective: making the sale. Let me explain.

In one case, the more common of the two, marketers are given a product and told to go sell it. It's up to them to determine how to position the brand in a way that sets it apart from all the rest. In David Ogilvy's case, the product to be sold was a pretty nice one, but he had to start with a blank page, nonetheless. Loaded down with every conceivable fact and figure about the car, provided with a plethora of features and benefits, it was up to him and his team to cull from this laundry list the one simple, meaningful thing on which they could build a sustainable brand promise—a single notion that would represent to consumers what the Rolls-Royce brand was all about. After sifting and thinking, they recognized that, because of the vehicle's finely tuned mechanics, its airtight interior, airtight exterior, et cetera, et cetera, et cetera, the car drove so quietly and elegantly that, yes, the only thing one could hear was that clock ticking. For many years, this simple idea stood for the quality and workmanship that distinguished the Rolls-Royce brand from every other luxury brand of automobile.

What Mr. Ogilvy knew and followed were the rules of taking a brand from zero to success. You identify a simple selling point that differentiates the product or service from its competition in the minds of consumers and you use the branding to ensure that this selling point sticks. Fifty-two years after it was written, this headline is still on the top-ten list. For those faced with a product or service a tad more mundane than a $200,000 car, say a $1.00 brick, the same rules still apply. Identify something you can say about your product that is meaningfully different to consumers and make sure it has sticking power. For example, Liberty Mutual, charged with selling insurance, which is among the most commoditized of categories, determined that standing for "responsibility" would help its brand stand out in a sea of price quotes and same-old-same-old promises. Its strong growth in the industry is evidence of a successful mission. Sexier, but in no less a commodity category, Sephora took on both the over-the-counter department store cosmetic brands and the under-wraps drug store brands and created an open-sell environment as its distinguishing brand factor. Simple in concept and brilliant in its branding, from retail site to online service, the brand's reputation—and its sales—have soared since its inception.

On the other side of the sell-it spectrum is the product that sells itself, Exhibit A being the iPad (or any one of Apple's magical products, for that matter). How does this happen? A company identifies a gap in the marketplace—something that will meet a specific consumer need—or, in Apple's case, intuits a product that people will absolutely want and need after it's introduced. The company then develops the product or service to fill this need, generally in a first-mover advantage manner. In other words, there's no need to determine which bells or whistles or ticking clocks to focus on in order to make this kind of sale—simply use a de facto presentation of the story. Apple gets this, and its advertising lets its products do the talking. Its campaigns simply showcase the seemingly magical functionality that differentiates the Apple products from others in the category. While the iPad is the quintessential example of a product that simply sells itself by just being itself, consider, too, every product in the Method brand's line of environmentally friendly cleaning products, each created with the consumer's socially aware needs in mind. Think about Swiffer, Dyson vacuum cleaners, Garmin GPS, Teva waterproof footwear, Wikipedia, or Google. Each is unique in its category, and each is a self-seller because there is no story line required other than the one written by consumer desire.

If I were to enter the sell-a-brick contest, I'd obviously follow the rules relative to the first case marketing scenario: Find something that differentiates your brand of brick from any other. Make sure people care about what this is and will remember it as a result of its distinctive character and its equally distinctive branding. Oh yes, and one other thing, as you do your homework (which you should), don't confuse the razzle-dazzle effects of digital branding with the razzle-dazzle of the point you're trying to make. David Ogilvy had only a print ad with which to get his simple idea across, and this idea helped spawn a multimillion-dollar global communications firm. The clock's ticking. Get to work.

"AHA!" INNOVATION MEANS LOOKING BEYOND "GEE WHIZ"

You don't need to be either a technology guru or a parenting guru to know that a young child's experience with digital technology will be far different than that of his or her older siblings. I can see this phenomenon in my own household and in those of my friends and neighbors. The accelerating pace with which digital tools and behavior replace yesterday's models is mind boggling. Relative to technological advances, it's no longer 20 or even 10 years that separate generations, but two or three.

> *To survive, let alone gain a leading edge, identifying something that consumers have never seen before and that they can really use is essential.*

This fact hits harder each day as reports from Silicon Valley roll in with accounts of the newest mega-millionaire (usually a scrappy college student) who has come up with the latest and greatest digital gizmo or video game. From innovative products like the Elevation dock, a sleek stand for the iPhone, to the Brydge, which turns an iPad into a laptop, to Instagram, which magically tags the location of your smartphone photos, there seems to be no end to the cavalcade of brands hitting the shelves, virtual and otherwise. The key to long-term brand success in this all-new-all-the-time marketplace, however, is ensuring that whatever it is that's on the drawing board is something that people will really want or need. Sure, bells and whistles are fun, but if the newest devices or apps or even everyday packaged goods don't provide consumers with benefits they see as meaningfully different, or that make life truly better or more convenient in some significant way, the bottom line won't be fun to look at. This principle of brand building is no less true now than it has ever been. In fact, with the plethora of new products and services hitting the market and the speed with which they're being introduced, I suggest it's more important than ever. To survive, let alone gain a leading edge, identifying something that consumers have never seen before and that they can really use is essential.

So what's a marketer to do to find this elusive white space in a category? While there are many ways to do your homework, including sophisticated research and analysis of the consumer psyche, I'd advise those who want to cash in on

the next new thing to start from a more obvious position. Literally obvious. As in, "Gee, why didn't I think of that? It's so obvious." It's kind of akin to the old Jerry Seinfeld routine in which he'd ask a question like, "Ever wonder why they don't make muffin tops without the rest of the muffin?" Those who know branding will tell you that some of the most powerful and long-standing brands in the world have been built on something hiding in plain sight.

Green Mountain Coffee, for example, asked the question, "Ever wonder why people have to make a pot of freshly brewed coffee if they only want one cup?" Along came the Keurig K-Pod concept, which made its debut in 1998. It was founded on a simple idea by coffee lovers who understood that there are a whole lot of other coffee lovers out there who want to enjoy the same quality and consistency of their favorite coffeehouse brews right at home without the hassle of making an entire pot. Since its "aha!" moment, the company has become the leading manufacturer of single-serve coffee machines and individual gourmet-flavor portion packs, which now include teas, hot chocolates, and other single-serving beverage options, both hot and cold. While other companies have entered the category, including Kraft and its Tassimo brand and most recently Nestlé and its Nespresso single-serve machines, first-mover Keurig continues to dominate the market.

Another brilliant "aha!" moment led two scrappy college guys to come up with a line of products that is currently giving some of the biggest names in the brand world a run for their money. And, no, they're not operating in the digital realm. Rather, they're cleaning up with cleaning products after asking themselves a couple of "wonder whys," as in, "Ever wonder why the products you use to clean your body and your home have to be made with harsh, toxic chemicals?" or "Ever wonder why the cleaning products you use every day come in containers so unattractive you have to hide them under your sink?"

Ever since San Francisco–based Method first entered the category in 2001, founders Eric Ryan and Adam Lowry have achieved double-digit sales growth and become game-changing players in an ultra-competitive category. I've heard these guys speak at a number of industry events, and their tale of success never ceases to amaze me, for a couple of reasons. First, I used to work at Lever Brothers, a once-giant brand name in the cleaning products business. Even way back then, if someone had asked me if there was any "white space" in the detergent or soap category, I would have said "no." As their environmentally friendly products and designer-worthy packaging show, lo and behold, there was white space galore. You just had to know where to look.

Second, Ryan and Lowry never stop looking for opportunities to expand the brand, always in ways that are in keeping with their original promise to keep it green and ensure that whatever it cleans, it does as well as any competitor. As they told the audience in one conference I attended, "Disruptive innovation is the goal we strive for. Big companies talk about economies of scale. We want to make the category about something else." Method is about something else, a relevantly different something else—products that reflect a passion for caring for the environment and for beautiful design. Or, the way they sum it up, "to be a catalyst in a happy, healthy, home revolution that improves human health." Yes, the brand is still small compared with P&G, Unilever, and Clorox, but because of its laser focus on giving consumers what they want and need (clean and green, please), the big players have had to make major adjustments to their own lineup of eco-friendly cleaning products. Or, as the book Ryan and Lowry wrote with co-author Lucas Conley more aptly states in its title, *The Method Method: Seven Obsessions That Helped Our Scrappy Start-up Turn an Industry Upside Down.*

There is no doubt that the marketplace is being rapidly and overwhelmingly commoditized, pushing innovators and manufacturers to turn things upside down and inside out in their search for the next new thing. That this newest generation of products and services, be they digital or traditional in nature, is seen as relevantly different to the newest generation of users is an understatement. Consumers are savvier. They're more demanding. And their opinions are shaped by other consumers worldwide. There is always an opportunity for short-term sizzle. But brand success takes a long-term view and is built on what consumers really want and can genuinely use to make their lives better in some substantial way. While money and research can help in the quest, I suggest you try something else first: look at the obvious.

CHAPTER TWO

To Have an Edge, a Brand Must Start with a Simple Idea Based on "Who" and "Why," Not Just "What" and "How"

Quick. Who stands for "truth, justice, and the American way?" No, it's not your local politician. It is, of course, Superman: "Faster than a speeding bullet, more powerful than a locomotive, able to leap tall buildings in a single bound." It was a miserable time for America in 1938. The Great Depression and its impact had spread from one end of the country to another. Parents tried, often without luck, to find work to support their families. Gangsters made headlines every day. The specter of another war was materializing abroad. And President Roosevelt looked for ways to put a shattered nation back together. While FDR did what he could in the real world, two men from Cleveland, Ohio, found another way to give people a sense of optimism. They came up with a hero, someone not from anywhere on this planet. Oh no. He came from beyond the stars. To this day, Superman has endured as the classic symbol of, well, the superhero, recognized worldwide, holding a special place in our culture, if not our hearts.

Now, it's not because I'm a sucker for Superman that I bring up the talented guy as a way to introduce this chapter (actually, I'm more of a Trekkie). Rather, it's because Superman is a super example of the fact that to have an edge, a brand must start with a simple idea based not just on what it does or how it does it, but on who it is and why. As a brand, Superman is whole in body and spirit. We know how he'll behave in a given situation. We know when the evil Lex Luthor is making him do things that aren't "on brand." The familiar "S" on his red and blue outfit (the brand colors and logo) is ever the same. He radiates decency and integrity, but we know that he has humility, given that he was raised by a sweet old couple in the American heartland. When he's in his other guise, Clark Kent, we see his gentle side, cute and dorky as it is, and love him for that as well.

I can speak of Superman as if he were real because his brand is that well crafted. The craftees, Joe Shuster and Jerry Siegel, knew exactly what they wanted Superman to stand for, they knew exactly why—to give people a sense of hope—and they knew what this meant in terms of his demeanor and his actions. Although the phrase "truth, justice, and the American way" has been modified as necessary for reasons of political correctness (in the 2006 film, *Superman Returns,* character Perry White says, "truth, justice, and all that stuff"), everyone sees Superman—the brand anyway—as the force for good.

A brand with an edge has an inner force. It knows exactly what it stands for, whether it's "truth, justice, and the American way," or something a bit more down to earth, like FedEx's long-held promise to deliver peace of mind, or Discovery Communications' idea to satisfy people's curiosity, or the idea on which Virgin Atlantic Airways is built, to bring good times back to the skies. These ideas are all simple, they're focused, and they're memorable. They are ideas that the organizations' employees can grasp intuitively and that drive everything the brand does—the branding—from the design and colors on the packaging and labels to its behavior in the marketplace. Most important, these defining ideas do just that: they help define the brand's character, what makes it tick.

Just as it's becoming more and more challenging to find an idea on which to build a brand, that elusive gap in the category, it's becoming equally challenging to dimensionalize this idea. That is, to build out the brand's character in a way that will satisfy both those who do the branding and those who experience the branding—the wary consumers. The process requires way more than just coming up with a string of adjectives, which could very well apply to any company's mission statement and could be interpreted in a number of different ways. It takes what is sort of the equivalent of psychoanalysis. Now, of course, this process is easy, or easier anyway, for a company whose brand was founded by someone who is still strongly associated with the brand, say Steve Jobs, or Charles Schwab, or Ben and Jerry. These real-life characters imbued their companies and their brands with real-life personality traits that were, and continue to be, soaked up by the organization. The brand DNA is all natural. It's authentic. The people who work for these persona-led brands have an advantage. Instead of a virtual archetype, there's a leader who clearly delineated not just the "what" and the "how" of the brand, the rational stuff, but the "who" and the "why," the less tangible qualities.

As "who" and "why" have become more critical to a brand's success, so too has the process by which companies go about developing and codifying the traits therein. It can't be done by simply checking off the boxes on a questionnaire. It can't be done out of context. A brand's persona must be genuinely relevant to the brand. How it acts and expresses itself must be authentic. It might stem from a company's heritage or its leadership style or the audience for which it's intended. To influence the hearts and minds of consumers, a brand's persona has to stem from the hearts and minds of those in the organization. The stories and tips in this chapter all deal with the notion of purpose and, as such, with brands that know "who" they are and "why" they do what they do. Before you get into these accounts, however, you might want to take a look at the sidebar, which includes a bit of industry insight into how smart companies take on this brand psychoanalysis.

WHO AND WHY: A HOW-TO

It's an interesting exercise to get to the essence of a brand's character. It might be that you're starting out with a solid baseline, possibly your company's heritage, or a leader who, while not the brand's name, like Michael Dell, was highly influential in establishing its personality, like Fred Smith at FedEx or Mark Zuckerberg at Facebook. Whatever the case, here are four guidelines to help you become your brand's Dr. Freud. Once you spend time on each area, connect the dots and see "who" appears.

GET UNDER THE SKIN OF THE COMPANY

As you might imagine, this takes more than just a cursory walk down the halls. Walk down the halls and talk to people. Do they like what they're doing? What do they like best about what they're doing? Are they mostly cat owners or dog owners? What do they like to do in their spare time? How do they dress—corporate or jeans and T-shirts? What do the offices look like—corporate or the equivalent of jeans and T-shirts? If a celebrity worked at the company, which one would be the best fit? (And in which role: George Clooney in *Syriana* or George Clooney in *Ocean's Eleven?*) How are meetings conducted— with lots of spirit and interaction or with PowerPoint? How do internal memos go out—stiff and formal or breezy and friendly? If it's a customer-facing brand, what do the external venues look like? What goes on at the call centers? Are those who answer the phones given the freedom to make decisions or are they required to get a "supervisor"? To get under the skin of a company, you must be an astute observer and listener. It's often between the lines that you'll find "who" you're looking for.

DETERMINE WHAT THE BRAND ASPIRES TO STAND FOR

By this I don't mean "to be the best soft drink in the world." What are the brand's reasons for being that go beyond the obvious (and the mercantile)? What is the company's purpose beyond making tangible goods or providing good service? What other companies does it admire or aspire to be like? How can it change or reframe the category to influence how consumers think about the brand? What purpose will unite the people within the organization?

EXAMINE WHAT'S GOING ON IN THE MARKETPLACE

What are people talking about? What's important to the people the company cares about? Is there something being overlooked that is important to potential customers? What brands will you have to outsmart or out-execute in order to win? What do you need to do to credibly own the space? How can you take the lead? Most critical, is it feasible?

BE REAL

What is your company best at? Where can you create a competitive advantage? What are the company's inherent strengths and skill sets? Where can the company seize a long-term opportunity? Do the employees want to do it? Can they "be" it? Can they live it?

TOP TIPS: TO CONNECT WITH CONSUMERS, "WHO" IS AS CRITICAL AS "WHAT"

These days, consumers want to know more than just what a brand does, makes, or sells before they commit their time and money; they want to know "who" the brand is, what it stands for, and whether they are simpatico with its values. The stories in this chapter are about brands that have gained an edge because they know "who" they are, as do all the consumers who do business with them. It is in good part *why* they do business with them. People want brands that are authentic. Brands with an edge have tapped into their DNA and that comes across in everything they do. Here are a few tips to aid in the tapping of your inner brand:

- Defining "who" a brand is goes beyond coming up with a string of adjectives. It takes insight and rigor. You must be able to describe a brand the way you would a real person, with a well-rounded set of character traits—you must even be able to hold a casting call for it. (You wouldn't get into a relationship with a string of adjectives would you?)
- "Who" a brand is helps differentiate it in the marketplace and within your organization. Make sure it's someone you feel comfortable living with for the long term.
- To *redefine* "who" a brand is, go back to the fruits of your roots: What did those who launched the brand have in their hearts and minds? In fact, *who* were they and what motivated them?
- Once you define who your brand is, make sure your employees understand and grasp the meaning. They're the ones charged with bringing it to life.
- Authenticity cannot be underestimated. Gratuitous initiatives will be seen as gratuitous. "Like" real is *not* real.
- Hold your course. Follow your true north. Ensure that everything you do is consistently in line with who your brand is. In a transparent world, people can see the seams.

BEHIND EVERY GREAT ENTREPRENEUR IS A PERSON WHO WAS THEIR INSPIRATION (OR, IN ANNIE'S CASE, A BUNNY)

How can you not love a company whose logo is a cross-hatched pencil drawing of a bunny? The fact is, millions of people have come to love Bernie the bunny, whose picture appears on every package of Annie's Homegrown products, just as they've come to love all the yummy, organic, natural food inside the packages, from the original macaroni and cheese, to the array of kid-friendly snacks, to the everybody-friendly pizza. Annie's was co-founded by the very real Annie Withey and Andrew Martin in 1989 with the goal of showing, by example, that a successful business can also be socially responsible. Annie, who lives with her family on their working farm in Connecticut, had the simple mission of making good food that other moms could feel good about giving their families—down-to-earth foods that taste great and are easy to love. That Annie and a team of passionate employees continue to achieve this mission is evident both in the letters that pour in from happy parents and children, and in the fact that Annie's went public with a successful stock offering in the early spring of 2012. That the company's New York Stock Exchange ticker symbol is "BNNY" is very much in keeping with the brand's sunny, funny, organic nature.

Wanting to know more about this company and how it jumped to the top of every healthy family's shopping list, I called Sarah Bird, whose title at Annie's is SVP marketing and chief mom officer. In this transparent marketplace in which consumers want to know as much about who is behind a brand as what the brand makes, I thought it would be a good lesson learned to hear the story of the literal Annie and how she and her real gray and white Dutch bunny (who "Rabbit Approves" a product before it leaves for the stores) launched this company. Here is part of our fascinating conversation:

> **ALLEN ADAMSON:** Among the key factors for success in our current marketplace is being able to convey a clear persona—a sense of the "who" behind a brand. While there is a real Annie behind the Annie brand, it takes a lot more than just having a person's name on a package to express the brand persona in the genuine way that consumers

demand. Tell me about Annie and how the team brings her original ideal to life as a brand.

SARAH BIRD: To begin with, Annie had a very clear sense of what she wanted her brand to be about. Her title today is inspirational president and she is the grounding of the brand. The management team prides itself on ensuring that every action is in keeping with its real and pure and simple nature. It's about always taking the high ground. Across all touchpoints, from the organic ingredients to the family farmers from whom we get our ingredients, everything emanates from Annie's original vision.

AA: Some marketers call this having a "North Star" and know that to succeed you have to always follow the North Star to determine whether a branding initiative is on course with what the brand stands for.

SB: I agree. We've done a lot of equity research and know what's required to ensure that consumers continue to trust the goodness of the brand.

Consumers expect that all actions reflect the fact that there is a real person behind the brand, someone who, in the early days, put her own home phone number on the back of the packages so people could call and share their input on the products. While her phone number is not there anymore, Annie continues to write the personal letters that are printed on the back of the boxes and she continues to personally answer mail from consumers.

AA: So the commitment to listening, which is critical in this day and age, started with Annie. This action is just one of many that reflect the authenticity of the brand and everything it does, authenticity being another critical factor in winning consumer trust. I'm surprised Annie didn't put her picture on the label.

SB: She's shy and has a wonderful sense of humor. She didn't want to be in the limelight and recognized that other brands have "seals" of approval. She thought it would be more in keeping with the nature of the brand to have a "rabbit" of approval to include on the label— Bernie, her pet rabbit for many years. It's a playful way to give the company character without being slick or sophisticated, which aren't traits in our brand's DNA. Annie's brother drew the cross-hatched pencil drawing of Bernie, which makes the effort even more endearing.

AA: Understanding a brand's DNA—what is on-brand and what is not—is one of the things consumers look at as they judge companies. In fact, given that consumers have the ability to look deeper into a company, they can readily see any disconnect between the marketing, the product, the consumer care, and everything else that makes up the fabric of the brand.

SB: Our fabric is woven out of the intent to do well and do good at the same time. It's in our company culture, our DNA. Annie was a pioneer in the healthy, organic food business and it's been part of our culture from the get-go. In fact, we brought on a sustainability director to ensure that we continue to walk the talk and to grow our brand in a simple, organic fashion. We aim to keep it honest.

AA: This means having the innate ability to ensure that your left hand always knows what the right one is doing. It's a fact in branding today that a brand has to be true to who it is and that whatever this is has to permeate the culture of the company. How do you make sure that employees understand what the Annie's brand is about?

SB: We hope that everyone who works at Annie's cares about the impact their actions have on the world. We encourage this and support this by providing benefits that reinforce our (and hopefully their!) values, from health-care and wellness programs to programs that help them save energy and natural resources at home and in their transportation choices. Additionally, our office space very much reinforces our values. To succeed today you need to build authentic touchpoints for the brand because people can sense superficiality immediately. All of the people who work here know exactly what's required to reinforce the perception people have of our brand. For example, the person in charge of our Facebook page is quirky and fun and gets great conversations going with our customers. Our culture is very well defined, and our employees know our history and what makes us special.

AA: When you have a clear sense of purpose, of knowing who you are, managing a brand is easier, even as you get bigger.

SB: The Annie's team is steeped in the brand. Our culture comes to life naturally and it's what helps us create and innovate, never losing sight of where we started.

WHAT MADONNA CAN TEACH LADY GAGA

When you reach my age, you do not want to have it rubbed in with the news that the Rolling Stones are going to celebrate their fiftieth anniversary together. If they're that old, what does that make me? In any event, this news, together with Mick Jagger's appearance at a recent Grammy Awards (along with Bob Dylan, Barbra Streisand, and a relatively young lady whose surname is Gaga), got me thinking about the music business and what it can teach us about building brands. Yes, there is a lesson in here and it's this: music has evolved so much over the years, but the two types of approaches to building a brand haven't.

Let me explain. The Rolling Stones (along with Bob and Barbra) represent the first type of branding approach wherein you figure out what you want your brand to stand for in the minds of consumers and you consistently deliver on this promise year after year, and decade after decade, not straying too far from the expected executions. Yes, you make some changes to ensure that the brand remains relevant in the marketplace—in this case a new studio recording or different arrangement—but, essentially, you know what people expect and you meet their expectations with unwavering authenticity. Mick shakes it up, Bob warbles it out, and Barbra sounds just as lovely with each rendition of "Evergreen." These brands know "who" they are, and they remain timeless.

On the other hand, there's the brand from which consumers expect constant reinvention—it's in the brand's DNA. And, yes, while Lady Gaga is known for her quick-change artistry, it's not this mercurial miss who set the standard that branding meet the disposition of the cultural moment. Instead, it's a very talented marketing lady who, more or less, invented the category of brand reinvention in the contemporary music category—Madonna. Sensing changes in the public's mood for music, anticipating (creating?) the next trend, Madonna continues to change up her musical self. She's a genius at knowing how not to be too far out in front of the curve and being able to sense when what she's doing has run its course—both critical elements in this type of brand building. Equally important, she knows that, no matter the guise or disguise of the moment, she has to deliver on a core competency—in her case, a genuine talent for song and dance. Without it, no amount of artifice will help her win or keep fans. That

her latest release, *MDNA,* hit the Billboard 200 chart at number one the week it launched is evidence that the star still has pipes.

The different branding approaches of Coca-Cola and Pepsi, as discussed in chapter one, are a non-musical analogy to the above. Each brand knows what it stands for in the minds of consumers. Coke continues to build on its reputation as the classic, the "real thing," bringing to life the promise of happiness by way of a "Coke and a smile," or some variation on this timeless theme. Pepsi's claim to branding fame is being the "choice of a new generation." As such, its branding team is always on the lookout for daring and irreverent ways to communicate the hip Pepsi personality.

As a branding professional, I can tell you that, like Madonna, Pepsi has the harder branding challenge. It takes a well-honed sixth sense to understand what the next new trend or happening thing might be and to be able to move quickly enough to catch it before consumers have moved on to the next wave, while at the same time keeping in close alignment with your brand's core DNA. And this is a lesson that Lady Gaga can take away from Madonna's success. If she wants to follow Madonna's route to building her brand, let her have at it. I wish her well. As a classically trained musician she's definitely got the core competency. She must understand, however, that to succeed in the category, as Madonna did, she'll need to watch the waves. She can change it up all she wants, but she should make sure it's the change her fans want and can relate to.

CREATIVE CAPITALISM: BRANDING LESSONS FROM NEWMAN'S OWN

It would be hard to find anyone who doesn't think Paul Newman was a super movie star. It would also be hard to find anyone in the marketing business who doesn't think Paul Newman was a super branding guy.

When he launched his line of Newman's Own products in 1982, he understood that clearly defining a brand's purpose would help differentiate it in the minds of consumers, especially in categories as commoditized as those in which he competed, like salad dressing, lemonade, and pasta sauce.

This thought came to me when I read about a concert being held at Avery Fisher Hall with performances by Paul Simon and Trisha Yearwood, Josh Groban, and many others who were coming together to pay tribute to Newman, who died in 2008, and to raise money for his Hole in the Wall Gang Camp, a magical place he developed where kids with serious medical conditions can come and play and just be kids. The company's long-standing and simple purpose is to make stuff that tastes really good and to use the profits to do really good things for people, like letting kids just be kids. While I admit that it certainly helps to have Paul's charming, irreverent countenance on all of the brand packaging, I still maintain that there is a lot we can learn from this master of branding that has nothing to do with being a Hollywood idol or a major philanthropist.

To begin with, Newman's Own is built on a simple, believable promise. The products that Paul concocted with his buddy, author A. E. Hotchner, are his *own* old family recipes that taste really good. In fact, the company got its start after friends suggested that the two fellows market the delicious salad dressing they had been making and bottling at home and giving out as gifts. The products that followed are also in categories as credible as being homemade. It's easy to imagine P. L. and A. E., as they billed themselves, hard at it in the kitchen discussing the best recipe for a chocolate chip cookie or a spicy marinara sauce and then donning aprons and getting down to the business at hand. It makes a nifty mental picture.

Also nifty is the way this simple promise has been executed across all points of customer touch, another measure of powerful branding well understood by this company. Everything having to do with the brand has been brought to life in perfect alignment with its promise, starting with the name: Newman's Own. Having his signature on every wrapper underscores this point. The packaging itself looks like it was designed in the same kitchen in which the food was cooked up—no hint of slickness or artificiality, literal or figurative. Most important is that the food tastes great (although our family pet would have to vouch for the dog food!). And when you're selling food, ensuring that the taste of the food—the "table stakes"—meets expectations is a given. Delivering on a core competency is another of the basic tenets of smart branding being followed by the folks who successfully carry on in Paul's stead.

Perhaps most interesting when looking at why the Newman's Own brand is successful, even after its founder's passing, is how ahead of his time the actor-brander was in linking his brand promise to its purpose and making this the hallmark of his endeavor. He understood that he needed a purpose for his organization beyond the actual food and the shiny name under which it was

marketed. While many companies are philanthropic, especially in this hyper-socially conscious era, Newman's Own is defined by its philanthropic purpose. Consumers are deeply aware of what the brand stands for, and they care deeply about it, which is central to its continuing success.

Even back in 1982, when the number of product and media choices were far fewer, Paul Newman recognized that he couldn't compete on good-tasting products alone. There had to be another way to differentiate his brand of pretzels and coffee and frozen pizza from all the rest. Good food that does good is how most people think about this brand. Given his cheeky humor, Paul, without any false pretense, put it forward as "Shameless exploitation in pursuit of the common good," a tagline that's as on-brand as every other of the company's branding initiatives.

Now, with all due respect, we are talking about Paul Newman. He got the Sundance Kid to jump off a cliff. He conned Doyle Lonnegan into falling for his sting. He would certainly have been able to get a number of consumers to buy whatever goodies he was selling. However, the point is that he knew he would need more than his baby blues to build and maintain a winning brand. He started with a simple, believable promise that was relevant to people. He made sure this promise was executed brilliantly in all aspects of the branding. And he aligned his promise with a purpose that helped differentiate it in a highly competitive marketplace.

Four years after his death, Paul Newman's vision for new structure and leadership keeps the company's "shameless exploitation in pursuit of the common good" alive and well. Paul personally donated to charities an average of $9.6 million in after-tax net profits per year during his 25 years as the private benefactor of the company. Recognizing that this unstructured business model was not sustainable without his presence, Paul worked with long-time friend Robert Forrester to establish the Newman's Own Foundation in 2005.

Since Newman's death, Forrester has worked, as CEO of the company and president of the foundation, to marry Paul's whimsical attitude toward business with a more structured model. He is responsible for changes such as replacing the non-existent advertising with the likes of the brilliant, very Paul-esque advertising mentioned earlier. Under the direction of loved ones who carry on Paul's original vision, values, and spirit through a new business model, the company has a new average donation of $21.5 million per year. The exploitation continues, stronger than ever.

While Paul Newman's name and stature as a star might have helped at the beginning of the brand's run, it was adhering to the basic rules of branding that made this company a star on supermarket shelves.

MARK ZUCKERBERG'S CLARITY OF VISION CONTINUES TO DRIVE THE BRAND—AND ITS SUCCESS

Let me take you back to the Silicon Valley of 1939 (yes, it existed, albeit not yet in the way we think about it today). In any event, it was way back then that two very smart and incredibly prescient people started a business focused on making a contribution to society through technology. They didn't refer to it as a brand purpose, per se, but the idea on which William Hewlett and David Packard launched their very powerful brand—HP—was, as Hewlett said, "to operate on the assumption that if we made a contribution to society, rewards would follow." This was a pretty revolutionary thought back in 1939. But, today, as more and more companies come to the stark realization that consumers are judging brands not just on what they make, but on who they are, it's brands *without* a purpose that are in catch-up mode. While it may sound a bit like Philosophy 101, a company whose employees can answer the question, "Why are we here?" will be the company that makes stronger connections with consumers.

This notion was reinforced, literally and figuratively, in a recent conversation I had with David Kirkpatrick, author of *The Facebook Effect: The Inside Story of the Company That Is Connecting the World.* In this seminal story of the company founded by another very smart and incredibly prescient person, David makes exceptionally clear that Mark Zuckerberg was of the same mind as Misters Hewlett and Packard when he envisioned his company: He had a strong sense of the social impact he wanted it to have on the world. He began with not just a brand promise, but a brand purpose that continues to drive the company and everyone in it. What follows is just part of the fascinating conversation David and I had about his work chronicling Mark Zuckerberg and the newest generation of Silicon Valley denizens.

> **ALLEN ADAMSON:** You say in a recent article that it may be helpful to think of Facebook as a movement, which is a word Mark himself has used since 2007. You state that to understand his company and where he may take it, one should think of him more as a social revolutionary than a businessperson. Tell me more about this and how it relates to the notion of brand purpose.

DAVID KIRKPATRICK: Mark Zuckerberg's personal brand is one of tremendous conviction, commitment, and vision. He began with and continues to have a very consistent sense of the social impact he wants his company to have. It's the idea that a business ought to have a function in the world more than making money. Now, that a company should have a vision beyond making money is not new, but to have a CEO who believes it so fervently and has done so from the beginning is a critical factor in the company's success. Mark absolutely believes in the idea of changing the world for the better by making it more open and connected. Having a clear, simple vision is not dissimilar to how revolutionaries of earlier eras convinced societies to change. The single biggest reason that Facebook is such a strong brand is that Mark had a clarity of vision that he was able to articulate inside the company from the beginning, and to this day.

AA: Articulating a CEO's vision is not about printing your company's mission on a laminated card. To be successful it has to be driven into the company and become part of the company DNA. Mark and the people who work with him live the vision—of Facebook's social impact being the ultimate determinant of its success.

DK: Yes, and of course you need to have the financial wherewithal to drive this social impact—the more social impact, the more financial success. It's a virtuous circle, and he's built a great economic engine. But, if he honestly thought that he was building an advertising business, he'd walk away. He's a man of his era and his generation. In fact, if you ask ordinary people what they think the role of business is, they'd tell you it should be about more than making money. Facebook has had the fast valuation of any company because it's a company that abides by this vision. He believes that as long as he sticks to his social vision, or his purpose, his shareholders will be okay.

AA: A typical challenge for companies in which a CEO has such a strong vision is to ensure that the culture stays the same as it gets bigger. How does Mark make sure that when people come on board they "get it"?

DK: This is a very important point. One thing that he's done is have Andrew Bosworth, a senior engineer and someone very close to Mark, hold a half-day session with every single incoming hire, be it a coder, a marketing person, a salesperson, or a janitor. Part of the session is a lecture on what's referred to as the "hacker ethos." The hacker way is the old Silicon Valley ideal of constant iteration, experimentation, never being satisfied. It's a watchword for constant invention. The objective is that someone who works at Facebook must feel motivated to constantly rethink the nature of their actual function. In other words, is there a better way to do it?

AA: It's like setting the employee GPS to stay in constant alignment with where the company's going. Consumers today are increasingly locked onto a company's intrinsic values. It should be among a company's highest priorities to continually reinforce these values, to make sure the message is conveyed.

DK: You could argue that the mere fact that I know all of this is a reflection of the values. When I told Mark in January of 2008 that I wanted to write a book about Facebook, he said, "Go for it." He made himself available and encouraged everyone in the company to cooperate. It's not common for such a young company to be so open. But Mark was hoping I could help crystallize his vision. He really knew that it was important for someone to record the company's history because he wasn't going to.

AA: I know that Mark is still with the same woman he was with before he started Facebook. I've also heard that he's very close to his parents and his sisters. The guy has some real touchstones in his life, which leads me to believe he's very grounded.

DK: He stays connected and real, and it's this balance that his employees observe, which adds to the degree of respect he has. The only way he can continue to convey the values as the company grows is to maintain credibility.

AA: The concept that a brand is as a brand does has taken on enormous importance in the marketplace, given its transparency. You can't fake it and succeed.

DK: We are living in what you marketers refer to as the "age of authenticity." You cannot fake anything. You cannot hide anything. It will become obvious, and Mark is giving a lesson to the world in this respect, that being the extent you have to go to make it real, to align the brand with its culture.

AA: What's also evident about the Facebook culture, as you said earlier, is the inherent understanding of how critical it is to constantly look at everything with fresh eyes. It's a culture of reinvention, which is essential in the tech space. It's Andy Grove, founder of Intel, and his remark that "only the paranoid survive."

DK: Mark truly believes that his biggest risk is someone else out there in a dorm room or a garage. He keeps his eagle eye on what's happening out there, and it's part of why he decided to buy Instagram. He's obsessively worried, but in a healthy way. He's totally convinced that if Facebook stops moving for one second, it will die. He can't put it on autopilot. He's perfectly aware of the fact that it was the fastest growing company in history, and could just as easily become the fastest disappearing company. An interesting phenomenon, if you take a look, is that over the course of history the Facebook logo has gotten progressively smaller on the website. That's because as they build out the platform more and more, and embrace their long-term destiny as a set of services, it's a signal that what's important is the user's experience, not the logo.

AMAZON, DISNEY, THE GAP, AND JUSTIN BIEBER
KNOW THE ONE BEST BRANDING LESSON

As my kids have recently discovered *Star Wars,* it's been a treat for me to watch the movies again. And as I can't help but see a brand lesson in everything in life, doing so made me think about how apt a concept one of the series' most enduring lines is for brands today: "May the force be with you." Here's the connection.

With the advent of digital technology, the number of backseat drivers has increased, that is, the number of consumers who have something to say about companies and their brands. Not only that, they have the ability to share their opinions with whoever is a friend on Facebook, a fellow tweeter, or a reader of blogs and product reviews (which would be millions of people). Now, this is not a bad thing. Good companies listen to what's being said. But good companies also push the envelope to stay relevant. They'll try new things and invent new wheels, and in doing so, mistakes will be made. Or, mistakes as far as the backseat drivers are concerned.

Looking back on the marketing events of 2011 and 2012, there were multiple reminders of the increasing power of the people to call the mistakes as they saw them. From demands that Bank of America get rid of the charge for debit card usage, to demands that Netflix readjust its pricing for DVD rentals, to demands that the Gap go back to its original logo, consumers had their say and, in many cases, got their way. This is all well and good, to a point. Companies must, of course, listen to what's important to their customers in order to meet their needs.

But they also need to do something more than just listen, which is where that connection comes in. All companies with an edge keep in mind the "force" on which their brand is based. Another celestial metaphor: they have a North Star and they follow it. While most of their actions will please most of the people most of the time, mistakes, as I mentioned, will be made. If they get the message that a particular action or behavior on their part is off-brand, that it doesn't live up to what the brand stands for, they should change direction, retract a policy, go back to a well-loved package or logo. But only if they feel it is in keeping with the meaning of the brand as originally intended. If this is the case, the company should move as quickly as possible to admit its error and fix it just as quickly and move on. The short-term cost of dealing with an issue will be far less than the long-term cost of ignoring it.

All companies with an edge keep in mind the "force" on which their brand is based.

On the other hand, if a brand's management bends to the will of every disgruntled customer, that is, if it tries to make everyone happy, the brand will veer off course, lose its force. Or, back to the other metaphor, if your goal as a brand is to please all of the people all of the time, you'll forever be looking for your North Star. This is true for any and all types of brands, be it in the realm of consumer-packaged goods or in the world of politics. As we've seen in the press, a candidate who changes views with each read of the daily tea leaves is going to struggle to have a platform to stand on when Election Day rolls around. If you stand for everything, you stand for nothing.

The idea that a brand must stay focused on its core message and deliver it authentically becomes both more critical and more challenging as the brand gets bigger and the number of customers grows along with its profits. That a brand must have the stamina to stay the course is equally important. Take Amazon, for example. The brand took a few punches of late from investors who bemoaned its short-term results stemming from a few less than complimentary reviews of its e-reader, the Kindle Fire. CEO Jeff Bezos set the record straight when he made clear that the company manages for the long term, that its initiatives are based on what its most loyal customers want and need, and that it will not stray from its course of action—a position, by the way, that keeps Amazon among the world's leading growth companies.

On a personal note, the point of this chapter was brought home during a recent family visit to Disney World. Yes, there were lines and throngs of people, but they (we) were also happy, smiling people. The experience that Walt Disney envisioned so many years ago remains alive and well and thriving because even as the company has grown bigger, as it has expanded globally and added new businesses to its original stock in trade—that noble-hearted mouse—the folks at

the helm have never lost sight of what the brand represents; as Walt said, "a source of joy and inspiration."

The best brands have a sense of what they are and the sense to stay focused on it, whether it's Justin Bieber, who kept his sweet boy nature in the face of a silly baby-mama drama, or Bank of America, which admitted that its extra fees were not in line with its user-friendly promise. If a brand wants to stay ahead, it has to know what it stands for and stay the course. (Okay, I'll say it, "May the force be with you.")

IBM CONNECTS BRANDING INITIATIVE TO BRAND PURPOSE AS ONLY IBM COULD

Do you know what to do with all that heat that comes off your computer when it's not in use? IBM knows. The big, smart brand has figured out a way to pool the idle computer time of the thousands of members of its "People for a Smarter Planet" campaign on Facebook and use it to fight childhood cancer, find treatments for AIDS, research clean energy solutions, and support many other things that will benefit humanity. I heard about this big, smart initiative at an Advertising Week CMO Roundtable I attended during which Ben Edwards, VP of digital strategy and development for IBM, was among a number of folks who talked about their company's latest marketing projects.

What struck me about IBM's project was not just how fascinating the whole idea sounded, but how brilliantly the idea linked to the IBM brand purpose, which, in a nutshell, is to use its technological smarts to help make the planet work better in areas like health care, education, environmental causes, and other areas of critical need. Now, lots of companies have a brand purpose, as they should. But what gives IBM its edge is the number of proof points it has—initiatives that bring its purpose to life in very simple ways and in ways that capture the imagination with their "wow" factor. In a world where "a brand is as a brand does," IBM proves this maxim very well.

For example, there's your computer sitting on your desk, all alone in the room, blinking and binging, as you walk out the door. Join People for a Smarter Planet and this blinking and binging computer can help you do good deeds while you're out doing other things. How smart is that, not to mention easy? Or, as the site on Facebook states, "Each of our activities lets you con-tribute your brain power, your data-gathering ability or your idle computer time to help crack a problem that matters to you . . . and shows you the impact you're making in real time." Say "IBM," and the first thing people will think is "computers, networking, or connectivity." What makes the People for a Smarter Planet initiative so effective is that it builds on this association. It's aligned with what consumers already associate with the IBM brand, which in this case is to use technological connectivity to literally connect thousands

of people to build a super computer of ideas for solving the planet's most pressing issues.

On the "wow" side are proof points that we may only read about and that don't influence us directly but that are credible because we know IBM has the skill set to make them happen. (Hey, it built a computer that competed on *Jeopardy!*) For instance, IBM and the Vermont Electric Power Company (VELCO) announced an agreement to build an intelligent fiber optic and Carrier Ethernet communications and control network across the state of Vermont. Spanning more than 1,000 miles, this advanced fiber communication network will connect transmission substations to Vermont's distribution utilities, delivering reliable electric services and the capabilities required for the state's future Smart Grid—an innovative model for the rest of the country to build twenty-first-century Smart Grids. A little farther south, in Florida, fans who attend Miami Dolphins football games and other events at the Sun Life Stadium will find more-organized traffic, better services, and an improved experience thanks to the on-the-spot data analysis provided through an IBM Intelligent Operations Center on the IBM SmartCloud. And, for those attending a different level of athletic event, Rio de Janeiro is transforming its emergency response system in preparation for its hosting of the World Cup and the Olympics, all with the help of IBM's smart solutions.

A company's purpose is to help people understand not just what it sells, but what its brand stands for. IBM makes clear that its purpose is to solve problems that affect all of us, day in and day out, in ways small and very, very big, across the planet. A smart brand and incredibly smart branding.

> *A company's purpose is to help people understand not just what it sells, but what its brand stands for.*

WHY, ALTHOUGH HE'S MISSED DEARLY, APPLE WILL DO PERFECTLY FINE WITHOUT STEVE JOBS

The guard may have changed at Apple with the reins being handed to Tim Cook just prior to Steve Jobs's passing. And the world may be vigilantly watching every move made by this megabrand's new guardian, from the naming of the new iPad to his choice of clothing, to his decisions to dip into Apple's incredible stash of cash to pay out dividends. Some critics claim that, without Jobs's direction, Apple will become just another retail company, vulnerable to the quickly rising competition. From this branding professional's (and Apple advocate's) point of view, I say hold your horses.

Remember way, way, way back, when, in 2006, Apple launched a branding campaign called "Get a Mac?" Seems like eons ago, which in technology years it is, but in this specific initiative, it was proved that the Apple brand was so sure of its brand's voice and personality that it could go out and do a casting call for it. In this case, it was able to capture its "who" in the real persona of actor Justin Long, who pleasantly and with great assurance took on an inept "PC Guy" to point out the difference between Apple technology and its users and PC technology and its users. I bring this up to make a point about what makes a strong brand strong and why I think that the Apple brand will succeed even without Steve Jobs.

While any brand can come up with a list of adjectives to describe its "brand-ness," Apple has gone deeper in its psychological assessment. Long before it became the right thing to do in terms of brand building, Apple answered the questions "who" and "why" about itself. While we might define the Apple brand as cool, innovative, and friendly, the reason the brand resonates the way it does is that those who work inside the organization have a greater recognition of the brand-ness than can be summed up in just four or five words. As a brand, its self-awareness is first rate. In fact, after the launch of the "Get a Mac" campaign, *Advertising Age* ran an article about a study undertaken by the interactive research firm Mindset Media, which demonstrated that in its casting, the Apple brand team knew just what kind of person would represent the Mac and the Mac user. It had to be a person

who showed openness to new ideas and new ways of doing things. These are people who "Think Differently," as an Apple campaign from the prehistoric era of the 1990s illustrated. Apple customers are people who are intellectually curious and more comfortable with emotions than the average person. They are people who are more likely to drive hybrids and buy organic food, and they probably replace their sneakers more than other people do. Oh, and they're perfectionists.

Most organizations have a set of guidelines for tone and manner and color and typeface. This all helps, but unless everyone in the organization can live what makes up the "ness" of its brand and deliver on it brilliantly in the marketplace, chances are the brand will have a difficult time helping consumers get a sense of "who" they're dealing with. Steve Jobs not only created a strong vision for the company, he instilled his vision into the culture of the company: passion for the perfect marriage of design and functionality, and passion for ensuring perfection in everything Apple does. Apple's is a culture built around delighting the customer. As long as those who carry on continue to live the brand as Steve Jobs lived it, I don't think Apple enthusiasts will have anything to worry about. No one can predict what will happen, but I'm not turning in my (new) iPad anytime soon.

MARKETERS THINK PINK IN OCTOBER

In the month of October, leaf-peepers enjoy vivid reds and yellows, and trick-or-treaters favor spooky oranges and blacks. But for brand builders, the color of the month is pink—a powerful link to breast cancer awareness. Hundreds of brands have incorporated breast cancer awareness into their October marketing efforts. From applesauce to appliances, power tools to paper towels, in packaging and product design, pink branding is everywhere.

In 1974, First Lady Betty Ford began talking openly about breast cancer. Since then, the struggle for a cure has become a successful and dynamic brand story. The reason? There has been a relentless focus on the most basic rules of brand management, from the single-mindedness of its purpose, to the support of relevant brand partners, and, not least of all, to the strategic use of the color pink as an incredibly powerful branding application. It is, perhaps, because of this pretty color that the goal of curing breast cancer has become more well known than any other philanthropic cause in its attempt to generate awareness and advocacy.

Anyone in the brand business will tell you that the first step in gaining an edge is to start with a simple promise that is meaningfully different to the consumers you want to reach. In this case, it's the clear and singular fight to eradicate breast cancer—not cancer in general—that is at the core of this brand's promise. Add to this promise the unfortunate fact that there is almost no one, myself included, who hasn't been personally affected by watching a loved one do battle with the disease, and you've got a strong and motivated target audience for the message. The mastery of the initiative, however, is in the branding—the "-ing" being the key. A brand is what something stands for in the minds of consumers; the branding, the symbols, and the activities bring the idea to life in order to reinforce this association. What separates the good brands from the really terrific brands is an understanding of where and how to use a branding application to its greatest advantage. These are called "power apps" for obvious reasons.

And that is where pink comes in.

Susan G. Komen for the Cure introduced the color in 1982, but pink as the mother of all colorful power apps really took off in 1992 when Estée Lauder began distributing pink satin ribbons in stores. Year after year, the branding has been consistent and, as a result of some enduring strategic partnerships, has grown in strength and recognition. Estée Lauder's Breast Cancer Awareness Campaign is only one of several major corporate initiatives at work for the purpose of "pink." Avon, with its tag line "the company for women," has raised more than $500 million over the last two decades through the Avon Foundation Breast Cancer Crusade. The Avon Walk for Breast Cancer is one of its most significant and inspiring branding events. Yoplait, which targets women ages 35 to 54, also aligns its business strategy with a pink, cause-related branding strategy. Its Save Lids to Save Lives campaign has been tremendously successful in raising awareness of the disease while raising millions of dollars for research.

And with the keen understanding that husbands, boyfriends, sons, and fathers are part of the breast cancer demographic equation, the NFL has also committed

to pink as a branding application, reaching millions of viewers with its message every weekend. As part of the program called "A Crucial Catch," which encourages mammograms for all women over the age of 40, players and on-field personnel draw attention to the issue by wearing pink headgear, footwear, and other accessories during the month of October.

There is increasing evidence that companies want their brands to be seen as having a purpose beyond the products or services they provide. There is also increasing evidence that the companies that succeed best in these endeavors ensure that there is a meaningful link between what they stand for and the purpose they espouse. But the reason breast cancer awareness as a brand purpose has been supported by consumers is as simple as Branding 101: The promise is simple to understand. The message is relevant to an audience that is ready to listen and participate. And the branding—anchored in the ownership of the color pink—is consistently emphasized from usage to usage. While all of us would like to see a cure for this disease, the fact that the brand and its branding have been successful in raising both awareness and funding is a step in the right direction.

HYUNDAI'S CHALLENGE TO MERCEDES: SHOULD
EITHER BRAND BE NERVOUS?

When I travel on business I like to rent different types of cars to see what's out there. What astounds me is that no matter what brand or model, the features on the insides of the cars are all pretty much the same: satellite radio, navigation systems, heated seats, air controls for both driver and passenger. It's hard to remember what you're driving. Now, the auto industry is much like many other categories of brand in that it's hard to distinguish one from another based on just the product features. A company's got to do something really different to set itself apart, something beyond just the table stakes. That's why it caught my attention when Hyundai came out with the Equus. The Korean automaker's new luxury car comes equipped with standard features—the standard features of a Mercedes-Benz S550 with one, no, make that two, exceptions: the Mercedes brand price tag, and the Mercedes brand name.

A number of folks asked me whether I thought this was a smart move for Hyundai, a brand known more for its affordability than anything else, and whether Mercedes, or any other luxury car brand for that matter, should start to worry. It's an interesting, not to mention long-winded question, but from my branding point of view, the answer—or answers—are pretty straightforward.

First question first. I do think this is a smart move for Hyundai. Even if the company sells ten of these well-equipped models, it will have gotten consumers to think of its brand within a whole new framework. "Wow, did you hear about that Equus? It's got everything a Mercedes has and it's $20,000 less!" When you're a challenger brand, which Hyundai is (against companies like Honda, Toyota, and Ford, that is), it takes a bold step to move up in the minds of consumers. People will now have another metric against which to compare auto brands. Hyundai can put the same stuff into its cars that Mercedes does, but for less, which says something about the company's engineering acumen. The Equus, if nothing else, will help differentiate Hyundai from others in its league. And in a world where competition in every brand category is only increasing, identifying a relevant way to set your brand apart can only help.

As for the second part of the question, well, a car has never been about the "stuff," all those standard features. A car, like clothing, jewelry, boats, or kitchen appliances, is more than the sum of its parts. It's about what the stuff *says* about the person driving it. It's the intangibles that differentiate one brand of car from another. Cars fall into what those in the industry call badge brands. Those who drive a Mercedes-Benz make a conscious decision to pay top dollar for their badge-brand of prestige.

This is not to say that the Mercedes-Benz isn't a fantastically engineered machine, full of luxurious details, and an absolute pleasure to drive. However, the branding lesson for this top-notch company, or any other luxury car company for that matter, is that it cannot rest on its laurels. As features like sophisticated sound systems, heated seats, multiple airbags, and GPS become standard features, Mercedes is going to have to keep a couple of steps ahead in its innovation. Complacency is not an option for any leader brand. Look what happened to Sony. It thought Samsung could never catch up, and Samsung is now one of the hottest brand names in Sony's category.

On a similar note, in this era of non-conspicuous consumption, when Target and Walmart have become brand badges for those who can afford Saks and Neiman Marcus, companies that represent prestige brands are going to have to work extra hard to make sure that the entire experience of the brand is worth its weighty title and price tag. Consumers' expectations for special treatment will only rise as prices on similarly featured goods and services fall. They'll want the reassurance that, however intangible, the price-to-value ratio of their purchase is significant.

Bottom line, kudos to Hyundai for doing what challenger brands should do. It takes a bold move to help consumers see a brand from a different perspective. And, it's a bold move to compare your brand to another that sells for tens of thousands of dollars more. Only time will tell if the number of consumers who flaunt Equus badges can change the meaning of prestige in the eyes of car buyers. Until then, if I were Mercedes-Benz, I'm not sure I'd lose any sleep. I would be careful, however, not to fall asleep at the wheel of innovation or superior service.

AMERIPRISE UNDERSTANDS THAT TRUST IS THE TRIGGER POINT IN EVERY RELATIONSHIP AND FOR EVERY BRAND

Given my profession, lots of studies, reports, and white papers cross my desk. While many are worth reading, occasionally there is one that really strikes a chord, so much so that it's worth writing about. In this case, it was the summation of a survey taken by the global public relations firm Weber Shandwick having to do with consumer trust in companies (or lack thereof). The findings revealed that nearly 70 percent of consumers would avoid buying a product if they did not like or trust the parent company. Over 67 percent of people now check labels to see who the parent company is, and over 56 percent do research on a company before they set out to make a purchase. In another report of equal note, this one put together by Y&R, it was found that between 2009 and 2011, the average trust factor for corporations fell from 51 percent of the population to a pitiful 23 percent. Pitiful, but not shocking. The fact that brand names in the financial sector were the hardest hit also came as no shock. Times, we all know, have changed. Where trust was once seen as a "must-have" for a brand to be relevant to consumers, today it's a way for a brand to differentiate itself.

With this notion in mind, I put in a call to Kim Sharan, the president of financial planning and wealth strategies, and chief marketing officer at Ameriprise, America's largest financial planning company and an institution that, by the way, never took a bailout or asked for one and is doing just fine. I wanted to get her take on the marketplace, specifically relative to brands in the financial services industry, and learn how Ameriprise has been able to keep its cool and its clients, even in the most recent rocky economic times.

> **ALLEN ADAMSON:** Given all that's happened over the past decade, I believe that authenticity plays a much more critical role in how a company is perceived. Who a company is, what it stands for, must register as absolutely genuine, especially in a relationship-driven business such as yours. Tell me how Ameriprise sees itself in this respect and how you came to where you are.
>
> **KIM SHARAN:** In our research, we've found that consumers are looking for someone and something to believe in. As we started looking at our

story, at the company that is Ameriprise, we found that by going back to our beginnings, we had an interesting and entirely relevant story on which to build our brand. We felt that having gone through many evolutions and so many name changes, it was time to tell this story. Ameriprise got its start soon after the Panic of 1893. John Tappan, a 24-year-old lawyer, had a dream to help ordinary Americans plan for a secure financial future. He founded the company in 1894, and we use this strong, simple idea as the basis for our current brand campaign. It's entirely relevant to what's happening in our country today.

AA: So when you think about what you stand for to consumers today, it goes back to where you started—helping average people recognize their financial goals. It's authentic to your company, part of your DNA, which makes it believable. More than this, it's such a fundamentally simple idea, which means that not only is it easier for consumers to understand what you represent but, more important, perhaps it helps the people inside Ameriprise know what and how to deliver on the promise.

KS: That's right. If you find something that's already real and true about your brand and build on it as opposed to saying, "Hey, what do we need to be today?" it flows naturally from the inside out. And this "inside-out" dynamic has taken on a whole new meaning at Ameriprise. Over the last couple of years, we have focused maniacally on creating a great brand experience for the three key constituents we serve, beginning with our employees and our advisors. They're the face of our brand. If they're not true believers, if they're not advocating for the brand, it doesn't matter what I or anyone else here says. What matters is their perception of the Ameriprise brand.

AA: Very often a company looks to define itself with adjectives—accessible, user-friendly, intelligent, and such. This doesn't go nearly far enough to crystallize who the brand is, especially a brand built on individual relationships.

KS: Everything we do is about relationships, especially a client's relationship with money. Money is a funny thing. It's an emotional topic. In 2006 we introduced our unique approach to financial planning, and one of the things our advisors do better than anyone on the street is listen. In that very first connection with a client, an advisor listens and learns about this individual's relationship with money. It's a key part of our process. When we look at how our clients experience us, it's through the relationship they have with their advisors. It's a completely different marketing challenge than, say, with a packaged goods brand where the product is a tangible asset. The key tenets of Ameriprise are embedded in the idea of the relationship, the individual experience. Everyone's dream is personal and everyone deserves a personal plan. It's not about filling out a data sheet. It's about listening and putting the clients' needs first. And trust is the trigger.

SNL, THE MUPPETS, AND *SESAME STREET* KNOW
PURPOSE IS AT THE HEART OF GREAT BRANDS

"When people go to a Muppet movie, they don't say, 'Gee, I can't wait to see a human.'" Oh, Kermit, you've always been so smart. Smart, too, are the branding folks who have monitored this group of merry characters over the past many decades. Introduced to the world at large on both *Sesame Street* and *Saturday Night Live* (*SNL*), these "marionette/puppets," created by the wonderful Jim Henson, have endured as a brand for a great many reasons. But it struck me as I watched their performance on a recent *SNL* that the primary reason the Muppets, as a brand, have endured so powerfully is the same reason that brands like *SNL* and *Sesame Street* continue to endure so powerfully. Simply said, they are brands that know what they stand for, who they are, why they do what they do, and why it's important—a branding dynamic that branding professionals have identified as being paramount to long-term brand success.

I remember first being introduced to Kermit, Miss Piggy, Elmo, and the rest of the bunch while watching *Sesame Street* with my kids about, well, just one decade ago. My kids loved this ragtag bunch because they were engaging and funny, and just the right kind of funny-looking. These characters had personalities my kids could relate to in one sweet or silly way or another. I, and most adults I know, love the Muppets because they're engaging and funny and take on the travails of the world with just the right kind of optimism and determination. They have personalities *we* can relate to. The Muppet brand has carried on, now under the watchful eye of the Walt Disney Company, as a result of knowing what it represents to people and never wavering in its brilliant execution or veering from its purpose to make us laugh at ourselves through the idiosyncratic behavior of its denizens.

Now back to where I originally met Grover and Big Bird and Fozzie Bear. My kids loved *Sesame Street* because it was spirited and filled with age-appropriate humor, along with delightful music and storytelling. I loved *Sesame Street* because it made my kids giggle and helped give them a love of learning. (I knew they were learning, even if they weren't aware of this benefit.) Over the years, as its friendly neighborhood locals have moved in and out, and as the world

has changed around it, this PBS mainstay has stayed relevant to every new era of preschooler, evolving its cultural references and format to fit its audiences' needs. The brand's purpose, to help children become better prepared for school—and life—has never veered off course.

On the other end of the audience spectrum, the *SNL* brand continues to win acclaim for the same reason: it knows its purpose, why it's on the air, and why it's important to its long-standing fans. For those who've worked the Saturday evening night shift, *SNL* is, of course, the sketch comedy and variety show that, long before Jon Stewart and Stephen Colbert, took on the role of TV standard-bearer for poking fun at American culture and, especially, politics. Almost as long running as *Sesame Street* (36 years and counting), those managing the brand know that pushing the envelope on edgy parody is what's expected. With the exception of a couple of early seasons (when those at the top learned what happens when you go *off*-brand), the show has hit the mark, its consistently high ratings as solid evidence. To this day, there's no better barometer of who and what is hot (or not) in our crazy world than the *SNL* line-up of hosts, skits, and musical talent.

And this brings me full circle: Jason Segel, very hot actor, musician, and, yes, puppeteer who, along with the motley costars of the newest Muppet movie (which he cowrote), hosted the *SNL* that inspired me to write this. While singing a song together with Kermit, Miss Piggy, Rowlf, Fozzie, and Gonzie, he helplessly tries to explain to them that he's supposed to be hosting the show alone. The sketch brought a smile to my face, a smile to the face of my two post–*Sesame Street*–age kids, and, I can only assume, a smile to the face of everyone else watching. Three brands, all very successful because each knows who it is and why it does what it does: each consistently delivers on its simple purpose in fresh and relevant ways to each new (and old) generation of viewers. Pigs in space, anyone?

PROMOTING GOOD WORKS IN GOOD TIMES (AND BAD)

When the economy goes bad, can companies still afford to be good? This is a question that comes up every time there's a dip in the Dow. It's a question that has rational underpinnings, of course. When a company is in the midst of cost cutting and downsizing to keep its shareholders happy, shouldn't it be shelving initiatives that have to do with corporate responsibility until better times return? The answer, as if you hadn't guessed, is no. In fact, during times of economic doubt and uncertainty, as consumers compare and contrast brands and carefully deliberate where to spend their dollars, they're taking into consideration not simply value as in "price-value," but the intrinsic values of the company. This trend toward good citizenry on the part of corporations has been trending up for quite a while, and there are two critical reasons.

First of all, consumers can see everything, not just the product on the shelf, but the ingredients that go into the product (are they environmentally friendly?), the ingredients in the packaging (are they environmentally friendly?), and the way the products get to the store (was the truck environmentally friendly?). While corporate infrastructure and operations used to be invisible, there is nothing in the world today that is invisible. What goes on behind the scenes is not only visible, it's illuminated. Second, although it may have started with the younger generation, consumers of all ages are becoming more passionate about supporting companies that do the right thing. They vote with their wallets. Not only this, they want to work for companies that do the right thing. The best and brightest college graduates will select employers based not just on what the company does, but on who it is, and why it does what it does—what the company believes in, its values.

The bottom line is that in a market where one cereal is not all that different from another, where one insurance company differs only by degree from another, who a company is and what it stands for can play a significant strategic role in helping consumers make purchase decisions. It helps them differentiate beyond product benefits. And it helps brands set themselves apart as people look for solutions to the social, environmental, and educational

challenges that affect the planet and its citizens. Good citizenry has become a critical dimension in ensuring that a brand gains the leading edge.

Now, let's be clear. I'm not talking about gratuitous gestures or acts of kindness. If you are going to incorporate a goodness dimension into your brand promise, like any aspect of branding, it has to be appropriate to your brand's character and linked intrinsically to your business strategy. It has to be a genuinely good fit and be seen as authentic. For example, while the refreshing taste of Coca-Cola will always be at the heart of the brand experience, the folks at the company understand that consumers are making brand choices based on criteria that go beyond how its iconic beverage tastes. Talking about the need to make social initiatives central to its business and its long-term branding strategy, Neville Isdell, chairman of the board of Coca-Cola, made this point evident. "The key ingredient in Coca-Cola is water," he said during a speaking engagement, "so that's our number one priority. With regard to reducing our footprint and expanding our handprint, we are making clean water available to the communities we serve through partnerships" with organizations that include the World Wildlife Fund, the US Agency for International Development, and the Gates Foundation.

Acknowledging in word and deed that companies must shoulder some of the responsibility, Coca-Cola has made a strategic business decision to link what it makes to making the world a better place. It has become part of "who" the company is and what it wants to be known for. The objective of this alignment of philanthropy and business is to help consumers differentiate the brand from the others in the beverage aisles.

A literal and figurative smart move, too, is IBM's linkage of its business model and do-good efforts as a way to differentiate its brand of technology. With its promise to "build a smarter planet," IBM launched a forward-thinking initiative that continues to actively demonstrate its use of technology and brain power to find smart solutions for everything from traffic, to food and health care, to energy and infrastructure. IBM's goodness strategy and its business strategy are one and the same. The same can be said of GE. It was among the first companies to understand the benefits, planetary and otherwise, of connecting what it does to "who" it is, its values, as a way to set its brand apart in the minds of consumers. Its "Ecomagination" efforts have cast a bright and proprietary halo over everything having to do with the company and its many brands. From innovative, energy-saving household appliances, to alternative energy sources, to cleaner jet engines, there is no question that consumers see its constructive and inventive environmental efforts as part and parcel of the GE brand.

Although not quite as overt, similar endeavors are being undertaken by Clorox as a way to set its brand apart from the multitude of cleaning products available. In a session on sustainability and corporate responsibility, Katherine Hagan, marketing director of environmental sustainability for the company, made the point that "going green only works if there is a business case that can be made as well." Most of Clorox's packaging is made from recycled materials, and its line of Green Works, products made with natural, biodegradable ingredients that clean powerfully without harsh chemical fumes or residue, continues to grow, and grow more popular with environmentally conscious consumers.

Smart companies know that doing the right thing is increasingly becoming the right thing to do, and the resulting efforts should not be stopped and started based on economic conditions. Consumers can see behind the curtain and want to align themselves with brands that align themselves with initiatives that make the world a better place. To be effective, "goodness" must be undertaken as a way to help consumers differentiate the brand from others in its category. It must be tied honestly to both the brand and its business, and it must be undertaken for the long term. Companies whose goodness is woven into the fabric of their brands will be those who will do best.

> *Consumers can see behind the curtain and want to align themselves with brands that align themselves with initiatives that make the world a better place.*

FAITH POPCORN PREDICTS A SHE-CHANGE IN
HOW GREAT BRANDS ARE BUILT

Fact: Today, young single women purchase twice as many homes as young single men. **Fact:** Two thirds of undergraduate degrees and 60 percent of master's degrees are going to women. **Fact:** In 2011, all three winners of Google's Science Fair were women. **Fact:** Women currently own 35 percent of start-up businesses. **Fact:** Single women between the ages of 22 and 30 earned 8 percent more than men in that age range in most US cities, and, in a recent survey, 73 percent of men said they had no problem with their spouses being the primary breadwinners.

Get where I'm going? Actually, get where women are going, or actually, have been going for quite some time? The sea change taking place relative to the way women, especially young women, are influencing society, the economy, and our culture is among the many very interesting topics being explored by futurist, author, and CEO of the marketing firm BrainReserve, Faith Popcorn. In her January 2012 issue of *What's Popping @ Faith Popcorn's Brain Reserve*, where she shares the facts stated above, Faith refers to the sea change as a "She-change." Based on her copious research, she says it's exactly what society needs right now, especially after years of roiling markets and boiling mad consumers. Her strong belief is that we need to rely on compassion more than competition and innovation more than invasion. Her prediction is that "the introduction of this new feminine power into all aspects of our lives will bring about a new era of productivity and peace." More than a little intrigued (actually, *really* intrigued) by her findings and her predictions, I decided to give Faith Popcorn a call and find out what she had to say about what "She-change" means for those, be they men or women, whose jobs include building leading-edge brands. Our conversation was, to say the least, lively and very informative.

> **ALLEN ADAMSON:** Part of what it takes for a company to gain an edge in the marketplace is being able to see what's coming around the corner before the competition sees it. Given that this is your business, tell me about "She-change" and what it means in the marketing arena.

FAITH POPCORN: I started talking about the topic of marketing to women over 12 years ago and wrote about it in my book *EVEolution*. People, marketers, didn't want to believe that women would be ascending the way they are. As time went on, and we started to watch the numbers—more women than men going to college, women making more money than men in many instances, the global buying power of women increasing—it became clear that women have loads of money, but that no one is talking to them. It's ridiculous.

AA: Is it about creating separate brands targeted to women, or is it about making a brand's center of gravity female-based?

FP: It's about making a brand, in general, more compassionate, more rounded, creating an opportunity for more communication back and forth. Women love to know the person behind the brand. I'd say Tom's shoes is a female brand. Apple is a female brand.

AA: Why would you say Apple is a female brand?

FP: We did a whole study in which we asked people whether they thought a brand was male or female. We found that 100 percent of respondents thought of Apple as female because its products are beautiful, it's a service-oriented company—people come up to you in the store, they talk to you, they joke with you, they're nice to you. That's a female brand.

AA: Why have most brands been so slow to adapt, especially given the economic indicators regarding women?

FP: I think it's because companies are run mostly by men. I think there's a big fear of women's ascendency, which may be subconscious, and we've found that even some women are uncomfortable with the idea.

AA: Is there a story you can share about a brand you've worked with that has shifted its thinking from masculine to more feminine that has paid out?

FP: Absolutely. We repositioned Jiffy Lube. What we did first was alert management that over 70 percent of the cars that come for an oil change are being driven in by females and that what these women find when they come into the shop is that the toilet seats in the rest rooms are left up, there are *Hustler* magazines in the waiting room, the service guys reach across the laps of these women drivers to check the odometers, they ask them to take sleeping babies out of the car. Things like that. Not just old boy, but rough old boy. So what we did was create maps of the Jiffy Lube retail space to show them what these spaces should look like to be female friendly; keep them extremely clean, have a variety of great stuff to read, have a TV on the wall with appropriate programs. Then, we told them how to change their business practices in small, but meaningful ways, like allowing a sleeping baby to stay in the car while the oil is being changed.

AA: So the company didn't have to make one big audacious promise, but rather a string of small unbroken promises that clearly demonstrated the change.

FP: Women don't believe big promises. They buy peripherally, from the side. I always tell my clients it's like going on a date. You don't ring the doorbell and tell the woman as soon as she opens the door that you want to have sex. She'll slam the door in your face. What you do when she opens the door is tell her how pretty she looks, or tell her that you'd like to have dinner with her. Women do not like to be sold directly. They hate that.

AA: We all know that certain categories are just more male focused than others, except for beauty and maybe fashion.

FP: Yes, but even in fashion there's a male presence. We undertook a project for Nike Women, for example. Nike's tag line is "Just do it." When we asked women what this meant to them, they said it's the male lingo for having sex. If you watch women when they're at the gym, they spend a lot of time looking in the mirror at their booty. They want to look beautiful. So we repositioned the brand idea as "Sweat Beauty" and helped create a line of clothing and shoes that reflected the notion that women aren't just men with little feet. For the record, Nike still doesn't have a maternity line. I guess they don't think of having a baby as a performance sport.

AA: If you were teaching a business class, how would you sum up the lessons learned from your research? How would you counsel branding professionals to incorporate this trend into their business thinking?

FP: I have what I call the Eight Truths of EVEolution: First of all, *are you connecting your female consumers to each other?* Women are more into social networking than men. Helping them connect to each other connects them to your brand. And, second, *if you're marketing to just one of her lives, you're missing all the others.*

AA: Meaning that women wear a lot of hats. They're pulled in multiple directions, and you have to know when and how to talk to them given their many roles.

FP: Exactly. And tap into a woman's economic strength. There's a terrific group of companies called Fifth & Pacific, which includes Juicy Couture and Kate Spade among others, that offers its company stock, with no fees, directly to its customers on its website as part of what is known as a Customer Stock Ownership Plan. It lets women invest in the company.

AA: The really great branding strategy being that if your customer owns stock in your company, she's motivated to want it to do well. So what is the next of your Eight Truths?

FP: *If she has to ask, it's too late.* Ask any husband and you'll know what this means. If she has to *ask* for a birthday present, it's not the same. It's like the way Amazon can predict what a consumer wants next. It's just plain smart. So, the next truth is what we talked about earlier: *market to her peripheral vision and she'll see you in a whole new light.*

AA: Don't make a big promise that you may not be able to keep. This aligns with the fact that in a transparent market you can't fake anything. You can't do cosmetic things to get your point across. Everything has to be authentic.

FP: Women have a sixth sense for detecting when something isn't real. Your brand actions have to be in line with its promise. Okay, next truth is this: *walk, run, go to her, and secure her loyalty forever.* For example, Burger King just launched a fleet of 40 delivery trucks. For a woman stuck at home with a baby and no babysitter, this can make a real difference. Moving on, the sixth truth is that *this generation of women consumers will lead you to the next.*

AA: Not just because they're more socially connected, but because consumers trust other consumers more than they trust brands. Given the enormous strength of social media today, it's even more important to have a story people feel good about sharing.

FP: Right, which leads to the next truth: *co-parenting is the best way to raise a brand.* Create conversations. Ask your customers what's important to them, what they want from your brand. And, finally, *everything matters.* Everything you do counts. You can't hide behind your logo.

AA: A brand is as a brand does. Any brand that looks in the rearview mirror will see this. But, as you know, it's looking ahead that matters.

CHAPTER THREE

To Have an Edge, a Brand's Actions Must Tell Its Story

On a recent evening a little after 8:30 p.m., my son was packing for a two-day field trip with his school that would take him a fair distance from home. He was leaving the following morning. As I walked into the room to see how things were progressing, he informed me that his cell phone wasn't charging. After trying it myself a couple of times (I'm a guy, what can I say?), I realized his cell phone wasn't charging. Had he not been going to be a fair distance from home, I would have waited until the next day to look into the situation, but this was one of those moments when a parent really wants his kid to have a cell phone. I grabbed the phone and ran down the street to the local Verizon store. After examining the phone, the fellow behind the counter told me the input was broken and couldn't be fixed. I'd have to buy a new phone. I agreed, and so he started doing all the things that need to be done when someone buys a new phone, including downloading saved names and numbers. It was now almost 9:00 p.m., and the manager (who was not the fellow behind the counter) went over to lock the front door. At 9:15 my son called me on my cell phone and told me not to forget to have all his photos downloaded. This proved a bit more troublesome and took more time. It was now close to 9:30, and the store had been officially closed for 30 minutes. It was then that I realized that one of the other features that had been on my son's broken phone was the Verizon Family Locator app, which allows, say, a parent, to go to any device with an Internet connection and locate a child. It's a super app. When I told the fellow behind the counter, he said, "No problem," and proceeded to not just install the app, but make sure I could connect to it. It was now 9:50 p.m. During this whole episode, there was never one moment when the fellow who helped me out glanced at his watch, rolled his eyes, or did anything else to express agitation. He did what he needed to do. No, actually, he went beyond what he *needed* to do. He did whatever it took to ensure a great brand experience that went beyond normal expectations.

As you can probably guess, the reason for this little family tale is to make a very important point about building a brand today. A company can talk the talk, but if it doesn't walk the walk, there is no amount of talking that will matter. The Verizon employee in my neighborhood did more than any Verizon advertisement or promotion could have even done to win my loyalty. His actions sold me on the brand.

In this day and age, as consumers become more skeptical, when they have more choices and when they can see and readily share their interactions, smart companies live by the maxim "A brand is as a brand does." The experience of a brand says more to consumers about what the brand stands for than anything else. In what might be called the "experience age," brands that use their actions as a way to communicate their message have a much better chance of gaining an edge—if, of course, their actions are positive ones.

Smart marketers also recognize that this notion, demonstrating intent through action, extends far beyond just doing the right thing in terms of the funda-mental delivery of the brand. As I wrote in the Introduction, there is increas-ing proof that consumers of all ages want a better world and are becoming more motivated to choose brands that improve lives beyond their own. They're actively seeking out brands that do right by the world. Consumers want to do business with companies with which they share values or some deeper purpose. It is critical to this purpose that it isn't a fad or a cause du jour. It has to be intrinsically linked to the idea on which the brand is built. To be effective it must identify some social good that is relevant to the business and its customers and create the actions that bring about this social good on a sustainable, long-term basis. The belief is that companies that link "goodness" with their brands' essential meaning—what it stands for in the minds of consumers, employees, and shareholders—will be companies whose brands experience both stronger brand equity and long-term financial gain.

I received a round of support for this idea during a conversation I had with Marc Pritchard, global brand-building officer for Procter & Gamble. "People are definitely embracing brands that are purpose inspired and benefit driven," he said. "As such, over the years, we've taken the mantle of corporate social responsibility and put it into brand action. That is, we've looked at how to make the social benefit of the brand congruent with its core equity." By way of example, Marc told me about P&G's initiatives with its Pampers brand, the Pampers-UNICEF program, which focuses on eliminating maternal and neonatal tetanus in developing countries. "The benefits of the Pampers product are fitness, dryness, and comfort," Marc explained. "This makes for happier, healthier babies. It makes their lives better and it makes moms' lives better. With the Pampers-UNICEF program, for every package of Pampers a parent buys, P&G will donate the cost of one tetanus vaccine to save the life of a child. What's important to take away from this is that we've aligned the core benefit of the brand—healthy babies—with the societal benefit of the program. If you can't tie the benefit of your actions to the essential DNA of the brand, it doesn't help your revenue or the brand's equity with consumers." Marc's last point is vital to success and vital to a brand's purpose being accepted as genuine, not gratuitous, by consumers. If consumers don't see the intrinsic link between what the brand stands for and its social purpose, they won't buy it, literally or figuratively.

The stories in this chapter showcase companies that fully grasp the meaning of "A brand is as a brand does" and, as such, have gained an edge in the market. Some of these stories have to do with day-to-day branding initiatives that bring life to the brand's inherent benefits, much like my Verizon experience, and others are about companies that show what their brands are for—and about—through their social, or purpose-driven, actions. For those looking for a few pointers on the latter aspect of this subject, take a look at the sidebar.

A BRAND IS AS A BRAND DOES "GOOD"

Purpose, extending a brand's idea to encompass the common good, cannot be looked at as a short-lived activity or a way of taking advantage of a current trend. To be effective, the initiative must address the following questions:

- **Can our social good become a business good? And, can our business good become a social good?**
  The GE brand is built on the idea of "imagination at work," which drives its business units, its people, and the approach to the people it serves. Seeing a natural extension of this idea as a way to solve a broadening social challenge, it has undertaken a significant initiative to revitalize manufacturing in the United States: "GE works by providing jobs for thousands of Americans."

- **What is it that our company does best? What do our customers really care about?**
  To be effective, it is essential to identify some social good that is relevant to your business and customers and through which you can create a competitive advantage. For instance, everything Pedigree does is "for the love of dogs," from basic nutrition to health care. It has instituted a number of purpose-driven actions, from donating food to animal shelters to providing assistance with dog adoptions— very warm fuzzies for pets and the people who love them.

- **Where can you seize a long-term opportunity? How can your actions build sustainable equity?**
  From launching its brand on the simple idea "Think," to its evolution "Building a smarter planet," IBM has looked for ways to use its smarts to change the world for the better in areas ranging from health care to energy to public safety. To make good on its commitment to *do* good, it has embarked on a long-term initiative to help governments—of cities, states, and countries—become more "citizen centric" by reorienting their information technology systems and policies to be more accommodating and user friendly.

- **Is this initiative authentic for us? Will it feel natural for our employees to live it?**
Purpose is not simply a marketing program and should not be perceived or communicated as such. Whole companies are built on purpose, including Whole Foods, which was built on the commitment to sell only the most natural and organic products available. The incredibly successful company has proven that it is possible to do good and do well, if, yes, it comes naturally.

TOP TIPS: LET YOUR ACTIONS TELL YOUR STORY

There's not much explanation required here: In a marketplace where everything can be seen and shared, a brand's actions speak volumes about what it stands for. Experience is all. A brand is as a brand does. The stories in this chapter are about brands that have the edge because of how they behave, not simply what they say. The tips below are meant as guidelines, but if your brand doesn't practice what it preaches, my preaching won't help your case.

- Establish a clear understanding of your brand's purpose. Ensure that your branding unlocks this purpose in ways that exceed consumer expectations.
- Remember that a brand experience must align with a brand's purpose to be seen as credible.
- Feel the data. Use research to guide your branding initiatives, but use your gut to determine what's on brand or off.
- Clarity of brand meaning is efficient. Lack of clarity is expensive. Make sure everyone in your organization understands what it means to "be the brand."
- Brilliant execution eats strategy for lunch. Make sure your brand idea is brought to life in a powerful way across all points of touch, no matter the scale or scope.
- One unfortunate experience with a brand can erase one hundred good ones.
- Don't let your competition define you. Let your actions define you.
- Great branding is like conducting an orchestra. Everything must come together in harmony. Just because you have a great first violin doesn't mean you'll sell tickets.

GENERAL MILLS WALKS THE TALK OF SOCIAL RESPONSIBILITY, AND SCHOOLS EVERYWHERE ARE THE BENEFICIARIES

What university has 90,000 active alumni? What university has brought in over $400 million in contributions since 1996? What university has a rolling event every year that goes from city to city to city across the country and for which registration by joyful enrollees only continues to increase in popularity? That would be Box Tops University. It was introduced by General Mills as part of its extraordinary Box Tops for Education program through which millions of dollars are raised every year to help schools across the country get more of what they need—from books to computers to playground equipment—to meet the educational needs of the children they serve.

The hundreds of thousands of families, friends, and community members who take part in Box Tops for Education, and the hundreds of coordinators who

enroll in Box Top University, are passionate about helping schools succeed and giving students more opportunities to learn. General Mills continues to be passionate about its role in making this possible. From its initial launch, Box Tops for Education has taken off like a rocket as more and more people have looked for ways to make a difference in their communities and as General Mills has expanded the program to make it easier and more fun for them to do so. The company's objective is twofold. First, it's to open a dialog with consumers, to listen, and to learn about what's important to them, their families, and their communities. And, second, it's to sell consumers on the greater benefits of products by linking the products to what General Mills knows is meaningful to consumers.

Smart branding today means knowing what your brand stands for and understanding its purpose beyond the facts and figures. And if there's any company that knows smart branding, it's General Mills, whose iconic brands from Pillsbury to Green Giant to Cheerios and Betty Crocker can be found in the kitchen cabinets of families around the world. General Mills cares about the role its products play in consumers' lives, and it was with this notion in mind that I spoke to Mark Addicks, SVP and chief marketing officer of this world-class company. Here is just part of our conversation about its mega-successful Box Tops for Education program.

> **ALLEN ADAMSON:** There is no doubt that consumers want to do business with companies that have a sense of social responsibility. Sure they care if a product tastes good, or if a battery lasts a long time, or if a car gets super-efficient mileage, but they also care about what the company is doing to make the world a better place, its imprint on the community, so to speak. Before consumers bring a brand into their homes, they want to know everything they can about it. Tell me about how Box Tops for Education got its start and if this was the impetus.

> **MARK ADDICKS:** Box Tops For Education started out as a traditional promotion to address the buy rate and market penetration of what was then called Big G cereals in a small area of Los Angeles. Schools there were financially challenged, and we saw this as a way to tie a promotion to our products and raise money for the schools. You clip a physical coupon from the top of a cereal box, and when you redeem it, money goes to a school. It was immediately successful. Consumers

loved it. Being who we are, the team stepped back and asked *why* it was so successful. It was only when we began to look at the program as a brand, and not as a promotion or a tactic, that it really began to take off. Its brand presence, or purpose, was to give parents a way to invest in their kids' schools, to demonstrate that they cared about and were participating in their children's education. There was a core meaning to this "brand."

AA: So, by looking at it as a brand and not a promotion, you were able to connect with consumers at a deeper level—with their hearts and their communities. There was a benefit that transcended the product.

MA: Right. We saw that if we thought about Box Tops as a brand, it could help us develop a more powerful relationship with our customers, something that went far beyond anything that a coupon or a frequent-buyer program could possibly do. It forced us to think about how General Mills could be more useful to its customers.

AA: There's nothing else like this, and it just keeps growing. How do you keep it moving forward? What do you do to ensure that you keep the momentum going?

MA: Our customers tell us. It's not a matter of adding any particular bells and whistles. They want more brands added to the list of participants in the program. So we've created a marketing platform that's open-sourced. It's not just General Mills' box tops that help raise money for schools, but those from over 175 brands, including companies like Kimberly-Clark and SC Johnson. We also have a digital marketplace where you can earn money for your school while shopping at online stores like Apple, Barnes & Noble, Crate & Barrel, Home Depot, Nike, and others. It's a community-based program that, as you said, tran-scends any one product or company. The beauty is that we touch a lot of households, roughly 34 million. That's a third of US households, and they're not just households with children in school. We have some really wonderful stories of friends, neighbors, and other interested members of the community who wanted a way to "give back" to the community. We've made it easy for them to do it.

AA: Word of mouth has always been one of the most powerful branding applications among parents, especially moms. The Internet and all the tools of digital communication must be having a huge influence on the success of this program.

MA: General Mills, and specifically Box Tops for Education, is hot-wired to social media. We're fully aware that with the evolution of social media, the consumer is in total control. They can raise their hands and give you instant feedback. It's our responsibility to listen, to engage in conversations, and to give them information they want to pass along and share. People will share things that they're engaged in and, more so, that are meaningful to them. Box Tops for Education is not just meaningful, it adds real, tangible value to people's lives. It's another way the General Mills brand nourishes people's lives.

STEVE STOUTE KNOWS JAY-Z AND LADY GAGA, AND HE KNOWS WHAT MAKES FOR POWERFUL BRANDING

I don't know much about rock and roll, let alone rap or hip-hop, but I do know a lot about building strong brands. So it was interesting to hear what Steve Stoute, former music business executive and now marketing executive, had to say about his transition from one challenging industry to the other. Seems that the lessons he learned advancing box-office favorites (including Mariah Carey, Will Smith, Eminem, and U2) put him in very good stead to advance Wall Street favorites. (Stoute was the brains behind Jay-Z's winning Reebok sneaker initiative, Justin Timberlake's "I'm Lovin' It" jingle for McDonald's, and Beyoncé's partnership with Samsung.) From his advice to "feel the data" to his avowal that authenticity is critical in a transparent world, the stories he shared with the audience at a recent Forbes marketing forum were not only fun and fascinating, but struck just the right note (yes, pun intended).

As those of us in the branding business know, getting a sense for what's real, or as Stoute put it, being able to "feel the data," is not something that can be taught in an MBA class. You've got to be hard-wired to appreciate not just what is, but what is about to be. In other words, being able to pick the next Grammy star from the thousands of talented kids out there takes the same well-honed instincts as knowing what great new technological gizmo consumers will need—or want—before they do. To that end, I might just be imagining it, but it seems that since the death of Steve Jobs, there has been more and more talk about intuition as a criterion for success in our overly commoditized, increasingly competitive marketplace. In a column in the October 29, 2011, *New York Times* Sunday Review, for instance, Walter Isaacson, Jobs's authorized biographer, made the distinction between intelligence and genius when it comes to being tuned into the next new thing. Jobs's success wasn't the result of conventional learning, Isaacson wrote, but of experiential wisdom. In other words, numbers won't tell you where to go; you've got to feel it in your gut.

> **More than ever before, authenticity is essential; a brand must stay true to its values and not try to be something it's not.**

Something else Stoute was able to take from the record industry and easily apply to the branding arena is the fact that, more than ever before, authenticity is essential; a brand must stay true to its values and not try to be something it's not. Being both savvier and more skeptical than in times past, consumers definitely call it as they see it—and they see and share everything. Stoute used the latest Kodak branding campaign to illustrate his point. In this initiative, he explained, the company brought on hip-hop stars Pitbull, Rihanna, and Trey Songz, among others, to tout one of its new cameras—a camera that can send your nifty pix directly to Facebook. As Stoute told an appreciative audience, "There's already a camera that does this. It's called a smartphone!"

All kidding aside, Stoute went on to say that when a company tries to present itself as "cool" simply by aligning itself with cool celebrities, it's totally not a cool thing. It's inauthentic, sort of like a nerdy guy going to a frat party filled with football heroes thinking all the girls will assume he's a football hero. (And, this, in part, points to why Kodak filed Chapter 11. Although an iconic brand name, its internal culture didn't allow it to adapt to changes in broader cultural and technological trends.)

Finally, the music industry provided Stoute with yet another significant insight that he's been able to translate successfully into his work with brands: "You can't put consumers in silos." In his book *The Tanning of America: How the Culture of Hip-Hop Rewrote the Rules of the New Economy,* Stoute explains that before hip-hop emerged in the late 1970s, ethnic and racial barriers were rigid and defined by cultural boundaries. Since the popularization of hip-hop, and as the result of other dynamics as well, the lines between races and cultures have become less visible. With stars like Jay-Z, Pharrell, and Lady Gaga, and hip-hop's mainstreaming, there's been a blurring of these cultural and demographic lines, laying a new foundation for marketing. Stoute advised the branding people in the room to look at the market the way music people do: "There's a cultural shift happening. The latest census data shouldn't have surprised us. When people are totally out of sync with what tomorrow looks like, it causes brand damage." From this brand guy's perspective, that's definitely not a cool place to be.

HOW NOT TO SCREW UP A CELEBRITY-BRAND MATCH

Dead celebrities are big business. That's why it came as no surprise to me to learn that more than one billion cans of Pepsi would be adorned with a silhouette of Michael Jackson. While the decision was not without its critics, this announcement came on the heels of a new global partnership between Pepsi and the estate of Michael Jackson. Besides the design on the soda cans, the Pepsi promotion was to include live events and opportunities for fans to get special-edition merchandise. It was as a result of this, and other "accelerated nostalgic" marketing initiatives, that Michael Jackson was able to pay off a substantial portion of his half-billion dollar debt after he passed away. Well, not actually Michael, but his estate, which was able to cash in on the phenomenal Michael Jackson brand name with music sales, concert films, and other super deals. While most people read about this news from a star-gazer's point of view, I, of course, viewed it from a brand-gazer's point of view, the topic being deceased celebrity branding—or, "delebs," as they are called.

The agencies that deal most successfully with deceased celebrities—with their brands, of course—know exactly what will make their initiatives successful. It's not just that a celebrity was a celebrity, but that the celebrity was associated with some image that has a natural relationship with what a particular brand stands for (think of Marilyn as a sex symbol associated with beauty products, Elvis as a rock idol associated with fringed jackets, Lou Gehrig as a baseball legend associated with sports equipment, Einstein as a wild-haired genius associated with educational toys). Those who do the best job on the stage of celebrity branding know what the specific celebrity stood for (and continues to stand for) in the minds of consumers, and they link it to a brand with a similar persona. It's sort of like the marketers who manage Mr. Speedy, the Alka-Seltzer man, Tony the Tiger, or Colonel Sanders. They know what traits these "celebrities" are associated with and, therefore, what will be on-brand and off when they think of branding initiatives.

Now, celebrity endorsement is nothing new in brand building. In fact, using a well-known face, and the well-known character behind it, can be a great way to jump-start a brand and the associations you want consumers to have with

it. I remember when Seagram's wanted to make its wine coolers look less like a product for ladies only and asked Bruce Willis to step in and convince men that the beverage was a very cool way to quench your manly thirst. When using a non-dead celeb, however, it's critical to ensure that the star doesn't do anything to disabuse the brand's reputation—like being stopped by a cop for having a little too much, uh, beverage.

There is something else relative to great branding that is practiced well by dead-celeb brand agents: Great branding doesn't happen when it's done by committee, but rather as the result of a singular focus and an intuitive sense as to what's right or wrong for the brand. Or, as master adman David Ogilvy said, "Much of the messy advertising we see on television these days is the product of committees. Committees can criticize advertisements, but they should never be allowed to create them." Building a powerful brand takes a long view and the absolute right view of what's right for the brand in question. Brands like Amazon, Southwest, Target, and Facebook continue to be leading-edge brands because those who lead their branding efforts remain vigilantly on cue about what's right or wrong for the image. You think Steve McQueen would make a good spokesperson for Pampers, or that Ingrid Bergman should be a virtual model for Juicy Couture? What about Fred Astaire as the perfect guy to introduce the new season of *Game of Thrones?* I think not, nor do those who represent these celebrity brand names. They know what these brands say to consumers, and they make sure to keep them in their proper branding places.

Whether the brand is Ella Fitzgerald or Disney, Elvis Presley or Apple, the same branding rules apply. Know what your brand represents to consumers. Ensure that your branding is consistently in brand character, is brilliantly executed, and delivers as promised. Said another way, smart branding is as much about saying "yes" as it is about saying "no." Back to Michael Jackson: He had a long history with Pepsi, starring in his first Pepsi campaign in 1983. Whether his image will make for a suitable link between Pepsi's past and Pepsi's future will be something only Pepsi's "new generation" can decide.

CAPITAL ONE KNOWS THAT IT'S NOT FUNNY ADS, BUT SERIOUS VALUE THAT WINS AND KEEPS CUSTOMERS

Comedy is hard, or so the saying goes in the theater world. It obviously takes a great deal more talent to make people laugh for all the right reasons than to make them cry. (I wouldn't know. I can't even do karaoke right.) Comedy is also hard in the world of branding. Sure, you can get consumers to laugh at an advertisement, but it's whether they take away what the sponsor of the ad wants them to take away about the intrinsic value of the product or service being touted that really counts. It's a dual challenge, and one that very few companies do effectively. Southwest Airlines is one brand that can pull off this interesting branding paradox: quirky on the outside, but all business when and where it really matters. Capital One is another brand that knows how to use humor to get its point across, at the same time making it clear that the company is serious

about offering no-nonsense financial products designed to make life easier and more rewarding for its customers.

With this concept as a backdrop, I decided to call Jackie Pyke, senior director of brand marketing at Capital One. I should note that I had the pleasure of working with Capital One on a variety of branding projects, so my conversation with Jackie naturally focused around its branding initiatives and the challenge of using humor to build a brand, especially in often-less-than-funny economic times.

> **ALLEN ADAMSON:** I like the Capital One advertising because it's funny but, more important, because it portrays your brand as approachable. It seems like there's a person behind the brand and not just a corporate entity. Given how skeptical consumers have become these days, and with good reason, there's as much attention being paid to the "who" of a brand as to "what" it offers. Tell me why you decided to use humor to help consumers understand "who" Capital One is and how you balance it with the verity of your business.

> **JACKIE PYKE:** Having a distinctive personality is an asset for us, not just because it helps us break through the "sea of sameness" in financial services advertising but, to your point, because it helps us convey something about who we are as a company and as a brand. While we want consumers to think of us as forward thinking, as accessible and innovative, we also want to make sure we communicate that we're serious about the right stuff. One thing that many people may not know about us: As much as our funny commercials stand out from most advertising in our category, we are, paradoxically, a culture of pretty nerdy, analytical types. We test everything and put a great emphasis on metrics—advertising is no exception. We test all of our ads to make sure we are resonating with consumers.

> **AA:** What also comes through in your advertising is that you keep things simple, which is obviously critical in this day and age. Your rewards programs are pretty straightforward and easy to understand. The flexibility and relevance you build into your products speak to the fact that you know that consumers don't like surprises. They want to be able to use their rewards programs in the way that best works for them without too many rules or restrictions. This also underscores something about the persona of the Capital One brand.

JP: We know that the competitive landscape is always changing, and this not only forces us to look for ways to innovate, but to create the easiest, most transparent experience for our rewards customers, both while earning and while redeeming. We've also made it easy for our customers to combine the rewards they've earned through different product relationships. Our objective is to offer something both different from the competition and, of course, of great value. Our Venture Double Miles, our new Cash Rewards, and our High-Yield Checking are all products that represent this thinking. At the end of the day, we know it's the customer who rules and who fuels everything we do.

AA: It's become more and more evident that "a brand is as a brand does." What do you do to get your employees on board with what the Capital One brand stands for? How do you ensure that they deliver consistently across all your touchpoints?

JP: I think this is a really important question. I think 95 percent of this happens through product and experience design work. If we want to make things easy for our customers, we have to make it easy for our front-line associates to talk to them, essentially by creating fair terms and fair solutions to any questions. We succeed or fail largely before we ever get to the front-line associate. But taking it across the finish line does require internal training and raising awareness of how we see our position in the marketplace. Authenticity is so important—it can't be a Brand Department PR effort. In order to be believable, it has to be something that's embraced by and embodied in all of our leaders.

BRIAN WILLIAMS AND AL MICHAELS HAVE A NOSE FOR NEWS, BUT ALSO FOR WHAT MAKES A BRAND STRONG IN A HYPER-NEWS WORLD

As is the case with most conferences I attend, I get to hear what some of the smartest and most innovative chief marketing and branding officers in the business have to say about what's going on in our world. And those hosted by the Association of National Advertisers' Masters of Marketing are no exception. In the past I've had the privilege of hearing AT&T's Esther Lee speak about what's required of technology brands in such evolutionary times, IBM's Jon Iwata share lessons learned from the company's "Centennial" and "Smarter Planet" campaigns, and Cheryl Callan from Weight Watchers explain why the company's stock outperformed the S&P in a year when consumer confidence was at its third lowest level since 1952. All of the discussions bring forth some incredibly instructive perspectives on the intensely competitive business we're in. Not unexpected, certainly, but it's always a terrific venue in which to listen and learn.

What was unexpected, and downright fascinating, however, was when some powerful insight on brand building was offered up by two newscasters and a sports commentator. This occurred during a lively panel conversation about current events between Brian Williams, anchor of NBC's *Nightly News,* and Al Michaels of NBC's *Sunday Night Football,* moderated by Lester Holt, anchor of NBC's *Dateline.* It was noted by Mr. Williams that information, specifically news, is as much a commodity as anything else, or as he said, "We've choiced ourselves out of all creation." When asked by Mr. Holt how, in a world where there are thousands of news sources, what with bloggers and tweeters and myriad cable networks, NBC could possibly differentiate itself, Mr. Williams replied, "It's my super nova theory. We have the best and the brightest people, people who have a passion for journalism and who are authentic journalists. When given so many choices, people want what's simple and understandable, what's true and verifiable. Call it a flight to quality."

Mr. Holt asked the right question, and Mr. Williams gave an answer near and dear to the hearts of every branding professional in the room. In a world of overwhelming choice, consumers today are looking for brands that are not only the best and the brightest in terms of basic value, but that are true and

authentic, and whose employees are passionate about the brand and its purpose. They want brands with character and brands they can trust and believe in.
In other words, consumers are as interested in the "what" of the brand as in the
"who." Whether it's sneakers, diapers, automobiles, or the daily news at stake,
it's the "who" behind the brand that matters. Along with this idea, consumers
are seeking out brands that have a consistent and compelling story. Or as Al
Michaels said, "We've all got the same technology, the same side-line cameras
and such. The difference is in capturing the inherent drama of a sporting event.
As the technology gets more advanced, we need to ask ourselves, 'What's the
story?' We need to use the technology to tell the core story from our unique
perspective. Our people work hard to make it perfect."

Yes, news is news. A dictator is gone. A hurricane has battered the coast. The
Dow Jones is down. A movie star has misbehaved, again. The Green Bay Packers
have won, again. It's a commodity when you look at it from a commodity point
of view. But like all great companies and their CMOs, the folks at NBC don't

look at their offering as a commodity. They do what it takes to differentiate their programming in ways that people care about and that are meaningful and relevant to their audiences. They know that what's drawing people back to NBC is a "flight for quality" and authenticity. In terms of branding fundamentals, NBC has got it right. People want what's simple and understandable and believable. And while the news of the day may not be the best, the people behind the NBC news brand, the "who," definitely are.

RADIO SHACK GOES BACK TO GO FORWARD: BUILDING ON ITS AUTHENTIC "GEEKY" DNA SUPPORTS ITS CREDIBILITY AS AN EXPERT IN TECHNOLOGY

"Crazy Eddie, his prices are IN-SA-A-A-A-A-NE!!!" If you are not from the New York Tri-State area, and if you are younger than, say, 50 years old, you probably have no idea what this quote refers to. Well, it was the last line in a long-running and generally annoying series of television ads for a guy who went by the name of Crazy Eddie who opened a chain of electronics stores in 1971 and did pretty well with them until he didn't. Circuit City, an electronics retailer whose marketing was a bit less frenetic and whose business tactics were a bit more sound, did very well until about 2009, when it didn't and had to file for bankruptcy. Best Buy is now among the top of the brick-and-mortar brands that sell all manner of electronic and digital wares, but it, too, is having its share of challenges as consumers will often use its venues to try out the merchandise before

they go to online sources to make the purchase. Selling electronics, all the stuff that keeps us connected and tuned in, is an insane business these days, and it's not getting any easier. The category continues to confound even the best marketers in the category, what with all the places people can look for information about the latest equipment and all the places they can buy it.

While many retailers in this arena have come and gone, there is one place that still exists and has been in local shopping malls since the 1920s: Radio Shack. This feisty company was founded by two brothers who wanted to provide equipment for the then-nascent field of amateur, or ham, radio. They termed it "radio shack" after the small wooden structure that houses a ship's radio equipment. It was then that Radio Shack latched onto its reputation as the credible, friendly place to get "parts, pieces, wires, and batteries," all the ordinary, but necessary, things that make electronic stuff work.

Well, as we all know, electronic stuff is now digital stuff. And the parts, pieces, wires, and batteries are now being eclipsed by parts and pieces that are almost too small to see and that become obsolete in six months anyway. This change in the marketplace has become a mighty big challenge for Radio Shack, whose name alone doesn't lend much support to its quest to be in the consideration set for consumers seeking new-age technology and the assistance to keep it running. After I had the pleasure of hearing the former CMO of Radio Shack, Lee Applbaum, speak at an industry conference, I decided to get more input about this very daunting category challenge, and what the company is doing to regain its status as the place to go for expert geek assistance with any and all technological products and services. Intrigued by his comments, especially those having to do with the company's mission to reinvent itself by going back to its core DNA, I decided to give him a call to get more of the Radio Shack story. Here are a few bits and bytes of our fascinating conversation.

> **ALLEN ADAMSON:** At the CMO conference you talked quite candidly about how so much of a retail brand's reputation is based on the customer experience and how one of Radio Shack's greatest challenges is ensuring that the people on the front lines—behind the counter—understand what the brand is all about.
>
> **LEE APPLBAUM:** Radio Shack's credibility as a technology expert happens in the stores. This means that what it stands for has to be eternalized

and evangelized by the associates. Radio Shack wants to be seen as the trusted authority for today's technology requirements, and it can't happen if the people who work there don't have a passion and commitment to tinkering and technology.

AA: That's a tough one. It's one thing to be known for being an expert at finding the right battery. It's another to be known as the expert in everything digital.

LA: That's why, as it's moved forward, it's been looking for people who have a true fanaticism for today's technology. They need to be able to not just sell stuff, but to be excited about selling knowledge.

AA: And that's going back to the Radio Shack heritage. It's a point of differentiation that other technology retailers can't own.

LA: Exactly. Being able to advise people about electronics and technology is in the Radio Shack DNA. It's the source of its authenticity and credibility. When it started out in the rebranding efforts, much like Starbucks did, it recognized that it couldn't ignore its roots. It wanted to restore the company's heritage but, at the same time, embrace the reality of the present.

AA: In its efforts to contemporize, what were your thoughts relative to how you would reposition the Radio Shack brand in the minds of consumers who saw your stores as relatively small in square footage and equally small in the types of products you sell and service?

LA: Small played right into our new format. Mobile is small, and we are positioning Radio Shack as the *agnostic* mobile authority. It has all the best products and the best plans, and the associates are experts in the mobile category across the board. When you go into a big-box retailer, you look around for the right department. If you're in a Radio Shack store, you're in the department. The associates are focused on delivering the right product, the right features, and the right plan based on an individual customer's needs.

AA: Given how slowly brands turn, how do you get "mobility" into the brand promise, especially given that neither word in your brand's name implies mobility?

LA: It's been an uphill battle. While the marketplace has been rough, to say the least, Radio Shack has been very proud of its performance, particularly relative to the peer set and to broader retail in general. It's discovered that the challenge of the name has been outweighed by the inherent equity of the brand's authority in technology and electronics. What research showed was that Radio Shack stands for "knowledgeable, geeky associates who connect me with products and services that improve my life." When we launched the campaign "The Shack" a few years back, it was based on making people aware of the full spectrum of products the company sold and serviced. We didn't have to make them aware of its authenticity as experts in the technology field. We wanted people to know *what* they could now buy, not *why.*

AA: Authenticity in today's marketplace is the key to success. Everything is transparent and everyone has something to say and the means to say it. If you don't make good on your brand's promise, the whole world will know.

LA: That's why, to go back to the start of our conversation, Radio Shack is focusing its energies on its employees. They have to be knowledgeable about what they sell and passionate about what they do. It's the customer experience that will cement Radio Shack's credibility and its authenticity as the original geeks.

WHAT IT TAKES TO KEEP "BADGE" STATUS IN A ROCKY ECONOMY

Back during the last recession, when many luxury brands thought it was time to pack it up and go home, there was a cartoon in the *New Yorker* that hit home for many consumers. In it, a couple of ladies are looking at a store window plastered with "Half-price!" and "Big Sale!" signs. One says to the other, "Finally! Cheap is the new black."

This cartoon captured a universally held sentiment in the silly sophisticated way that has always distinguished this magazine's talented humorists and their take on social events. However, sentiments like these are no laughing matter for either the companies that are the target of the chuckles or the consumers who are made to feel embarrassed about the brands they once coveted and purchased.

What does a rocky economic landscape mean for companies whose brands go from being badges of the privileged lives their consumers lead to being badges of conspicuous consumption? What happens when well-heeled shoppers ask luxury store personnel to put their purchases in brown paper bags like some new form of pornography?

The best advice is not to jump to conclusions. Luxury brands like Hermès, Rolex, Frette, Porsche, and Graff have always had a place in the market. And they always will, if the consumers they want to attract consider the brands worth the exquisite price point. In other words, brands in this category must deliver on the brand's promise exquisitely. When the economy takes a dive, the wealthy will still make purchases, but they will not dive for their wallets unless luxury companies prove their value by delivering both a product and the service that complement the name on the tony label.

When the economic conditions are less than stable, this is the time for luxury brands, if anything, to up the ante. Put on the gloves—the white gloves, that is. Offer a level of service beyond expectations. Reestablish your right to be in the stratosphere. Taking a middling or waffling position will only muddy the waters. You'll be better off being considered a brilliant niche brand rather than a middling mass-market brand.

While long-standing luxury brands will most likely be fine if they continue to deliver tangible quality and the high level of service well-heeled consumers expect, some other brand categories that consumers see as badges of their status in life will find it increasingly difficult to survive in what has become the "new normal," the era of non-gratuitous spending. These are the brands that represent not just big money, but a big lack of concern for the environment and society. Suburban McMansions, houses that are expensive to build and main-tain and are big just for bigness' sake, are now seen as wasteful extravagances. (Small is the new big thing?) And, manufacturers of burly cars and trucks will probably find it almost impossible to convince drivers to feel anything but em-barrassed about a vehicle that gets four miles per gallon. It's amazing how many drivers once believed they needed SUVs and other gas guzzlers to keep ahead of the Joneses. This category, now on consumers' "least wanted" brand list, has been replaced by another sort of badge brand: the practical hybrid or the smart car, or even the luxury vehicle that's now known for getting great mileage.

The way consumers view brands always shifts with the economy. Given the transparency and speed of information exchange created by social media, consumers will become increasingly careful about their brand choices; however, value will always be a defining metric. There is nothing wrong with a company that offers a genuinely high-end product if it delivers what's expected and as promised. While there may be times when it's challenging to be in the luxury brand business, just stay the course and do what you need to do to prove your value. And, anyway, there will always be other things that will amuse the cartoonists at the *New Yorker.*

THE HARDEST PART OF UNITED'S MERGER WILL BE
MAKING PEOPLE HAPPY—THE EMPLOYEES, THAT IS

Mergers happen. It has been a marketplace dynamic as long as there have been markets. And it has always represented one of the thorniest of branding challenges, the merger between United Airlines and Continental Airlines being no exception. I've been flying on United since it joined forces with Continental in 2011, and I'd like to offer up my review of the situation, from a brand professional's side of the aisle, that is.

The first step in the merger of these two companies was the part no one but the bigwigs saw. Let's move on. I wasn't involved. After this, the news of the merger was announced and the press argued the pros and cons, with consumers adding their pros and cons relative to which airline they preferred. Next came the

cosmetic changes. The iconic United "tulip" logo was replaced by a combination of the Continental globe and the United name in its newest typeface. It appeared on airplanes, in airport signage, in frequent-flyer lounges, on websites, and everywhere else a logo is required. This was merely a tactical initiative, and other than griping from graphic artists and those in charge of the logistics, it wasn't that big a deal.

Then the real challenge began. The two airlines' infrastructures were merged, including operations, frequent-flyer systems, and online activities such as reservation and flight-status information. This step was more complicated than just making the cosmetic changes. There were blips in the new system that aggravated customers, especially those who were frequent flyers on one airline or the other, along with all the other annoyances one would expect in the mashing of logistics. This challenge, however, was easy compared to what marketers know is the most difficult part of the merger of two companies: deciding what will be the core idea of the new brand. What do you want consumers to associate with your brand and, most challenging of all, how are you going to instill this idea in your employees? It is with the employees that the rubber meets the road or, in this situation, where the friendly skies happen.

The most critical issue in this or any merger is to get the employees—new and renewed—on board. They've got to feel motivated to deliver whatever core idea is established for the brand, to get their heads and hearts around whatever this is. It's the employees who will be charged with delivering the brand experience. If they don't buy into the promise and feel personally engaged and excited, neither will the passengers.

> **The most critical issue in any merger is to get the employees—new and renewed—on board.**

I'd say that what United needs is an idea similar to the one that Avis used to build its brand when it saw the competition in the fast lane. The simple, sticky notion to "try harder" became the touchstone for employees and the impetus for all of their actions and initiatives with the customers. Another great model for United to consider is how UPS employees think about their brand. At the recent ANA conference, Christine Owens, senior vice president of communications and brand management, told her audience, "Manuals and methods don't tell our employees

what to do. Doing the right thing is just part of who they are. Before your customers can express their passion and affinity for their brand, it must connect to
an even more significant ambassador—your employees." Perfect.

However United Airlines chooses to redefine its new brand, the story has got to
be both a cultural and a business engine. While this is a tough enough task for
individual companies, in the case of the merger of two companies, it's exponentially harder. Even more critical, as consumers look to see what value they'll
derive from this marriage, especially when bigger is absolutely *not* deemed
better, scrutiny will be sharp. This is not a situation where the merger is between
two brands people consider equally magical, as was the case of Disney and
Pixar where each brought interlocking strengths to the table. Nor is it a merger
in which one brand definitely elicits more positive consumer response than the
other, as was the case when Hewlett-Packard merged with Compaq. Neither
Continental nor United was considered exponentially better or worse, let alone
any passenger's idea of an ideal airline brand.

The airline industry, generally speaking, has been a category filled with
over-promise and under-delivery. No one, be they from Wall Street or Main
Street, will assume that there is any difference between the old United brand
and the new one unless, of course, there is. There can be. If United finds the
right story and ensures that its employees get it and are provided with the necessary infrastructure to make it a *real-life* story, there will be a difference. Sure,
there will always be things out of the airlines' control. But if there's internal
motivation to make the journey as gratifying for passengers as possible, if employees are empowered to solve problems and the day-to-day experience of the
new United proves much better than the old United, the name will take on new
meaning. But before consumers have reason to believe, employees must get on
board first, with a story *they* can believe in.

THE TARGET BRAND GETS THE SIMPLE THINGS RIGHT (AND A LOT MORE)

Being a typical family man, one of my most frequent weekend activities is a trip to the local Target with, well, my family. We usually end up with a cart full of things, and the only objective I have other than replenishing household staples including paper towels and soap is to keep my kids out of the toy aisle. What makes the acquisition of these household staples more interesting than the mundane exercise it could be is that Target is such a delighting brand experience. I don't just mean because it stocks its shelves with an evolving array of merchandise from hip designers, or that these hip and trendy goods are offered at very competitive price points (cheap chic, I think is the buzz phrase). It's that Target makes even the most basic aspects of the shopping experience delightful. The aisles are wide and clutter-free, making the cart navigation easy. The stores are always bright and crisp and clean. There is always someone in a "red shirt" nearby to help you. And the lines at the check-out move along without long waits.

Now, lest you think I tell this tale of weekend activity just to shoot the breeze, there is, of course, another motive. And that, of course, is to make a point about branding: While building a brand is, without question, more challenging than it used to be given the torrent of new products and the deluge of new media opportunities, there are some things that haven't changed. Key among them is that when you make a promise to consumers, you must deliver consistently from one interaction to the next, down to even the simplest, often overlooked, things. A brand is as a brand does, and Target, in this case, does it all well.

This principle idea took on greater resonance when I attended an ANA Masters of Marketing Conference and, most notably, when I listened to Michael Francis, who was at the time the chief marketing officer of Target. The discount retailer's promise is summed up very nicely in its tagline, "Expect More. Pay Less," or as Mr. Francis put it during his presentation, it's the "balance between making our 'guests' aware of value while emphasizing superior merchandise and a pleasant shopping experience." A distinction such as using the word "guests" when referring to those who shop at Target is yet another example of the brand's ability to get the simplest things right.

Another example is its marketing. Even if you've never been to a Target store, you immediately pick up the Target vibe from watching any of its television ads or seeing any of its print or online marketing. The look is as crisp and clean as its stores, not to mention incredibly engaging, from the whimsical, yet stylish casting, to the music, to the sharp and contemporary production values. You just know it's a Target ad even without seeing the logo. In a world where it gets harder every day to distinguish one brand's message from another's, brilliant execution can be a huge differentiating factor. As can the use of an innovative strategy like Target's continuously updated problem-solution technique. In one series, within a quick ten-second spot, they've identified a common problem—needing a Band-Aid, some school supplies, a hat to hide your bad-hair day—and offered up the solution. Come on in, have a little fun, and take advantage of the extensive merchandise assortment without breaking the bank.

Another of the simple things Target gets right is the consistent use of color, the ubiquitous red and white. Color as a branding application is one of the most basic, but most powerful, ways to help consumers forge associations with a brand. Target ensures that its two-color palette registers well by using it consistently from signage and store décor to the packaging of its name-brand products and the packages it sends out the doors with customers. And, speaking of name-brand products, the super logical design of the easy-to-read and easy-to-open prescription bottles offered by Target pharmacies is such a simple, but delightful, experience you have to wonder why other companies didn't think of it. Well, other companies are not Target.

Until they choose to be occupied otherwise, I will continue taking my family to Target on weekends. And I can only assume, based on past excursions, that the Target experience will continue to delight (even when the kids outgrow the toy aisle). We do "Expect More and Pay Less," and the brand keeps delivering on this promise, down to the most simple of things. As far as being a leading-edge brand, Target is hitting the bull's eye.

WHAT REAL MAD MEN AND WOMEN CAN LEARN FROM THE TV SHOW

Like many marketing people of a certain age, in the early days of my career, I knew some authentic "mad men." For those of us who had this opportunity, the experience of watching the AMC television show is especially enjoyable. The producers and writers of *Mad Men* have captured all of the nuances of the ad agency world back when smoking, drinking, and political incorrectness were as common as thin-lapelled suits, skinny ties, and IBM Selectric typewriters. This authenticity, in combination with well-written dialog and plot lines that reflect current events, from LSD to the NAACP, is what makes *Mad Men* so compelling.

Authenticity is one of the benchmarks of brand success. From the inside out, the voice, the look, the texture, and the behavior of the most powerful brands never veer away from the original intent of the ideas on which they are based. If you were to cover the logo or the brand's packaging or website, mute the sound on a television ad, or hide the brand's name in a print campaign, or even in the design of a retail space, you would still be able to identify the brand. This is what I mean by authenticity.

Brands that get authenticity right work on a gut level. What they do relative to the brand is visceral and feels natural because it is natural. Why is this so important, especially fast-forwarded a couple of generations from the "mad men" days? The world has become increasingly cluttered with products and services, media channels and messaging. As the result of exponential advances in technology and communication, we can do business with billions of consumers from Bangkok to Bangalore faster and more easily than ever before. Companies that know how to get people to quickly and automatically understand what their brands stand for and why they are relevant have a distinct advantage. A company's goal in branding should be to make the meaning of the brand a no-brainer.

I talked about this notion with Thomas Friedman, a columnist for the *New York Times,* who wrote about the dynamics of globalization in one of his early books, *The World Is Flat.* He talked to me about his experiences traveling across this "flat new world" and what he discovered in conversations with corporate, cultural, and political leaders. "People listen with their gut, not their ears,"

MAD MEN

Friedman said. "If you connect with them on a gut level, they'll say 'Don't bother me with the details. I trust you with my gut. Go ahead.' If you don't connect with them viscerally, you can't offer them enough details or statistics to bring them around. You have to connect on a gut level first."

Looked at from a branding perspective, this means that you must be able to define your brand's meaning as crisply and precisely as possible. You must get to its core essence in such a way that you'd be able to do a casting call for the brand and know instinctively which actor to choose for the role. You'd be able to pick out the clothing this actor would wear. You could pick out the house or buy the furniture that would, without a doubt, represent the brand. It's only after you get to this crystallization, this core meaning, that you can align every expression of the brand against it. Once you do this, everything will hang together and give the brand the authenticity required to be seen as credible and authentic. Consumers know authenticity when they see it. And they know when it's missing.

While I hope the situation will have changed by the time this book goes to print, the Gap has been lagging in its category as the result of losing sight of its brand's essential meaning—what it stands for or wants to stand for in the minds of consumers. You can sense this lack of brand definition in the uncertainty of its merchandising, advertising, store designs, and window dressing. Ask someone to define a typical Gap outfit and they'll likely scratch their head. On the other hand, on a recent trip with my family to Orlando and the Universal Studios, I witnessed or, rather, experienced a brand that knows precisely what it stands for when I accompanied my kids to The Wizarding World of Harry Potter. From the corridors of Hogwarts castle, to the incredibly authentic "wand shop," to the Cauldron cakes and Butter Beer, everything was in magical alignment with the Harry Potter brand, including the actors who strolled the area portraying the iconic characters. It was the incredible attention to every detail, the way the whole experience was woven together, that delighted this branding professional. (The kids were equally delighted, of course.)

Another example of a brand that has gained an edge as the result of getting to a precise definition of its meaning: This year while attending a marketing conference in Greenville, South Carolina, I had the opportunity to spend an afternoon at the BMW Performance Driving School, which is close by one of their manufacturing plants. Now, in the spirit of full disclosure, I do not own a BMW, but it took only a short time behind the wheel of one of these incredible driving machines, whipping around curves, swerving back and forth between the cones on the track, skidding, and being able to fully control the spin on wet roads, to understand what makes BMW the "Ultimate Driving Machine." And it wasn't just the performance. From the inside out, the comfort of the seats, the dashboard design, how the stick shift felt in my hand, everything was tied to the idea that drives the BMW brand. The only advice I have for BMW is to consider putting a Performance Driving School in every area of the country.

But enough of a commercial break. The story line here is authenticity. Know what your brand stands for and be able to capture its essence in such a way that all of the branding will happen naturally. If your branding feels like it's coming from one place, if it works in harmony from one point of touch to the next, your brand will not only be seen as credible, but will stand out from the crowd. Despite their shenanigans, even the "mad men" knew this.

BOTH TREES *AND* BRANDING OPPORTUNITY
ARE LAID TO WASTE IN *THE LORAX*

So, despite pans by the movie critics for artistic merit (or lack thereof), *The Lorax*
did pretty well at the box office this past year. It seems that the marketing for
the film, a fable by Dr. Seuss about the need to protect the environment, did
its job. But did the marketing do anything positive for the more than 70 global
companies that wanted in on the eco-friendly message? This branding critic
would like to weigh in on this topic.

There is no question that social marketing can play an important part in any
company's branding strategy. What company doesn't want its brand to be associated with making the world a kinder, safer, cleaner place? The challenge
is to find a cause that fits appropriately with what the brand stands for in the

minds of consumers and then use it to strengthen these associations. It's got to be a genuine fit to help build brand equity, a branding truism being that the company you keep definitely has an effect on how your brand is perceived. For example, Dove and its "Campaign for Real Beauty" makes it clear to millions of girls and women that beauty is more than skin deep: that they should be able to feel good about themselves no matter how tall or short or plump or lean they may be. The fact that it sells hair- and skin-care products makes this message believable. In the same manner, it makes perfect sense that Lady Gaga (yes, she's a brand) would found Born This Way, a foundation to foster a more accepting society in which individuality is celebrated and differences are embraced. The folks at P&G also made a smart cause-marketing decision to showcase Dawn detergent's ability to get grease off dishes when it demonstrated how it was also able to get oil off fragile wildlife following major oil spills in our nations' waterways.

While there are few, if any, companies out there that don't want to be considered environmentally conscious and eco-friendly, there are only a few for whom connecting to *The Lorax* made smart brand-building sense. My opinion is that those in charge of managing the Dr. Seuss—or more specifically, *The Lorax*—brand should have been a bit more selective in their choice of partners for their marketing efforts and vice versa. Chances are the real Lorax would never have chosen to link his brand with Mazda or IHOP or the Pottery Barn. There's no obvious or natural connection. On the other hand, Seventh Generation, Whole Foods, and the US Forest Service are credible choices. Based on what they represent as brands, they're perfect tie-ins and show good brand management on the part of those involved.

Consumers are savvier and warier than ever before. They can see everything and share everything, and any branding initiative that appears less than authentic is bound to be met with skepticism. It's a lucky break for the producers of *The Lorax* movie that parents chose to overlook the Once-ler greediness in the decision to partner with any and every company that opted onto the environmental brand wagon. When Dr. Seuss wrote his prescient tale in 1971, I can only assume that he did not want it to be appropriated for inappropriate branding usage. While movie critics think that this film missed the mark in terms of creativity and inspiration, many branding critics think it also missed the mark in terms of worthwhile brand-building opportunities. To be a long-term asset, partnership marketing must be in alignment with what each partner brand stands for. Much as the Lorax saw his environment go to waste, so, too, may many marketers find signing on to this movie a wasted opportunity to build brand equity.

LRN EMBODIES THE MISSION AND MESSAGE:
A BRAND IS AS A BRAND DOES

They don't freeze. They don't prepackage. They don't over-process. They do things the old-fashioned way. And what they do comes across clearly in their name, in the consistent quality of their delicious products, and in the fast and friendly way the folks behind the counter operate. I'm talking about a family-founded chain of restaurants out west called In-N-Out Burger. People I know can't say enough good things about how incredibly good these burgers are. And that's mostly all that's on the In-N-Out Burger menu: variations of premium hamburgers, along with the stuff you'd naturally expect from a genuine burger joint, like fries and soda and shakes. While I can't comment on this incredibly successful company from a personal gastronomic point of view, I can comment on it purely from a branding professional's perspective. It is a simple and very good example of my maxim "A brand is as a brand does."

In a marketplace where everything, and I mean everything, is transparent, it's becoming increasingly important—make that imperative—for companies to do exactly what they promise they'll do, to "walk the walk," as another maxim goes. If a company isn't true to its word, doesn't deliver as expected, you can bet there will be lots of other words lighting up the digital communication net-work post-haste. And although In-N-Out Burger, as an example of a brand that succeeds by doing what it says it will do, is a small one, it speaks volumes about one of the biggest challenges faced by brands of every size. And it is about this challenge that I spoke to Dov Seidman, founder and CEO of LRN and author of the best-selling book *HOW: Why How We Do Anything Means Everything.*

LRN is a company that helps other companies "do the right thing." It oper-ates globally and reaches, works with, and helps shape winning organizational cultures by showing them how they can operate in both a principled and profit-able way. The inspired, and somewhat "meta," factor in their success is that LRN sees itself as what Dov refers to as a "human laboratory" for the practices it promotes and teaches. They work hard to authentically live their values, and then they pass on the learning in the form of new products and solutions to their client partners. It was during a very interesting conversation that Dov

shared an example of one his company's major initiatives. (Additional examples of *HOW* LRN does what it does can be found at www.LRN.com and www .HOWisTheAnswer.com.)

> **ALLEN ADAMSON:** So, you've explicitly deemed LRN a human laboratory, the impetus being that if you do something yourself before recommending actions to your clients, you'll have more credibility in the marketplace.

> **DOV SEIDMAN:** Three years ago, after 15 years of building a global business, I realized LRN needed to become a living, breathing laboratory, one in which we experimented with the governance, culture, and leadership necessary to thrive in the twenty-first century. We're trying to win by *outbehaving* the competition. How can we tell other companies what to do if we haven't examined our own company and tested our approaches? And one of the places we started was with our own culture. We've decided that the one thing the competition can't

copy is our culture. Business, any business, is about winning by gaining advantage, doing proprietary things. Just like my family can't copy your family, my culture can't copy your culture. We want to make culture a strategy for winning. We are going to translate our own ethos and our values into practices and processes and leadership models with individual customers by also doing it ourselves and learning from the experience.

AA: In other words, you can build your differentiation on trust and values. You'll compete on who you are and what you stand for. Tell me how you're going about this culture transformation.

DS: My colleagues and I had for years been on an up-and-down journey toward becoming an exemplar of living the values we promoted to the world. In this regard, we endeavored to become a flat organization. We had, for example, eliminated traditional approval processes for some capital expenditures and for all routine expense reimbursements. We never governed behavior exclusively with policies and procedures. And we long ago rejected performance evaluations based exclusively on "how much" outcomes that ignore the means by which colleagues achieved their objectives. We had long been rewarding colleagues for getting the job done the right way and had been doing a pretty good job of celebrating colleagues who lived our values. While we had come a long way in this regard, most of us began to feel and express that we were still far from where we needed to go. Going flat was one thing. Becoming truly self-governing is, as we would discover, quite another. There would be no middle ground. Over a six-month period, our colleagues set out to imagine what a self-governing organization would look like. Twenty teams around the globe formed to create the ideal organizational structure and operating model to be shared with everyone at a companywide meeting. I wrote an article for the *New York Times* in June 2012, in which I described ripping up our organizational chart in front of 300 LRN colleagues who work in the United States, Europe, and India, and proclaiming that none of us would report to a boss any more. From that point forward, we would all "report" to our company mission. Literally. No one would experience life at LRN as someone else's subordinate. My symbolic shredding, though subsequently supported by genuine changes, reflected a turning point; we actually called it our own "crossing of the Rubicon."

AA: It's one thing to proclaim you can do this and another thing to do the hard work—to embed the work into the operational DNA of the company. You're trying to figure out how to actually operational- ize the promise. What are some of the specific actions that you're undertaking?

DS: Any CEO can rip up an org chart. Putting in place new frameworks where colleagues are inspired—from within—to contribute their creativity and character and hold each other accountable for results would prove to be a monumental challenge. We still have not reached our desired destination, but we at least now know what we're striving for: self-governance. True self-governance is not only about becoming "flatter." It is not about a CEO "empowering" her employees or exhorting people to "think outside the box." We tried that, and it doesn't work. Empowering employees only reinforces power—a temporary gift bestowed from on high—as the most im- portant source of authority. Thinking outside the box leaves organi- zational boxes and silos in place rather than removing them entirely. In a self-governing organization, power and authority are wielded in a highly collaborative manner. Information is shared openly and immediately. Our employees make decisions and behave not in reaction to rules or a supervisor's directive, but in accordance with the company mission based on shared values. Power and author- ity still exist, but they stem from a genuine capacity to contribute and from the strength of the relationships rather than a hierarchical assignment.

AA: You don't tell people what they'll be doing based on a job description or the size of a desk. It sounds more like an organic culture rather than command and control.

DS: Exactly. Our mission is to advance our experiment within the company and also beyond its four walls, helping other organizations understand and embrace self-governance. Although the experiment included going flat, it encompasses much more: the rethinking of the corpora- tion so that the corporation's very character becomes its most valuable asset. We now run the company through elected employee councils that handle things like recruiting, performance, resource manage- ment, and conflict resolution. Although I hold the position of CEO and chairman of the executive council, my colleagues and I as a whole lead the company. I focus on contributing to our business and shaping our culture, not on my formal role.

AA: The on-boarding process at LRN must be very different from that at other companies. How do you go about hiring people?

DS: It's not conventional by any means. We're looking to see if people can demonstrate an authentic connection to our mission, not just that they're intrigued by us or like us. There has got to be something in their background, beyond practical skills, that suggests that LRN will be home to them. We ask them to read things or watch videos and write essays or comment on them. We see if they ask us what their role will be. We want to establish if they want to be here for the role or the mission. In other words, don't tell me what my title will be or how big my office will be, it's that I believe in what you're doing.

AA: I can only imagine that your performance assessments are unconventional. How do you determine how people are doing?

DS: We have shucked our traditional performance management and review approach. After selecting a personal network of 20 or so reviewers and a mentor to help the employee to reflect on and internalize annual feedback, colleagues give themselves their own annual performance ratings. We trust employees to weigh the feedback they collect into their own ratings. Self-ratings of all 300 employees are published internally. We trust each other to thoughtfully conduct what we call "principled performance reviews," and we pay bonuses based on colleagues' self-ratings.

AA: What about your own performance evaluation?

DS: I opened my own review process to anyone who wanted to weigh in on my performance. I then published the results of the assessments that 67 of my colleagues completed on my performance. While it was unnerving as a leader to have my performance appraisals published for all my colleagues to see, it also felt necessary and urgent if I want to lead my company to long-term success and significance.

AA: It's one thing to have a brand promise or mission. It's another thing to live it. You've got to translate your promise into real behavior for it to be perceived as credible. How would you rate your initiative, the self-governing organization, to date?

DS: It's been enlightening, frustrating, nerve-racking, authentic, and urgent. It's still a work in progress. But our mission remains to advance our experiment and help other organizations to embrace this concept as a key to long-term success and significance. Doing it ourselves, taking on the hard work, will give us currency in the marketplace. Recently, we put our theory of self-governance to the test. We conducted an unprecedented statistical analysis of the observations of more than 36,000 employees, from the C-Suite to the junior ranks, in 18 countries. Frankly, this was one of the biggest bets of my life. If the statistics didn't demonstrate that self-governing cultures inspire superior performance outcomes, my reputation would be pretty much toast. While the analysis was developed by LRN, it was independently conducted by the Boston Research Group in collaboration with Research Data Technology and the Center for Effective Organizations at the University of Southern California. The study found that self-governing organizations, while still rare, experience profound advantages in the marketplace, including the highest levels of resilience, employee loyalty, customer satisfaction, innovation, and financial performance.

AA: Do you see the move toward self-governance as part of a wider business trend?

DS: It's comforting that increasingly I see that we are not alone. Leaders of all stripes are alert to the fact that citizens and employees alike are clamoring for—and achieving!—an unprecedented level of freedom from old, outdated structures and conventions. Citizens who no longer want to live under oppressive regimes and dictators are toppling them from power. Employees who no longer want to work under command-and-control bosses are publishing their boss's behavior. Employees who no longer want corporate communications to tow the "company line" are speaking on behalf of the company through all of their social networks. And consumers who don't agree with price increases bolt in unison overnight. A particularly alert CEO of a large and well-respected company confided in me recently, saying, "Dov, it took 17 days for the Egyptians to get rid of Hosni Mubarak and he had a military. What if my consumers and employees decide to get rid of me because they don't like how I run this place or how my company treats them? What are the implications?" He was one of a growing chorus of CEOs and leaders who appreciate that they're in a new world where they need to fundamentally *rethink*—rather than simply reform or reset—how their organizations operate.

CHAPTER FOUR

To Have an Edge, a Brand's Customers Should Want to Tell Its Story

One of the books I read during the time I was working on *this* book was *The End of Illness* by David B. Agus, one of the world's leading cancer doctors, researchers, and technology innovators. The author, who had treated Steve Jobs and has been interviewed on numerous talk shows, including Jon Stewart's, writes about how, by doing some of the simplest things, we can live healthier lives. One of the concepts in his book that most resonated with me has to do with balance and, specifically, the effects of hyper-connectivity on our health and well-being. Our brains, it seems, have become hooked on the steady trickle of e-mail and tweets and streaming videos, and it's having a less-than-positive impact. With hundreds of technological "inputs" a day, we are, in essence, being driven to distraction. It's becoming harder not just to focus, but to let our minds wander, something critical to creative thinking and problem solving. It's not that we shouldn't stay connected to our friends and families with our phones and other devices, Agus counsels, but that we have to be smarter about it. Technology is like food. There's a time to step away from the table.

Now, among the many things Dr. Agus prescribed to help combat the ill effects of hyper-connectivity was something I could easily do: walk a dog. I already have a dog named Zoe. Actually, like many dogs in many families, Zoe came into our lives at the request of my daughter, so it's technically *her* dog. But because, as also happens in many families when kids get older, Zoe is the first one to greet me when I get home at night, she and I have, well, bonded. And it's a good thing. Taking her for her evening walk, actually getting pulled by her on our evening walks, I am forced to resist the impulse to speak on the phone, check e-mails, or surf the web. I physically can't do three things at once, and it's during our walks through the park that I do my best thinking. I can process information and reflect on everything in my mental "in-box." I mulled over some of the ideas in this book while being pulled by Zoe, including, ironically, one of the most challenging predicaments facing marketers today: Given that the current rage is all about word of mouth—getting consumers to become voluntary advocates for your brand and talk about it via social media—how do marketers who want to gain the edge get consumers to listen, how do they fuel a conversation, and how do they keep the conversation moving? In other words, what does it take to harness the word-of-mouth phenomenon that has taken on tsunami-like proportions? That I, as a branding professional, have learned the importance of being able to "disconnect" speaks volumes about this challenge.

Now, it's undisputed that word of mouth has always been an important part of building a brand. It's just that, prior to digital technology, it occurred on a more intimate face-to-face level, over the backyard fence, say, or on the front porch, on the bleachers of your kids' Little League games, or at cocktail parties. If people had a great experience with one product or another, they'd just naturally want to talk about it with others, and your brand would be the beneficiary at no cost. Social media platforms have given word-of-mouth marketing a scale and scope it's never had before, and, obviously, the upside potential is enormous. It's only natural that marketers would want to catch the wave of a message gone crazily viral to reach millions of potential customers in record time. But thinking that you can just buy yourself some "buzz" is akin to thinking that you'll win the mega-bucks lottery or be able to pick which new Hollywood release will break box office records.

What makes word-of-mouth marketing even more challenging is the "shiny new object" factor; herd mentality has taken hold, with even the smartest companies gravitating to the newest new thing without thinking about why. Watching this happen over the last couple of years reminds me of when my daughter (she of dog ownership) started playing soccer. All the little girls would run and cluster around the ball on the same end of the field, and there would be no one on defense. The answer this week is Facebook, it's foursquare, it's Pinterest, or it's user-generated YouTube content. Even before I finish writing this book, there will likely be more social media options for marketers, sites being launched by young kids whose enterprises are backed by only slightly younger venture capitalists, all with the same notion that their brilliantly must-have medium will be the one marketers will use to carry the million-dollar message to millions of others.

As if this weren't enough, also at work is something my colleague John Gerzema, executive chairman of BAV Consulting, refers to as "app-athy," which goes back to my notion of sensory overload and can be applied to any form of digital diversion. His very apt term (no pun intended) is based on a study conducted by Nielsen that found that, while 10 billion mobile apps have been sold on iStore to date, the top 50 account for 61 percent of the time spent. There are too few great apps, it seems, and too few "great customers." In other words, there are too many mobile apps out there chasing the finite amount of time people want or have to use them. In his article "Call it App-athy," which appears on the website JohnGerzema.com, John states, "According to the Pew Center, more adults own a smartphone than have a college degree. Telenav [a company that offers personalized GPS-based navigation assistance] found that one in three Americans would rather give up sex than their smartphones. Yet, despite that kind of passion, a phone is habitual and apps aren't really any different than which place you'd stop for coffee or what credit card you pull out at the cashier. Apps are fighting to be part of your routine. As such, for every Angry Birds and Fruit Ninjas, most apps are not profitable."

So then, with all the noise, the apps (and app-athy), and the continuous input, is there actually a recipe for success relative to how to get consumers to hear what you have to say and to spread your brand story for you? The answer, of course, is yes, or this chapter wouldn't exist, nor the stories in it. Having said this, the recipe is also, of course, easier said than done, given that you've got to get people when they're mentally and physically plugged in and in listening mode, and not out walking a dog. And the first ingredient is simply this: do the right thing all the time. Remember a few paragraphs back when I said that consumers will share experiences that they find worthy of sharing? Every point of touch with your brand should not just meet but exceed the criteria for making this happen. Every interaction a consumer has with a brand should be so surprising and delighting that they can't wait to tell their friends and family. Just being satisfied with a brand experience is no longer enough. You've got to have a message that's inherently newsworthy, something that people will spontaneously want to repeat. "Hey, you'll never believe what Zappos went through to get me the shoes I needed for my wedding, the unexpected upgrade we got at the Marriott this weekend, how the guy at Lowes spent three hours enthusiastically helping us design our new kitchen. It was awesome!" Consumers now control the story. Marketers can control if—and how—it's told by tapping into what the brand stands for and delivering on it. Social media should not be thought of as a separate line item on your marketing budget, nor should they be considered an afterthought or an à la carte enterprise. Social media should be the strategic underpinning of every brand interaction. Give consumers something of interest to talk about—interesting to them, that is—and they'll be more likely to pick up your message and want to share it.

The second ingredient in the recipe for getting your story told and heard is authenticity. For people to feel compelled to share a story for all the right reasons, it has to come across as credible. It must be aligned with what your brand stands for, not seen as a gratuitous gesture. People want to share their experiences with brands, and if you earn their trust by always doing the right thing (for the right reasons), they'll be *excited* to share them. Consumers have always trusted other consumers more than they've trusted any institution, and this factor carries far greater weight in today's ultra-skeptical, jaded environment. If an initiative doesn't feel like something that would come from the brand, it won't pass muster, let alone get passed along. This is as true for day-to-day branding initiatives—a great customer service experience or the wonderful way a product functions—as it is for advertising and public relations initiatives.

For example, the cable network TNT had great success with an initiative that drove home the point that, yes, "TNT Knows Drama." As a way of drawing attention to the launch of their new channel in Benelux (Belgium, the Netherlands, and Luxembourg), the marketing team produced a video campaign that showed not only how quickly drama can escalate, but how quickly consumers will spread the word for you if they feel a real connection to the brand. In the video, which gained 11 million viewers in two days, the creators had placed a big red button on a black-and-white striped pole in the middle of a typical town square in a typical Flemish town. A sign with the message "Push to add drama" invited people to push the button. Who could resist? Chaos ensues. First, an ambulance pulls up with sirens blaring. Two men jump out and grab a man on a gurney who they drop, pick up again, and put back into the ambulance. As they start to drive off, the man rolls out of the ambulance and another man on a bicycle runs into the front door of the ambulance, which has been flung open by the driver. The cyclist attacks the driver who tears off his shirt and begins beating the cyclist. Then a sexy woman wearing nothing but lingerie (hey, I'm paying attention to this, people) rolls by on a motorcycle. Black SUVs and a white van pull up, secret agent–types exit and start shooting at each other. Everyone, including the ambulance driver and the cyclist, jump into the SUVs and drive off, leaving a single agent remaining wounded in the street. Five football players run out of a nearby building, pick up the agent, and run inside with him. The lady in lingerie drives by once more and—finally—a large banner drops from a building in the square. It reads: "Your daily dose of drama from TNT."

Again, what's important to note about this initiative is that it was created to align with TNT's overarching promise. TNT has long been known to offer programs of dramatic proportions, so it would not have made sense, nor would it have been passed along with such enthusiasm, had it not been something already associated with the brand. What's fascinating about this video from another perspective is not just the precisely staged melee in the streets, but the startled looks on the faces of the people in the town square. It was a *Candid Camera* moment of capturing how people reacted to something so very out of the ordinary. And this, in essence, is yet another ingredient in the recipe for capturing the attention of a word-weary, world-weary consumer. If you create a moment that brings the core meaning of your brand to life in an extraordinary way, it's more likely to grab attention and be shared.

Just as with most things in life, there are very few guarantees in marketing. But it's by incorporating these simple ingredients into their thinking about social media that brands with an edge have been able to best take advantage of social media and get consumers to tell their stories. Before you get to their stories in this chapter, however, take a moment to read about why marketers should think of every day as Labor Day. I think you'll find it a very interesting conversation starter.

I think one of the most fundamental things a branding professional can take away from the world of politics relative to the importance of word of mouth is something we call the Labor Day Effect. The Republicans hold their presidential convention at the end of the summer. The Democrats hold their presidential convention at the end of the summer. Then, everyone goes off for the Labor Day holiday. It's the poll that we do after Labor Day, after people have had a chance to talk and share their opinions about what they've heard and learned from these conventions, that is the single most important poll we do. It's what happens after people talk to each other that matters most to brands. That means it's critical to give them the right things to think about before they begin talking.

- Make sure you have a theme or a point of view that clearly and succinctly represents your values.
- Know who your target is: who will care about what you have to say?
- Ensure that you set the context for authenticity: have a bio for your story that makes it credible and reinforces your values.
- Develop proof points (we call them issue ads) that support your story and help people understand what it is that is interesting about what you offer.
- Have a clear case as to why you're better than the competition.

THINK OF EVERY DAY AS LABOR DAY

Have you ever heard of the Labor Day Effect? Neither had I, until I talked to Mark Penn to get his thoughts on the topic of word-of-mouth marketing. Mark is the former CEO of the public relations firm Burson-Marsteller, which is part of the same family of companies with which Landor is associated, and he is also the former president of the polling firm Penn Schoen Berland. Among the many categories of brands with which he has extensive experience, and there have been quite a few, is the political brand, as in Bill and Hillary Clinton, and Tony Blair. Given that to be a successful politician you have to be able to encapsulate the most complex ideas in a very memorable manner in order to get legions of voters mobilized and motivated to share them with legions of other voters, I knew Mark would have some mobilizing and motivating input on the topic. And he did, including why every marketer should think of every day as Labor Day. Read on.

"The fact is, everyone today has the potential to be a broadcaster," he told me. "Where once politicians would think about what they communicated to the Washington Press Club, now they have to think about what they say to a group of visiting Norwegian high school students. Anything said on any channel can become a global story. Anything said on any channel can affect a brand anywhere. Look at the stock market. It has become a word-of-mouth game. You can find any opinion you want about any situation at any moment in time. At the end of the day, people have far greater access to information and far greater ability to consider the facts and make judgments on their own. A brand is no longer in the sole control of the marketer. People want to, and can, take greater control of information. Simple acts that were once taken for granted, like how much sugar is in soda, what's in the hamburger you're eating, or what kind of fat is used to make fast food French fries, now play significantly into how consumers make choices about brands. Suffice it to say, in this new era, social media has upped the ante for marketers."

TOP TIPS: LET YOUR CUSTOMERS TELL YOUR STORY

It's an absolute truth that talk value in building a brand is significant. The Internet and every device with an app have put the power of branding into the hands of anyone with a digital connection. Word of mouth has become supersized. The stories in this chapter are about brands that have gained an edge because they know how to use this power to their advantage and to the advantage of their customers. To ensure that you have the same advantage, here are a few tips to guide you:

- Word of mouth will happen with you or without you. Use it to learn what you're doing right. Use it to learn how you can improve the brand experience.
- Short jokes are easier to tell than long ones. Consumers can only tell your brand story the way you want it told if you've sharply defined it for them.
- Always remember that when something impacts a consumer's life on a personal level they're more likely to share it.
- For people to want to pass along a brand experience it must be extraordinary. Make sure you give them something to talk about.
- Make it easy for consumers to share your brand story with others. Give them a platform or forum to pass along their input.
- Consumers like to be recognized and thanked for their loyalty. Acknowledge consumers who have something nice to say about your brand. Reward their support.
- Consumers vote with their wallets. Treat your brand's advocates like the shareholders they are.

FORD'S INNOVATION FOR THE MILLIONS IS—AND ALWAYS HAS BEEN—AN AUTHENTIC PART OF ITS BRAND STORY

These days, when someone talks about an innovative company, it's likely they're referring to a small start-up, a couple of kids in a garage with a new idea that will revolutionize the way we do one thing or another, usually having to do with some far-out technology we didn't know we needed until we realized we did. Well, Henry Ford was a kid in a garage. He had an idea that revolutionized the very way we got from point A to point B. And while the life in the fast lane that used to be the automobile industry almost came to a standstill, the folks at Ford resisted the opportunity to take a government bailout and, instead, looked back to drive themselves forward. As is so often the case with big brands in search of a fresh beginning, Ford went back to what made it hot to begin with: Henry Ford's idea to democratize innovation—making the latest and greatest engineering, design, and technology available to everyone. Not only has Ford fared better in the recession than the other two big auto makers, it's doing all sorts of inventive things to ensure that a completely new generation of car owners falls in love with the iconic "blue oval."

Ford's innovative spirit goes far beyond just gears and crankshafts and cruise control. In the hands of Jim Farley, vice president of global marketing, sales, and service, it extends to the very way its cars are sold. Tapped by Ford CEO Alan Mulally to invigorate Ford's brands, Jim has "democratized" the conversation about Ford and its products, making efficient and effective use of social media to let consumers tell the company's story. While it has launched many initiatives that tap into the vocal power of the people, by far the most ambitious one was what Ford called the "Fiesta Movement," a grassroots social media campaign to promote the new Fiesta model in which 100 social "agents" were given cars, along with the freedom to share their opinions with the rest of the world, which they did through millions of tweets, YouTube videos, and blogs. That's a lot of advertising, all without spending a dollar on traditional media. Creating sharable experiences, making people the stars of the brand, comes naturally to Ford and is just part of what Jim and I talked about in a recent conversation. Here's a bit more of our very interesting exchange.

ALLEN ADAMSON: Every automobile company has the same basic set of bells and whistles. It's not about features anymore. Nor is it about marketing. How do you make it clear to the customer what makes the Ford brand different?

JIM FARLEY: In the past, you could have a marketing-oriented brand promise. Those days are over. The million-dollar question, getting to the brand promise, is being able to document the authentic truth at the heart of the company: what it is on a good day. In other words, what can we deliver that is credible versus just making it up? Research may tell you to do something, but if it's not part of the company's DNA, if it's not authentic, it won't work. To be honest, we had come to a crossroads at Ford because we had become a culture of personalities. We'd crank up or down depending on who was at the top. This isn't how to build a brand. When we started the process to restage the brand promise, we heard from a broad array of constituents—employees, suppliers, dealers, retirees—who all said the same thing. On a good day, Ford is all about innovation.

AA: This started with Henry Ford: innovation for the millions—streamlining production so that cars were accessible to anyone. It's very often that when a brand sets out to refresh its image, it succeeds when it goes back to its roots.

JF: Exactly. And this idea of accessibility or approachability is not just about customers, but about the people who work here. It's about people serving people. Let me tell you a story that illustrates this. One of the first things I did when I got to Ford after leaving Toyota was to ask the head of product development what made a Ford engineer different from a Toyota engineer. He told me to ask one of the engineers. The safety engineer to whom I spoke captured the whole idea of our global brand promise, "Go Further." When I approached him, he was working on this crash test instrument dummy that had a soft gel midsection, much like the abdomen of a twelve- or thirteen-year-old child. "I was a doctor at a Philadelphia children's hospital," he told me, "when my twelve-year-old daughter died in an automobile accident. Ford is the most innovative company, and I thought I could save more lives working at Ford than at a hospital. It gives me a better platform to impact people's lives." This is when I realized that it's the people at Ford who make the company different. They have a mission to serve others.

AA: This is a very different image of an American conglomerate. It's not the individual at the top, but the people on the ground.

JF: It was this insight that drove us to use real people in our ads and why we chose to use Mike Rowe in some of our advertising. He's believable and not overly slick in any way. It's also why we've invested so heavily in social media, or what we call credible media. We want people to tell their own stories, whether it's our customers or the people who work at Ford, like one of our engineers out on a test drive or the Fiesta Movement pre-launch campaign.

AA: In the old days you'd figure out what the customers wanted and just write an ad about it. Today you want to know what the customer wants, but it's a transparent marketplace where everyone can see everything, so the whole experience has to speak to the brand promise. This means you have to go into the company and figure out what you can authentically deliver on, where and how you can win for the long term.

JF: It's the stories that come from the inside, that they know are real, that connect with people. For example, everyone knows fuel economy is important. Every automobile manufacturer is working on turbo-charged smaller displacement engines for some of their vehicles. But we've put them in literally every one of our vehicles, from the Fiesta to the F150 and everything in between. We made a huge bet on our EcoBoost engine technology. It's not about making an electric car for a few thousand rich people. We wanted to impact the lives of millions of Americans with technology that none of our competitors had and across our entire line-up of vehicles. Being the fuel economy leader is a differentiator in the category, and it's authentically tied to our promise of democratizing innovation.

AA: It used to be that the engine decisions would be left to the engineers and the marketing decisions would be left to the marketing department. In your case, all decisions are part of the bigger brand story.

JF: We truly operate as a matrixed organization. We're structurally wired together in a way that promotes innovation. This has influenced everything from our engineering to our go-to-market strategy. For instance, we used to spend a ton of money on mass media after the product was available, but because we're an innovative company, we challenged ourselves to go to market more efficiently. We now pre-launch a product well before it's available. We use our time and money to generate a conversation. Then we make a traditional media buy contingent on what happens. What we've learned is that we can have six months of orders in the hopper before doing any mass media. With these new social media tools, new car buyers will self-select if they want more information. This has been a huge learning experience for our company. It has totally changed our way of doing things. We get people to talk. With so many new car launches every year, the choices and the media noise are overwhelming. If you slow-burn a launch before a product becomes available, it becomes cool to know about it. We've changed the game.

AA: You also get your employees into the public conversation. You have Ford engineers on Facebook answering questions about the Explorer, for example.

JF: We do the right thing for our brand. It has to be believable. Consumers are done with fluff. We let real people talk, we let our people talk. In other words, we put our brand in the hands of our customers and our employees.

HOW TO DETERMINE THE REAL WINNERS IN
THE SUPER BOWL BRANDING GAME

Every year, beginning in early January, the conversation starts. Who is going to win the Super Bowl and why? No, I'm not talking about whether it will be the Giants or the 49ers, the Packers or the Saints. I'm talking branding. Which companies are going to pay the big bucks to buy 60, or even 30, minutes of time, and which are going to win the battle of the buzz? That is, which brand's advertising will not only get talked about at the water cooler on Monday morning, but will get picked up and passed along on social media sites (the dollar value of which is almost incalculable).

> *Despite the flight to customized marketing, mass marketing, when you do it right, is still an incredible opportunity and remains a crucial part of brand building.*

In a world where buzz is critical, the Super Bowl is a critical venue for marketers. It's one of the last places where you can tell your brand story to more than one person at a time. Despite the flight to customized marketing, mass marketing, when you do it right, is still an incredible opportunity and remains a crucial part of brand building. Every year there's a winner of the actual Super Bowl. And every year there are winners and losers among the brands that choose to pay and play. So what does it take to win, to ensure that your brand isn't sacked by professional and, more important, consumer branding critics? Here are a few pointers.

1. **Play your game:** What's your brand's story? Don't get sucked into the "hey look at me" syndrome. Be authentic. Don't use borrowed interest. It's your one shot to let millions of people know all at the same time what your brand stands for. E-trade has been a long-standing winner in this regard. The clever "talking baby" spots continue to communicate clearly how the financial firm's easy-to-use tools and resources can help anyone pick out the right financial investments. No screaming (even by the babies) is necessary to get the brand message across. Every ad is built on a simple insight about what consumers want relative to their investment planning, and each keeps us engaged

because the kids are so damn cute and the way the points are made, so entertaining.

2. **Capture the force of the buzz:** Yes, you want your spot to become contagious, but not because it was so annoying. If you're using humor, make sure it's tied inextricably to your brand's benefit or what people already associate with your brand. You don't want to be the butt of your own joke or, on the other hand, have people at the water cooler talking about an ad that was funny—but they can't remember what it was for. Doritos are always funny in the right way, as are lots of adult beverage (that would be beer) companies. Ads that get passed around also have simple but engaging story lines. Take a recent VW spot, for example. In it, a little boy dressed in a Darth Vader outfit tries to use "The Force" to get his dog, his sister's doll, and his mother's dishwasher to do his bidding. No luck. Daddy comes home driving the new 2012 Volkswagen Passat. Kid runs out, ignores his dad, and stands in front of the car trying to get "The Force" to be with him one more time. All of a sudden

the car's sporty headlights beep and flash, the pint-sized Darth jumps back in awe, and dad, with a sly grin at mom and a quick glance down at the Passat's key fob in his hand, shows us wherein the force really lies. The spot isn't loud (did I mention it does not even have copy?). It doesn't rely on gratuitous high jinks to make its point, but, instead, gets our attention with a simple little plot that conveys something meaningfully different about the product, executed in a manner completely in sync with the brand's quirky yet familiar style. Cue the *Star Wars* soundtrack. This is branding at its best.

3. **Ensure that it's part of the long-term brand story:** The Super Bowl is not the venue for a Hail Mary pass. It's got to be in line with the pre-game and post-game show. Coca-Cola always gets extra points for this. Its spots are always innovative and fresh, and they're always tied to its long-standing promise of being the "real thing," the classic when it comes to inspiring moments of happiness. FedEx is another brand that performs well in this regard. We can count on something sharp and witty in the execution, but the story is always about delivering peace of mind.

Whether it's the Super Bowl, the Olympics, or the Academy Awards, it's not the time to shout louder, become (even more) outrageously sophomoric, or do something totally out of line with your brand's equity. Rather, it's the perfect opportunity to take advantage of the massive captive audience at your disposal and reinforce what you want them to think about your brand. With so many potential buyers out there in TV land, this is the time to put the shine on your branding game. Do the best job possible to tell the simple story tied to your brand's benefit. Clearly convey what makes your brand different and why people should care. And remember that while *you* may think your execution is brilliantly creative, if it doesn't make your point, what's the point? Game on.

IN THE WORLD OF TWITTER, YOUTUBE, AND FACEBOOK, DELL'S SOCIAL DNA SERVES ITS BRAND WELL

You don't have to be a parent to understand that there's a difference between just hearing and actually listening. This comment, at the beginning of the recent conversation I had with Karen Quintos, senior vice president and CMO at Dell Inc., summed up our shared opinion that a company can think it's being customer-centric when, in actuality, it's not. I had called Karen to talk to her about how social media have changed the way companies interact with customers and whether Dell, being quintessentially a customer-oriented brand from the get-go (as in, tell us how you want your computer built), had evolved as a result. What follows is a snippet of our very interesting dialog.

> **ALLEN ADAMSON:** Dell, as in Michael Dell, came up with the idea of involving customers in the building of their personal computers and, in doing so, built a differentiated brand name, customer-centric from the start—"customer-centric" being a buzz word, but an appropriate description nonetheless. How has Dell kept up with this concept given the advent and exponential growth of social media since your company was launched in 1984?
>
> **KAREN QUINTOS:** First of all, customer-centricity is and always has been part of the Dell DNA. It's not something we think about. It's the way we do business. It's like the difference between hearing and listening. Hearing is passive. You can hear someone say something, but it doesn't prompt any reaction. Listening, on the other hand, is active. You have a passion for the message and you take accountability to respond to what customers need. Listening is what we do at Dell, and social media have made it that much more effective and efficient.
>
> **AA:** I remember back to my "mad men" days in advertising when it was the research department that had the primary responsibility to look and listen and report back. It seems listening is the way Dell operates across the board.
>
> **KQ:** Absolutely. We have taken listening to a whole new level, and we use it in every aspect of the business—from product and solutions development to services to sales to customer support to marketing. A great

example of this is IdeaStorm, which we launched in 2007. IdeaStorm is a social community that allows customers to suggest new product and services ideas, and then we refine and prioritize those ideas within our organization. As another example, we have a very active group of storage technology enthusiasts. We leverage their knowledge to help us with new solutions and technical specifications.

AA: With social media, there is almost no option but to get things done in real time. The transparency dynamic prompted by digital technology has really brought to life the notion that "a brand is as a brand does."

KQ: Without a doubt. That's why we pay close attention to the conversations we have with our customers. We have what we call our Listening Command Center, which monitors conversations taking place about Dell on Twitter, Facebook, across all social media communities. The folks on this team can immediately triage a situation. They're able to trend data that shows us what issues people are latching onto, positive or negative, and then our teams deal with them accordingly. One

of the ways we respond to these conversations is through a program called DellCares (@DellCares on Twitter). DellCares is overseen by an enthusiastic group of customer support and technology people. Instead of just making notes and letting issues fester, this team is on top of addressing problems or questions promptly.

AA: Do you think Dell has a particular advantage over other companies because you started out as a brand with an inherent listening culture?

KQ: Yes and no. There is nothing new or novel about the notion of listening as a way of providing customers with what they want and need. It's so simple and so basic. But if you don't do it, you can't act on it. Listening enables superior customer outcomes. All of us at Dell, including Michael, start every staff meeting with a customer story, and then we talk about how we could have made the customer experience even better. If you fundamentally believe that being customer-centric is the right thing to do, opportunities will follow. But you have to believe in it.

FORGET SILVER LININGS. APPLE'S ICLOUD IS PURE GOLD

Technology gurus can cite chapter and verse about what makes Apple products so remarkable. Consumers can cite chapter and verse about what makes Apple products so magical. Authors of best-selling books can cite in chapter and verse what made Steve Jobs Steve Jobs. As a branding professional, let me take just a couple of paragraphs to explain what keeps the Apple brand at the head of the pack. And to do so, let me go back a few years to the Apple Worldwide Developers' Conference during which Steve Jobs unveiled the Apple iCloud. This presentation helped codify for me what this brand, its founder, and all who follow in his stead continue to do right in terms of not just building a brand, but owning a category.

To begin with, Apple picked a name for the product that communicates its benefit immediately. The name, in and of itself, made, and continues to keep, Apple the category owner. But wait. There is, of course, more to it than this. There's the logo, the simple little cloud that promises the experience will be fresh and light and simple. It is, because the functionality of the iCloud has been made as easy as the name and logo imply. You don't have to be a technology guru to set it up to do all the things that cloud computing is supposed to do. The way it works is invisible to the user. It's like magic. You just experience it.

Then, of course, there's the advertising. Again, it's simply and brilliantly elegant. An easy, breezy, clear-cut demonstration of what the iCloud does. You can start a project on one device and pick it up on another. Store pictures here, share them there. Your photos, songs, and documents are always where you want them, when you want them. This is not a Hollywood production but, rather, more akin to how the old country store manager showed you how to operate the things you bought. No gimmicks. No bells and whistles. The product is hero.

There are many companies that offer cloud storage functionality. Apple simply has the magical ability to make its product design, logo design, naming, and everything branding look so, well, simple. It's branding that's best-in-class and branding that continues to make Apple tough to catch. With more and more

consumers owning more and more Apple products, the company continues to ensure that they all work together in harmony. To this day, Apple understands the core requirement for succeeding in the technology category: find a simple idea, and execute it with brilliance—in this case, cloud service done right. Or as the slide Steve Jobs put up to close his presentation said, "It just works." A little silver cloud with a lovely silver lining? I'd say pure gold.

KLM, NIKE, AND CHIPOTLE ARE THRILLED TO BE CONTAGIOUS

Laughter is contagious. So, too, are the best ideas in technology, product design, advertising, and initiatives for social change, especially given our social media–driven marketplace. A colleague recently sent me a round-up of 2011's most contagious global trends pulled together by—who else?—the editors of *Contagious* magazine, with support from Yahoo! What is significant about this report is that it points out not just how hard it is to come up with a clutter-busting way to tell your brand's story, but how really hard it is to come up with an idea that millions of people feel compelled to share with each other. The branding idea goes, as they say, viral, because it touches a nerve, a funny bone, a place in the heart that resonates with people across the board and around the world. Like all great stories, these ideas are too good *not* to be shared.

> *Contagious ideas engage people and give them a reason to talk. And isn't that the point?*

Companies today are fully aware of the benefit of marketing initiatives that become contagious. Not only are they free publicity, but they enable people to see beyond the product and into the character of the brand. And while many marketers go to great lengths to concoct the secret sauce that will get their initiative picked up and passed along, most find it can be more miss than hit. If I had to guess at the recipe, I'd say it includes a dollop of what the brand already stands for in people's minds—that taste of authenticity. There's certainly a nugget of the understanding of human nature in the concoction—a piece of something that hits home on an emotional level. It also has to be wrapped inside a creatively brilliant execution, not necessarily of the Hollywood variety, but the DIY variety. To get picked up, relished, and passed along, it's got to be fresh and innovative and accessible. Contagious ideas engage people and give them a reason to talk. And isn't that the point?

Take KLM and its Meet & Seat program, for example. While it's hard to differentiate an airline experience these days—seats are all the same, food is all the same (peanuts are peanuts), the wait at the gate is all the same—KLM found a way to set its brand of airline apart. It has harnessed the fun and power of social media and created the Meet & Seat program, through which you can choose your seatmate after reviewing the social media profiles of passengers who have signed up and entered their information. The initiative was launched using online media, of course, and has literally and figuratively taken off. KLM is well known for its provocative campaigns, so it seemed natural that it would leverage the buzz factor of social media to differentiate the experience of flying on KLM versus other airlines. Ever wonder why nobody ever thought of a way to ensure you won't be sitting next to a screaming baby or a guy who thinks you'll enjoy hearing his life story during the entire six-hour flight to Amsterdam? KLM did. And the program—and its branding—has become contagious with those in the know. (So now, *you* know.)

Closer to the ground (and being a sci-fi fan), I was also struck by Nike's win in the design category as a result of its limited edition *Back to the Future*–inspired NIKE MAG shoes launched via an eBay auction. Proceeds from the shoes (only 1,500 pairs available) went directly to the Michael J. Fox Foundation

for Parkinson's Research, set up by the actor who played Marty McFly in the original *Future* trilogy. After having existed for 22 years only on Marty's feet, these extra-terrestrial shoes, based on the original movie prop, became available to any of the highest bidders. The strategic brilliance on Nike's part was that there was an authentic, and therefore credible, link to its brand imbuing the initiative with greater significance. In the promotional video with Christopher Lloyd, who reprised his role as Dr. Emmett Brown, you see him entering the Lone Pine Mall shoe store in search of some new Nike shoes. After being told by the employee, "not until 2015," Dr. Brown jumps into his DeLorean and sets the time circuits to 2015. The effort was a win-win for everyone. The Michael J. Fox Foundation, the lucky folks who got the innovative futuristic shoes, and Nike, whose branding idea was contagious and was seen by millions of sci-fi fans like me.

Food fans, on the other hand, made a contagious winner out of Chipotle's "Back to the Start" campaign. This Mexican restaurant chain integrated adver-tising, packaging, and its website to educate consumers about the company's core vision—food with integrity. The centerpiece of the effort, the initiative that got millions of clicks in no time, was an innovative stop-action film that was released both on the Internet and in movie theaters. It showcased the Chipotle commitment to finding the very best ingredients, all raised with respect for animals, the environment, and farmers. What made the spot truly transcendent, however, was the music, Coldplay's "The Scientist" covered by Willie Nelson. The video's story line, which tied directly to the brand's story line, was pulled together into a delighting and compelling branding effort. That Chipotle was one of the year's top contagious branding initiatives was proof that it knew the recipe for success. (And its food is good, too.)

SOMETIMES IT TAKES SCHWEDDY BALLS TO WIN THE BRANDING GAME

To say we live in interesting times is an understatement, specifically when it comes to brand building. The marketplace has never been as inundated with choices. The noise level has never been so high, the airwaves and fiber optic lines so cluttered. Nor has the promise quotient been so overwhelming. Just when you think, "Okay, we've seen everything and heard everything," along comes another election and its line-up of new characters and slogans or a line-up of new mobile devices with a steady stream of stealth spamming apps. If you're a legitimate marketer with a legitimately great story to tell, how can you possibly break through the clutter? From my perspective as a legitimate brand professional, I'd say it's the perfect time for the calculated risk. Before I explain, let me set the stage.

All companies (smart companies, anyway) understand that there are three critical factors involved in building strong brands in this digital age. Your brand has to stand for something different relative to other brands in your category. Moreover, this difference in meaning must be simple to understand for both consumers and those in your organization. The people responsible for the branding must be able to grasp the brand idea in order to execute it clearly and brilliantly. Aflac, for example, is based on the simple and effective brand idea that you'll get the supplemental money you need to pay for things not covered by major medical insurance should you be unable to work due to ill-ness or injury. Thanks to its quirky or, rather, quacky branding, people get this. Second, your brand idea has to be "sticky." It has to catch on and stay men-tally fixed in people's minds as the result of your clear and brilliant branding. GEICO's cheeky gecko, along with its other tongue-in-cheek initiatives, helps keep this brand firmly "stuck" in our heads. And then there's the "contagious factor." A brand's simple, sticky idea has to travel well. On-the-ball companies understand that digital technology is like word of mouth on steroids, and they ensure that their branding initiatives are worth sharing. Why pay for media when you can get it for free from your brand advocates? Isaiah Mustafa's starring role in the Old Spice "Smell Like a Man, Man" campaign had Twitter abuzz for months.

Nothing has changed relative to the basic rules of brand building. But sometimes, like right now, it may take a bit more to get people to sit up and take notice of a brand. And that's where the notion of taking a calculated risk comes in. "Calculated," because whatever you undertake must be strategically aligned with your core brand idea and authentic to what your brand stands for. If it's not, it will be quickly outed as the disingenuous action it is. As for "risk," well, because it must be somewhat risky, out of the box, nervy, edgy, provocative, an effort you'd never considered before. The launch of the new Ben & Jerry's ice cream flavor Schweddy Balls is a perfect example. In the midst of the increasing competition in the category, those wacky folks up in South Burlington, Vermont, decided to pay homage to a 13-year-old *Saturday Night Live* skit featuring Alec Baldwin as bakery owner Pete Schweddy, who offered a distinctive holiday dessert called Schweddy Balls. Ben & Jerry concocted this new flavor to get a conversation going (which it definitely did) and generate some buzz. That it linked its tasty confection to both Alec Baldwin and *SNL* was downright

clever, given that they're both cool brands compatible in nature with the Ben & Jerry's brand. That Ben & Jerry's is the only brand in the ice cream category that could have pulled this off is a key to the successful venture. The brand is known to be silly and all about fun. What other company could possibly get away with such a risky initiative? Oh, and by the way, the ice cream is delicious, also in keeping with the company's core brand idea and its core competency.

Another cool example of calculated risk taking in a challenging branding environment is Banana Republic's *Mad Men* fashion campaign. Created in collaboration with the show's Emmy-winning costume designer, the retailer is presenting a modern take on the '60s style that so many *Mad Men* fans have come to love and covet. Catering to those who want to dress like those naughty boys and girls of yesteryear, it's a super savvy branding move and one that's a sensational fit for the Banana Republic brand, known for its super savvy clothing. I can only assume this polished off-the-rack effort would impress even dandy Don Draper.

And while parodies are nothing new in advertising, T-Mobile's brilliant video execution of the most recent royal wedding—that would be Prince William and Kate Middleton—was just the right kind of naughty. T-Mobile is well known for its marketing campaigns that involve random members of the public breaking out with an impromptu musical performance. In this royal effort, it showcased actors impersonating members of the wedding, including the archbishop, dancing down the abbey aisle to the hip hit song "House of Love." People loved the spoofy spot, and it went crazy viral immediately. It was risky, yes, but it was calculated because the initiative was based on T-Mobile's core brand idea—"sharing life's moments." It captured all the things that make marketing these days successful: it was innovative, it was worth sharing, and it told the brand's story in a credible way.

Yes, we live in interesting times, and you don't need me to tell you that they're only going to get more interesting. In my estimation, marketers are going to have to get comfortable taking a little risk here and there. Just make sure that whatever it is supports what your brand already stands for, that it feels authentic to the brand, and that it supports your long-term efforts. You don't want to be left with Schweddy, well, you know.

MARTIN SORRELL TALKS ABOUT BRANDS AS THE SUM OF THEIR PEOPLE—AND THE PEOPLE WHO TALK ABOUT THEM

Eons ago, way back in the year 2000, there was a movie called *Cast Away* in which Tom Hanks played a FedEx systems engineer who was shipwrecked on an island after a FedEx plane crashed into the ocean. He was washed ashore with the remains of the wreckage, including a FedEx package. At the end of the movie, after years as a castaway on this island with no one to talk to but a volleyball he named Wilson, the guy managed to get off the island and, upon reaching home, made sure to deliver the FedEx package he'd been safeguarding. I was talking to one of our FedEx clients after seeing the movie, and she told me, "Not one person who saw the movie questioned this behavior. Given that he was a FedEx employee, it seems people knew that delivering the package was ingrained in his soul."

I bring up this long-ago movie (for which Tom Hanks was nominated for an Academy Award) to make a point about the importance of corporate culture in a marketplace that has been rocked by economic turmoil and in which the question of trust has become paramount in the minds of consumers. While employees are a critical factor in the success of any brand, employees and the corporate culture of which they're a part are even more critical in professional services brands, that unique species that includes everything from law firms and investment houses to architectural and medical practices to accounting, public relations, and communications firms. These are brands in which people and the expertise they bring to the table are the products. When your business is based on person-to-person interactions, it is critical that employees are able to understand and grasp the set of values that is at the heart of the brand promise. They must be able to live and breathe what the brand stands for in order for the brand to have a leading edge. Much as Tom Hanks's character literally delivered on the FedEx promise of "reliability," employees of professional service brands must know what it means to deliver as expected (although I would hazard a guess that senior management might be lenient in the case of a shipwreck).

Given that I work for a professional service brand, WPP to be exact, I decided to call upon Martin Sorrell, who is our chief executive, to get his view on this topic.

I wanted to see if he had any top "lessons learned" that he could share, not just with those tasked with the care and feeding of professional service brands, but with the care and feeding of any type of brand. Given that all brands are becoming more experiential and that consumers have the ability to share their experiences openly and freely, I thought his lessons would be applicable across the board. And they were.

> **ALLEN ADAMSON:** Building a professional service brand is difficult in that its product is a function of its people. It depends on a perception of not just experience and hard work, but of trustworthiness, which is getting harder and harder to do, what with all the challenges faced by the market over the last few years.
>
> **MARTIN SORRELL:** A professional service firm is built on human relationships—it *is* the sum of its people and their ability to live and to deliver the culture. That said, an employee can't deliver on a culture if it hasn't been defined for them. A strong company must determine what

makes its brand unique and make whatever this is very clear. Those doing the hiring must be able to articulate this culture and find people who can embrace the culture and do whatever it takes to bring it into their relationships with their clients. Employees must be able to make the story their own. In the end, quite rightly, a company will be judged both internally and externally, not by what it says about itself but by what it actually does and how it does it. If there's an obvious gap between rhetoric and behavior, the "culture" will be seen by everyone to be phony—and that's even worse than not having one.

AA: Are there professional service brands that you personally admire?

MS: I think Goldman Sachs and McKinsey & Company are two firms that do an extraordinary job. They are among the best because they understand what it takes to cultivate and sustain a professional services organization. They attract, recruit, and develop the best people, and they invest in them—they keep them motivated. It's also because they haven't made any big acquisitions, but have grown organically, promoting from within. They are tough about maintaining their culture and know that it's only by dedicating themselves to their people that they'll be able to best serve their clients.

AA: So it's almost an apprentice approach. Even as the founders move on—those who were responsible for establishing the ethos—companies that have been able to institutionalize their culture are able to more effectively attract and instill in their employees the skills and methodologies required to deliver a consistent experience with the customers. This is as true for professional service brands as for any other category of brand. It's like FedEx and the "purple promise," a commitment to service excellence that is intrinsic to their employee culture.

MS: Yes, and as a company gets bigger, as it achieves scale, this gets harder to do. It takes keeping people focused on whatever it is they need to do to ensure their clients' success. If they grasp the company's core values, they can make decisions that reflect well on the organization. You must do whatever you can do to keep people focused on client success—it's the North Star. Client recommendations are the best way to tell the brand's story.

AA: It's what consumers tell each other about your brand that matters most in establishing trust. And in more and more cases, this depends on what consumers say about the people who work in the organization. When you deal with an organization in which employees truly believe in what they're doing and live the values, you can feel the difference. When employees are on board with what their brand stands for, it translates to a better, more consistent experience.

MS: Which in turn builds loyalty and business. For a brand to succeed, you have to build your own culture, live by it, and take the long view. It must be sustainable. People should *absorb* a culture rather than have it thrust down their throats. You recruit the best people and motivate them. It's a way to communicate important truths about a company. And it helps clients understand and share with others why they use your services.

CHAPTER FIVE

To Have an Edge, Gear Up for a Marathon, Not a Sprint

In 1979, N. W. Ayer & Son, one of America's oldest advertising agencies, needed to come up with a creative approach to help AT&T, one of America's oldest brands, find a way to get consumers over the hurdle of making long-distance calls. The "Reach Out and Touch Someone" campaign ran for four years and was then launched anew in 2003 to draw attention to AT&T's wireless communications. It's amazing to think that there was a time that a phone company had to give consumers permission to pick up the phone to "just say hi." It's also amazing to think about how the telephone category has morphed over just the past couple of decades and that for the players, those still playing, how the bar for success has not been raised, so to speak, but keeps moving forward.

There is no question that branding is a marathon event. For companies that want to go the distance, this means taking the long view, planning ahead, and being just the right amount of paranoid. That is, always assuming that the other brand is nipping at your heels. (Believe me, it is.) Companies with an edge keep their eye on the horizon while keeping their eye on the prize: knowing what their brand stands for and why it's meaningful to their customers. The telecommunications industry is one of the fastest-growing categories in a marketplace that seems to move and change faster every day. With this in mind, I talked to Stewart Owen, a former colleague from Landor, and now chief strategic officer at the advertising firm mcgarrybowen, about his experience with this category and to get his input on the notion of marathon branding.

"The key challenge a brand has is how to increase its dominance," he told me. "Almost all successful brands begin with a simple idea, something to stand for, and ensure that it's different and better in a meaningful way. They never lose sight of their core meaning to people, but they need to keep identifying ways to stay competitive as the market moves forward. In the phone industry, the basis for differentiation has changed repeatedly. First, it was all about price. People were paying forty dollars to call family overseas. AT&T came out with its 'Reach Out and Touch Someone' campaign to tell consumers that it didn't have to be a special occasion to make a call. Then, the basis for differentiation moved to bundling. People had multiple phones and received multiple bills. One-stop shopping became the mantra. Then, when cell phones came out, but, pre-iPhone, it became signal strength, best illustrated by Verizon's 'Can you hear me now?' campaign. Post-iPhone, it's morphed a couple of times. First, it was which brand has the coolest devices and now, which one has the ability to offer the best content and make it easiest to access. The most powerful companies, those that move forward with the greatest success, are those that are smart and acute enough to see what's coming up next, what consumers want and need, and nimble enough to cover the turf, all the while keeping in mind who they are and what they represent as brands. It's why MCI and Nextel aren't in the competition anymore and why AT&T, Verizon, and T-Mobile are."

Stewart is absolutely right about the need to be both prescient and agile while keeping in mind what your brand stands for to consumers. The marathon event that is branding requires that you keep your balance. It's no longer enough to do what you did last year, just more of it; rather, it's a matter of continually looking at the world with fresh eyes to figure out how your brand can stay connected with your customers. And it's not just that products are changing, it's that the way people shop and live and everything else is changing. Hitting the default button, "If it ain't broke, don't fix it," doesn't work for even the most iconic companies, and that is why these companies stay iconic.

Take General Mills and its Pillsbury brand, for instance. To ensure that the brand was meeting the evolving needs of consumers, the smart folks at this company took a look outside the traditional box and had what CMO Mark Addicks called a "reinvention insight." "The brand was growing well," he told me in a recent conversation, "but we realized that there was something more we could do. When we went back and listened to what consumers were really telling us, we saw it was time to make a change in the Pillsbury brand. That change came down to a letter. Instead of looking at it as a 'baking' company, we began to look at it as a 'making' company. This change of a single letter opened up a whole new way of going to market. Where baking is functional and limiting, you bake biscuits and rolls or piecrust, making things for—and with—your family using Pillsbury products creates endless possibilities. It's what people were looking for: delicious and innovative ways to feed their families. We took the product from a commodity to a means of making life more fun, teaching your children while you create new things for dinner, making cooking a family event. In essence, we changed the frame of reference to a bigger arena, opened the funnel to include more than dinner rolls."

If you look at the Pillsbury website, you can see first-hand what Mark is talking about (and if you're like me, you'll get hungry). Pillsbury Grands!, for instance, aren't just the biscuits your grandma served at Thanksgiving dinner; they're also strawberry shortcake, chicken-bacon quesadillas, cinnamon pull-apart bread, sloppy joe casserole, and sausage calzones. To keep ahead in the marathon, to keep the edge as a brand, you've got to continually look at the world and your product from different perspectives; step back and see other ways your brand can fit into people's lives, and see if there is something bigger your brand can stand for. Among the many words of advice Mark offered up on this topic were these: "Be careful about the definitions and restrictions you put on your brand. You put the same shackles on audience interest. By narrowly defining your brand, you too narrowly define your audience."

Opening up a brand to a totally different audience is something that the oldest newsmagazine on television, *60 Minutes,* also did to keep ahead of the other, almost overwhelming, options people have for getting their news. Purposely, but almost imperceptibly, the CBS News program, the most successful in its category, has become younger in look and feel by peppering into the mix of long-standing and well-respected slate of correspondents, like Steve Kroft and Lesley

Stahl, new, and yes, younger, contributors, including Lara Logan and Anderson Cooper. In a category in which it's hard to keep up, let alone grow and evolve, *60 Minutes* has increased its viewership by appealing to the next generation. At the same time, it continues to appeal to its loyal fan base. That's because its producers never forget what the brand stands for. Viewers of *every* age have come to expect the reporting and the storytelling to be done at the highest levels, and they are. And viewers of every age appreciate that these stories are still kept to 20 minutes, just the appropriate length of time, even in this age of constant distraction. The show set the standard for the genre and continues to get better at its own game, Sunday after Sunday.

As Stewart Owen said, a brand must start out by identifying something to stand for that is different in a way that matters to the consumers it wants to reach. It is being able to take whatever this is and carefully update it over time to meet the changing needs of customers and the changes in the marketplace that makes for the greatest challenge in managing a brand. To win the branding marathon, you must start strong, but think about the entirety of the race at every step along the way. To be honest, I should add that a branding marathon doesn't really have a finish line, unless consumers deem that it does. Stay alert, and enjoy the stories that follow, each illustrative of what it takes to stay the course.

TOP TIPS: IT'S A MARATHON, NOT A SPRINT

The stories in this chapter are about gearing up for the long haul, because that's what it takes to build a brand with an edge. Success is not a one-time thing. Powerful brands have the nerve, the verve, and the agility to go the distance. They assess the competition relentlessly, and they assess the consumer mind-set relentlessly. Here are a few tips from brands that keep on moving forward:

- Being around a long time is only an asset if your brand maintains its relevance.
- Consumers can rarely tell you what they want. Do your homework. Keep going back to square one to look at your category from a fresh perspective.
- Live life in beta mode. Constantly tweak your "versions." Reinvention is not just for brands in the technology lane, but in every lane.
- You can't drive by looking at the curb. Look at the horizon in front of you. Be ready to zig when others zag.
- While evolution is critical to success, keep your balance. Don't lose sight of your core brand meaning.
- If you think there's a finish line, there will be.

IT'S *NOT* JUST TV ANYMORE, AND HBO KNOWS WHAT'S REQUIRED TO STAY AHEAD IN THE BRANDING MARATHON

Many critics have asserted that the show was the greatest and most ground-breaking television series of all time. They cite the acting, the direct-ing, and the writing, as well as the cinematography and the musical choices as reasons for their praise. It was among the first of many television shows to deal with difficult and controversial subjects, and its artistic contributors handled the subject matter with graphic, unflinching realism. A contributor to *Vanity Fair* magazine called it "perhaps the greatest pop-culture masterpiece of its day," and the *New Yorker* editor David Remnick called the show "the richest achieve-ment in the history of television," while the *New York Times* stated that this 86-episode series just may be "the greatest work of American popular culture of the last quarter century." I'm referring, if you hadn't guessed, to *The Sopranos,* one of *my* favorite shows ever (although the only people who listen to my enter-tainment critiques are my family members, two of whom are too young to have watched this epic HBO series).

But, while I have your attention, I think David Chase, the creator of this incredibly successful show, was one of the only writers at the time it was pro-duced to use television to its full potential to make a grand thematic statement about the American family (double entendre intended), and he never wavered from its core premise. Nor, for that matter, has HBO, the premium cable net-work that produced and aired the show. Since then, HBO has brought to the screen other entertainment that is groundbreaking for many reasons, from *The Pacific, Boardwalk Empire,* and *True Blood* to *Big Love* and *Sex and the City,* to *Deadwood* and *The Wire,* to miniseries including *Band of Brothers* and *Angels in America,* to the current hits *Girls* and, my latest must-watch, *Game of Thrones,* a high fantasy about seven nobles who are in a fight for control of the mythical land of Westeros.

Never wavering from the core essence of a brand, staying true to what it stands for in the minds of consumers, is what makes the best brands so powerful. But ensuring that the brand stays fresh and relevant is another of the factors that contributes to a brand's ongoing success and keeps it out in front of its competition. It's part of the marathon effort that separates leading brands from followers, and a topic that I decided to pursue further with Eric Kessler, who is the COO of HBO. Since its launch in 1972, HBO has done the required legwork to stay ahead and on top of what consumers want in terms of "groundbreaking" entertainment. Here is a part of our very lively discussion.

> **ALLEN ADAMSON:** For a brand to win over the long term, it means constantly finding ways to reinvent, to stay relevant to your audience. How has HBO looked at television and been able to consistently prepare for the future?
>
> **ERIC KESSLER:** Let's look at it this way. There had been very few significant changes in the way people watched television since its invention in 1946 until just a few years ago. There was the introduction of color in 1951. Then there was the introduction of HD in 2000. The box itself changed from a big set sitting on a table to a wall-mounted unit. But over the course of 50 years, there was one device on which people watched television and they were tethered to their home if they wanted to watch. Now, over the course of just the last five years, we've seen multiple devices hit the market on which people can get entertainment, including television shows. Computers, the iPad, and smartphones have fundamentally changed the way people think about watching television.
>
> **AA:** And it's the younger generation that is leading this change and this charge—a huge segment of the population that is determining how content should be delivered now and into the future.
>
> **EK:** Absolutely. For HBO to stay relevant to this audience, which is a critical audience, not only do we have to create content that speaks to them, like *Girls,* which has become a huge success, but we have to figure out how to deliver this content in a way that is relevant to them. The biggest danger for us is to become like your father's Oldsmobile, the advertising analog to falling behind the curve.
>
> **AA:** I assume that the development of HBO GO was, in part, an answer to this challenge. It allows people to watch HBO shows anytime and anywhere it's convenient for them.
>
> **EK:** HBO GO does exactly that. It's the integration of delivery and content through technology created specifically to meet audience needs. The concept is simple. An HBO subscriber should have the ability to

see whatever they want whenever they want at no additional cost. They've paid for the content. They should be able to watch it on their terms.

AA: So, basically, it's an un-tethering of the audience from the couch at home. If I have a subscription to HBO, I'm more likely to keep renewing it if I get to watch the stuff I want when I want it. My premium cable is a discretionary purchase. If you give me more access, I'll be more satisfied with the brand experience and become more loyal.

EK: It's an initiative that reflects the new definition of television. For the younger generation, it's *not* television, it's the iPad. I think the iPad has changed the business model of television and its once associated behaviors forever. You can physically interact with an iPad. No matter how sophisticated your remote control is, it will never do what the iPad does in terms of user engagement with content. If you take this further, as we have, it's changed the whole competitive set for television and for HBO. You had the consumer sitting at home on the couch watching HBO or another network. To move ahead, we had to evaluate this experience within the context of both programming and technology. Beyond individual networks, for example, you now have content aggregators including Hulu, Netflix, and Amazon. The key for HBO was to look at the competitive set and see it as inclusive of technology and myriad new content options.

AA: You have to think of yourselves differently and assess your brand promise on a different set of skill sets. You're no longer just being compared to network content providers, but to technology companies. This means that in addition to asking yourselves whether your programming is intriguing or creative or engaging enough, you have to ask yourselves is it easy enough to navigate, is it quick enough, or intuitive enough for users to access?

EK: To stay relevant we must continually evaluate the HBO brand not like a television network brand, but way beyond. While we're in 1.0 mode, we have to be thinking about 2.0, 3.0. More than this, we've had to really take advantage of social media and use it the way it should be used as a marketing tool. It used to be that before we'd launch a new show, we'd create a few teaser ads and run them a month or two before the start of the show. Then, maybe we'd keep them running a week or two after the show began to air. We'd let word of mouth run its course. Now, dialog about entertainment is ongoing. We see it as our responsibility to cultivate the dialog and keep it going. We have a whole team of people who tap into what viewers are talking about and generate more conversations about specific shows. Social media present a great opportunity for marketers. They have to know how to leverage it.

AA: HBO has done a great job of broadening its brand while staying true to its essence. As we've been discussing, what you do *has* to progress, but you've also got to balance your equities. With the pace of change in your category, this will only continue to be incredibly challenging.

EK: And this is one of the reasons we've morphed our tagline from "It's not TV. It's HBO." to simply, "It's HBO." It's in recognition of the fact that the category is not just about TV anymore. We have not deviated from our "true north," providing groundbreaking programming with only the highest level of production values, from the writing to the acting and directing. *Game of Thrones* couldn't be anywhere else but HBO. We have a vision and we will continue to bring it to the screen, albeit not just a television screen. This is not to say there isn't other great stuff out there. There is. It just pushes us to raise our game.

MCDONALD'S HEALTHIER HAPPY MEALS ARE JUST A FIRST STEP IN A BRANDING MARATHON

Less filling. Tastes great. No, it's not beer. For those of you who pay scant attention to what's happening under the "golden arches," McDonald's has made a significant commitment to help its customers—especially children and families—make healthier eating choices. It also wants to broaden its appeal to those who haven't, to date, made the mega-fast-food chain part of its consideration set when hunger sets in while on the road. McDonald's believes that there are many people who would stop by if they felt better about the product. And they've embarked on their mission with the right branding mind-set. They know it's not a single step that will change how consumers feel about the brand, like lowering the fat and sodium content of its Happy Meals, the menu item that became a flash point for those waging a battle against childhood obesity. Rather,

they are well aware that it will require a marathon of initiatives to continually reinforce what the brand is about, or wants to be about. That said, there is no powerful brand today that doesn't understand that keeping the edge is a marathon event.

The fact of the matter is that in branding there is no final destination. It's a journey. A smart company starts the journey by identifying something for its brand to stand for in the minds of consumers that is different in a way people care about. A smart company also knows that it must be able to evolve what its brand stands for over time without losing sight of what it was that made consumers love the brand in the first place. For example, a car company may want to be known for having greater fuel efficiency, but it doesn't want to lose whatever it was that drove its success to begin with, whether this was being seen as the sexiest, safest, or most powerful ride on the road. Discount retailers want to maintain their reputation for value, but they also want to keep up with what consumers want from the style side of the aisle. In the case of McDonald's, its claim was fast food, fun food, and tasty food. To stay a category leader, it knows it can't dismiss this promise, but it must carefully move away from being known as categorically unhealthy in order to meet changing attitudes toward food and nutrition.

> **The fact of the matter is that in branding there is no final destination. It's a journey.**

Although the notion is pretty simple, as a branding process, it's easier said than done. It takes time to change how people think about a brand, especially a brand with as deep a mental anchor as the McDonald's brand. While McDonald's has been on a journey to add healthier choices for a long time—it's had salads on its menus for years—to change its fundamental perception as a brand goes beyond re-jiggering its Happy Meals, adding a few apple slices, or replacing whole milk with skim. That's why, in addition to its new "delicious choices" campaign, which includes other more nutritionally beneficial menu items, it is literally and figuratively remodeling its more substantial branding points of touch, like its restaurants, for instance. Over the past year, the company has introduced Wi-Fi, IKEA-like furniture, and in some venues, flat-screen TVs, making the establishments look more like cool Starbucks than typical cafeteria-like fast-food joints. Some of its restaurants have even added solar panels and eco-friendly LED lights to the décor. Beverage choices have also been refreshed. McDonald's smoothies and espresso drinks have become a multibillion-dollar business in the United States.

While these steps have been critical in helping McDonald's change its image to meet the changing world, there's another step that has helped it make even greater strides: courting mothers. Given that mothers are often those most intent on the healthfulness of what their kids eat, McDonald's has made a concerted effort to get them actively involved in sharing their opinions with the company—and with other mothers—through well-publicized blogging forums and on Twitter. While it is not always ecstatic about the commentary, the company is gaining an advantage by making clear that it's listening, and mothers are pleased that they are being listened to and that their opinions are being taken into consideration. McDonald's has found that, in a transparent marketplace, this openness can be as potent a force as decreasing the size of the french fries portion in a Happy Meal.

That the average McDonald's restaurant in the United States generated nearly $2.6 million in sales in 2011, an increase of almost 13 percent since 2008, is an indication that its marathon initiatives to best the competition are on course. The company has demonstrated that it wants to step out in front of the national obesity issue and, in general, present a greener, more healthful image. Yes, there are a lot of people who loved McDonald's just the way it was. The key to its long-term leadership in the category, however, is to appeal to an entirely different bunch of consumers. As a smart brand, it recognizes that this will not happen in a single step, but in many steps over time. As it moves forward, the company must do whatever it takes not to lose sight of what made it a household name to begin with while meeting the needs of those for whom happiness is a healthier Happy Meal.

SEPHORA GIVES ITSELF A MAKEOVER TO KEEP
ITS EDGE AS A CATEGORY CHANGER

It happens to the best of them. They get a little tired looking. They just don't have that spark anymore. The blush, so to speak, is off the rose. I am, of course, talking about brands. And, any brand that's been around for a while is going to get to a point along its journey when it realizes that its game isn't as fresh as it should be. It's at this point that the best brands stop for a moment, take a good hard look at themselves and an equally hard look at the competition, and figure out what's required not to just get their mojo back, but to get back in the lead. While staying out front in the marathon that is branding is a challenge in every category, it is, perhaps, even more challenging in the fashion and beauty category where one season too many spent looking like last year's model can have major repercussions.

It was with this topic in mind that I called upon Antonio Belloni, a former client of mine at P&G and now group managing director of LVMH, the well-known purveyor of fashion and luxury goods, for insight.

It wasn't just that I knew he could tell me what it takes for a brand to keep up appearances in this arena, but that he and his team were in the midst of an overhaul of the Sephora brand. Now, just for some quick context (and for those who may not be in the fashion know), until Sephora came along, there were, generally, two ways for women to experience the world of cosmetics. One was the high-end department store, where everything was in glass-enclosed counters separating the customer from the products and for which you had to ask the price. And then there was the mass-market way, where cosmetic packaging was hung on wall racks and you played the color guessing game. Sephora introduced a third, category-transforming way in which women could experience cosmetics and beauty as they should be experienced. In essence, it opened up the cosmetics floor and let women play with the products. In fact, it broke with two industry conventions: prestige brands sold at individual brand counters staffed by commissioned representatives and mass-market brands sold in hard plastic packages with no service component at all. Sephora changed the business model, the category, and the customer experience in one beautiful move.

The retailer, which opened its first US store in the trendy SoHo neighborhood in New York City in 1998, is using this store and three others in Manhattan as launching sites for the brand's contemporary makeover. Manhattan is such a priority in the US market that the company actually refers to it internally as "the United States of Manhattan." Or, as Antonio told me in our conversation, it is where Sephora wants to put on its best face. What follows is just part of the fascinating conversation I had with him about the next steps in the marathon to keep this brand out in front.

> **ALLEN ADAMSON:** Sephora has grown so rapidly over the past decade. It's obvious that you touched a chord with women worldwide, enabling them to experience cosmetics the way they should be experienced. What did you see that prompted you to take on this brand makeover?
> **ANTONIO BELLONI:** Well, let's go back to 2009. In general, the market conditions were tough, but more than this, I walked into a couple of our stores in Manhattan and started to pick up signals that had

nothing to do with the economy. Sales were okay, but the energy level was down, the store fixtures tired, the experience predictable. As I went on to visit competitors, it struck me that not only had we lost some of the excitement that was associated with the brand, but other retailers were catching up. I went into Bloomingdale's on Fifty-Ninth and saw that they had made some impressive investments in design, in technology solutions, in the total experience. It made our stores feel dusty. I went to Abercrombie and Fitch on Fifth Avenue and saw some of their people dancing in the store. A bulb went off. I knew that we had to do something to refresh our experience and that if there was one place to show off our best efforts it was New York. It's where the opinion leaders are. Whatever people see here will count and be shared around the globe. I engaged the team on this challenge.

AA: Your brand is based on the idea of accessibility. Everything is accessible, both emotionally and physically—women can touch and try the products, personnel are not on commission, but are there solely to assist the customer without any affiliation with one product or another, and prices are clearly marked. You created Sephora with the idea that it should be a fun and enjoyable experience. What are you doing to reinvigorate the brand without losing sight of this core idea?

AB: It's systemic. Sephora is not about any individual product. It's about the total experience and enhancing the sense of fun and accessibility. When we set out for this renewal, we made sure we looked at how all the pieces, all the little things, would come together to meet this goal, from the physical nature of the store—the visuals, colors, and layout—to the attitude of our teams in the store to our beauty studios and nail polish bars to the uniforms, which were created by a fresh, young fashion designer. We also revamped our approach to e-commerce. We overhauled our website, we developed an official integration with Pinterest so customers can more easily "pin up" and share their favorite products, and we're installing iPads in some of our stores. We've even got Sephora TV on YouTube. Most important, the entire team of Sephora got energized on this elevation strategy. We asked the people who work in the stores for ideas. The key to our success was to get them engaged and motivated. They wanted to be reinvigorated and asked us to get involved. Only the people close to the brand and customers have the intimate knowledge and passion to come up with great, creative, surprising solutions. If the people who work for you feel passionate about what they do, if they make it their own, it will create a buzz and a sense of energy that could never be generated simply with communications from the top. They helped us rediscover and reenergize the core Sephora attitude to "make it fun."

AA: Buzz has become both literally and figuratively critical to staying out in front. People walk around with their smartphones and can instantly share their experiences with a brand. When a shopper feels excited, it's no longer a matter of sharing something on a one-to-one basis, but on a one-to-many basis. It's how you orchestrate things so beautifully that generates word of mouth, that tells the Sephora story.

AB: I agree. We need to be different and sell this totally different experience to our customers, especially being in the beauty industry where it's essential to be of the moment. Commodity is our enemy. Consumers can always find something cheaper. They can always buy a product somewhere else. That's not what Sephora is about. It's a system of activity that works together harmoniously. As such, it's something other stores just can't copy. In this market you can't afford to be complacent. We used the difficult market conditions, taking our core idea and making it exciting again.

DO SLOGANS HAVE ANY RELEVANCE IN A TWITTER-DRIVEN WORLD?

There have been myriad news reports about how Twitter is forcing people to get their ideas and thoughts across quickly and concisely. It's certainly an agile tool for communication and has been credited with everything from felling evil dictators to outing everyday politicians behaving badly. It's an always-on data stream from people around the world and is a wonderfully useful way, for those so inclined, to follow earth-shattering global events and life-changing personal events, as well as extraordinarily mundane events. And, yes, it does have its place in branding, especially when consumers can let thousands of friends and family members know in an instant that some experience with one brand or another has been less than great. A question many brand professionals ask, however, is whether a tweet will ever replace a brand slogan. The question was actually the topic of a very interesting edition of the daily newsletter 4A's *SmartBrief* that I read recently. And in just a few more than 140 characters, let me share my opinion.

Conventional wisdom says that it takes a long time to build a brand. What may appear to be overnight success doesn't really happen overnight. While many might think that digital technology makes this conventional wisdom, well, too conventional—given how quickly information can be shared—I say hold the phone. A tweet is a cool and efficient way to share information of immediate significance, a quick sound bite, as it were, but it doesn't come close to conveying what a brand stands for at its core. As much as I like the coolness and efficiency of social media, I also know that the coolness and efficiency of great brand lines take more than seven seconds to establish.

The success of a brand is determined in large part by its relevance to a specific group of people and its differentiation from competitors. Companies gain an edge because they use an assortment of tools and processes to capture the essence of its brand's meaning knowing that it will have to drive all of its branding efforts. A successful brand line, slogan, tagline, call it what you will, sums up concisely and effectively the essence of the whole brand story: Think Bounty's "Quicker picker-upper," FTD's "Say it with flowers," BMW's "Ultimate Driving Machine," or Hallmark's "When you care enough to send the very best." Not

here today and gone tomorrow, but a statement of purpose that is able to support and drive the branding for the long term.

Tweets done right are a fantastic way to get a quick thought across, well, quickly. Done right, they're also eminently sharable—a great media buy. But in my book, a tweet, even when pithy and articulate, doesn't carry the same weight as a strong, well-considered brand line built on a strong, well-considered, and actionable promise to consumers. A tweet lasts for maybe seven seconds. A brand line is a solid, meaningfully distinctive platform on which to stand as long as it's necessary. Tweet with your comments.

ACCENTURE NOT ONLY STAYS THE COURSE THAT IS BRANDING, BUT LEADS THE WAY

Running a marathon and winning is hard. Running a marathon and winning when significant hurdles are suddenly tossed into your path is harder still. Accenture, the global management consulting, technology services, and outsourcing company, has had a couple of well-documented branding hurdles thrown into its path over the last several years and yet it remains at the top of its game, the leader in its field, and, in fact, it gets stronger as it goes. For those who may not know the story, Accenture, initially called Andersen Consulting, was formally established in 1989 when a group of partners from the Consulting Division of the various Arthur Andersen firms around the world formed a new organization. By 2000, the company had achieved tremendous growth, with net revenues exceeding $9.5 billion and more than 70,000 professionals serving clients in over 46 countries. Enter branding hurdle number one: In August 2000, as the result of an arbitration decision, the company was required to change its name from Andersen Consulting, and it undertook one of the largest rebranding campaigns in corporate history. A few years later, enter branding hurdle number two: An iconic golfer who was the star of Accenture's very successful advertising campaign hit a bump in his own road to fame, and the company was forced to make yet another critical course correction (Tiger Woods, anyone?).

It was as a result of that arbitrator's decision that I and my colleagues at Landor first had the pleasure of meeting the folks from Accenture. We did some of the rebranding work for them, and the process was both incredibly challenging (we had five months to make it happen) and a lot of fun. Wanting to catch up on some of the latest initiatives being undertaken by Accenture's marketing team, I decided to touch base with Roxanne Taylor, who is the company's chief marketing and communications officer. She and I had the opportunity to reminisce about the crazy name-change period in Accenture's history and to talk in more depth about what it takes for a company to keep its edge in a fast-moving marketplace. Here is just one part of our interesting conversation.

ALLEN ADAMSON: Let's start with some facts about Accenture and about branding. With so many employees in so many locations around the

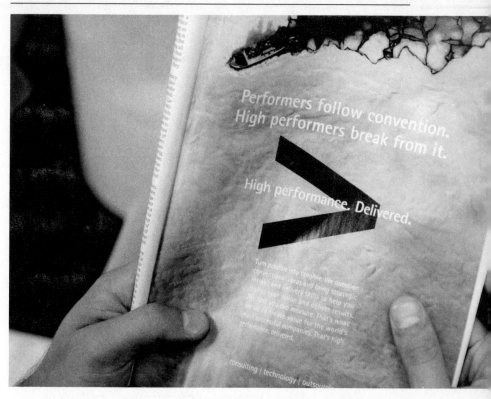

world, one of your biggest challenges must be getting people to understand who Accenture is as a brand, who they are relative to the brand, and how they need to engage.

ROXANNE TAYLOR: We're hiring 60,000 people a year. So, yes, it is important that we get all these people to understand our core values, what we stand for, and our business code of conduct. But it's also very important as we bring new people on board to recognize that, because they come from different countries and cultures, and because our business continues to change and evolve, you have to hold true to your core brand attributes and at the same time be sort of a living, breathing entity. You have to be organic to evolve.

AA: Do you think that you have an advantage and that you continue to be successful because you have such a clear point of view about your brand, how you manifest it and talk about it—"High Performance. Delivered." It's definitely not a fuzzy statement. It's a pretty focused promise.

RT: It does give us an advantage. Essentially, what we have done over time is build one global brand, and having a single global brand concept allows us to be efficient with our spending, certainly, but it also keeps us together in a way that speaks to both our clients and our employees. It's allowed us to go further than we would have if we had allowed ourselves to go off in different areas as different brands.

AA: Professional services are especially hard to brand because they're all in the problem-solution business. Your simple idea of what sort of solution you want to deliver has been consistent even as it's evolved over time.

RT: When I step away and think about what we've been able to do, when you go back to the year 2000 when Andersen Consulting officially separated 100 percent from Arthur Andersen, we had to relinquish a name that we had spent time building up—we had traction in the marketplace—and we went to a blank slate. Then we had this tiny period of time to come up with a new name and then transition all the brand equity we had built up under Andersen Consulting to that new name. We had from August 7 to January 1 to find a new name and get it into the marketplace. It was an incredible effort, and while we engaged Landor, we also engaged our people, and I think this is something that really differentiated us and continues to differentiate us. We get our people involved.

AA: And it was one of your own people who actually came up with the name Accenture. That was fantastic.

RT: I still remember the employee's submission like it was yesterday. "Accenture, it rhymes with adventure," he wrote. He told us how he thought of the idea while he was playing with his kids. It was so true to the culture of our company. Instead of being wedded to something that was created by someone from the outside, we were willing to chart our path based on something that was created by this young man in Norway. We all agreed on the name in October and then officially had everything rebranded by the first of January. It shows you how fast we were moving.

AA: And in situations like these, speed often helps. If you have a short amount of time, you're forced to focus and get it done as opposed to dragging it out and debating forever. You had to act quickly and you did.

RT: We called it "brand-storming," and we turned it into an exercise that was really fun. I think we were blessed by the fact that we had to move fast, especially coming from a big organization in which you can debate forever. There's something wonderful about being able to get all the facts on the table, debate to a degree, and then know you just have to move forward. This is something people don't know about our culture, our heritage. Accenture is a huge company, but it is nimble. It is characteristic of our company. Our name change, ensuring it worked in as many countries as we operate, that the concept behind the name translated well into many different languages, that we took care of all the branding including the digital components, it was the fastest rebranding that's ever been undertaken in a company our size.

AA: You had to really understand what your brand stood for and then transfer all the brand equity you had established to this new name.

RT: It was amazing. We debuted on Interbrand's list of great brands. It was "High performance. Delivered." And then the Tiger Woods thing happened. People sometimes say to me that they don't know how we acted so quickly to make our decision to move away from Tiger Woods, but it was with the same speed and decisiveness as when we changed from Andersen Consulting to Accenture. It is characteristic of who we are. We get things done. We live the brand.

AA: Tiger must have been hard to walk away from. He was the personification of someone who was performing and delivering. You could have debated, but you had to pull off the Band-Aid very fast.

RT: It's the culture of the company to be ready. When I began my job as CMO, way before the Tiger episode, I pulled everyone together and said let's look at a non-Tiger campaign. Everything was going great with Tiger, but I wanted to see creative work that didn't depend on Tiger, and I wanted to test it, and I wanted to keep testing new things because you never know what is going to happen. If we had to make a rapid change, I didn't want to be sitting there without a body of research and creative ideas we could quickly execute. It was a great exercise, and, at first, people were not taking it all that seriously, but we knew we always needed to be testing to see if Tiger still worked for us. It was a very expensive proposition to leverage his equity, and we wanted to make sure it continued to be the right thing.

AA: So, as a result of this, you were well positioned when everything hit the media. You got your first hint on a Wednesday night, and by Friday things were going down very rapidly.

RT: We were on alert. It wasn't just what *can* we do, but what will be the tasteful thing to do. By that Monday we had testing that went into the market, Tiger work and non-Tiger work. By Wednesday we sensed, through the testing, that there was a mood that Tiger was becoming very controversial. The market had shifted. We kept testing and we kept evaluating. We were able to make an informed decision very quickly and moved to end our relationship with Tiger. It was the same situation we were faced with during the name change. We were prepared. I'm a big believer in scenario planning. You need to have options. You have to always be thinking about the scenarios that could come to be and be protected on the downside. And that's what we did. We executed a scenario that was well thought out. We were able to move rapidly and launch something very quickly. And, we got kudos from our clients, by the way, who said, "wow," look at this company and how quickly and decisively—and with principle—it can make a decision and execute.

AA: It's all about your brand. A brand is as a brand does. So, if you're trying to sell this benefit to a client and they see you can do it yourself, it makes you more credible.

RT: That really is the case. I think that there is real value in putting a characteristic on your brand that makes you human. People may assume you're a big behemoth company that can only move slowly. But when they see you acting swiftly and decisively, it changes their perception.

AA: This is a strong promise in your space. There are a lot of smart people who do consulting, but at the end of the day, your position is about being smart and being able to get it done. It really is about high performance delivered. Tell me about how you've moved forward since then.

RT: It's been a challenging environment for everyone since 2008. So in 2009, we moved quickly to our "animals" campaign. We wanted our ads to have lightness to them, but also stopping power. Most of our clients are large global players. They travel a lot. They're always on planes and running through airports. They look up at our ads and smile. By making people smile, especially at a time when everything is bad news, I think it has made our company more human and accessible. The new campaign, which was launched in November 2011, gets to the heart of what we do and reflects the depth and breadth of our capability. The full spectrum of what we offer. It is important to remember, however, that underlying these creative campaigns is our consistent "High Performance. Delivered." brand positioning, which we have not changed and which continues to be a powerful differentiator for our audiences.

AA: Your mission is to try and differentiate what you do—to bring the idea of high performance delivered to life in a disruptive but meaningful way. You made incredible use of your logo in this present initiative, and in a way that's dead simple.

RT: Exactly. We have this amazing logo that includes a unique "greater than" symbol. It was right there and has been part of the company's logo for more than ten years. The campaign is based on the idea of working with our clients to help them be "greater than." However, it's not just relevant to our clients; the proposition works for our people as well. It's something that all people get. It's not convoluted. We bring the idea to life with disruptive colors and bright visuals and a bit of humor. There's a real human element to it. One of my personal favorite ads is the one that features Marriott and the kid in flip-flops in the swimming pool. You see it and know immediately that it's Accenture. What's really exciting is how well our employees have connected to these ads. They take photos of them on their travels around the world. They feel proud of the message and how it connects to what they do.

AA: So the campaign accomplishes two jobs. It expresses the work you do in human terms making the client the hero, and it energizes your employees. You want your clients to succeed, and it's your employees who help them improve their performance. What lessons learned would you pass along to other companies regarding the idea of brand building being a marathon?

RT: You can't see the future, but you have to plan for it. You have to keep asking yourself what you want to achieve. We have 249,000 employees, and we're all about making them feel proud about being here and supporting our clients. It's about creating value for our clients for the long term.

THE SECRET BEHIND JUSTIN BIEBER'S BRAND SUCCESS

Building a pop-star brand is not a new thing. I was reminded of this fact when I heard news of the death of Davy Jones, one of the members of The Monkees, a group that was initially cast by TV producers who wanted to create a series about an actual rock 'n' roll band. The series, the group, and Jones, in particular, exploded in popularity, succeeding beyond anyone's expectations. Dubbed the "pre-fab four" by critics, the group rebelled against its management in an effort to take greater control of its destiny. Pre-fab or not, the group scored a handful of No. 1 songs and four No. 1 albums. Not bad for band brand management. Not bad either, in fact, incredibly powerful, is the brand management of Justin Bieber, the latest teeny-bopper (am I dating myself?) heartthrob.

A year or two ago, as almost everyone in the movie theater for the showing of the documentary *Never Say Never* (including my eight-year-old daughter) watched in awe while hot-topic Justin Bieber flipped that wonderful hair off his wonderfully cherubic face, I watched in awe as his first-class management team, including Usher and Scooter Braun, skillfully carried out the tenets of Branding 101. It's not without good reason that this flop-top pop star has become the successful brand he has and that his YouTube videos, like *Boyfriend,* get almost 18 million views in the week after their release. The reason or, rather, reasons are as follows.

OVERNIGHT NEVER HAPPENS OVERNIGHT

While it may seem that Justin Bieber and any number of other strong brands appear magically overnight, this is not the case. It takes laser focus on a clear objective delivered consistently and with due diligence over a period of time to win hearts and wallets, especially in this very competitive, noisy marketplace (*American Idol, The Voice, Glee,* anyone?). Justin did his time playing in shopping malls and in parking lots from Cleveland to Syracuse, and visiting radio station after radio station with his finely tuned act, all the while remaining conscientiously attentive to his musical concept. A brand that succeeds, be it a Kashi or a Southwest, a Boyz II Men or a Bieber, does so because it steadily and reliably sticks to cementing what it stands for in the minds of consumers.

NO DETAIL IS TOO SMALL

The experience—and reputation—of a brand is the sum of its parts, no matter how big or small the parts may be. Even with its breadth and depth of inventory, Zappos wouldn't be Zappos without the quick and friendly e-mail follow-up or its super-easy return process. Whether it's his vocal coaching, his hair stylist, his back-up singers, or his choice of public relations initiatives, those in charge of the Justin Bieber brand, including Justin himself, know that one inauthentic move, one missed detail, one non-Bieber incident, could make non-Beliebers out of his fans.

TELL YOUR OWN STORY

If you don't say it, who will? Maybe the millions of people on YouTube or with Twitter accounts. The best brands grab hold of the message they want to communicate, and they communicate it in a style commensurate with the image they want to evoke. Take Unilever's Dove brand, for instance. It started with the brilliant video *Evolution,* in which a lovely young woman morphs into a stunning but unrecognizable version of herself by means of make-up and heavy photoshopping. The idea is that every woman deserves to feel beautiful just the way she is, and the Dove brand team continues to build on that idea. It's a campaign that has lasted and, more important, outlasted its many online parodies. *Never Say Never* was a brilliant way for the Bieber brand team to tell its story and, just as brilliantly, to get it out there when the media wind was at its back. When you're on a roll, do what you can to keep the momentum going. Since the launch of his movie, Bieber has released a couple of full-length studio albums, including *My World 2.0* and *Under the Mistletoe,* which both debuted at No. 1 on the Billboard 200 chart. His music video *Baby* is among the top-ranked and discussed YouTube videos.

KEEP GOOD COMPANY

Or, said another way, the company you keep can help define your brand. Gatorade gets a burst of branding energy from its association with professional sports brands, and Visa receives a healthy lift from being associated with the Olympics brand. These alignments are smart because they're in line with how these brands want to be—and are—perceived. In a similar spirit, Justin Bieber's brand image gets serious street cred from his association with American recording artist, dancer, and all-around superstar Usher, not to mention the likes of Miley Cyrus, Jaden Smith, and Ludacris.

> *The company you keep can help define your brand.*

OH, YES. MAKE SURE YOU'VE GOT A GOOD PRODUCT

I did say I enjoyed watching *Never Say Never,* didn't I? And although it was partly because I appreciated the branding acumen of the Bieber team, the kid can sing. He's personable. He's professional. All in all, he's good at what he does, and he is what he says he is. At the end of the day, if a brand can't deliver on expectations and do what it's supposed to do competently, if not better than all the rest, well, it should keep its day job. Justin, in my branding book, you're doing okay. (Your 20 million followers on Twitter think so, too.)

"GE WORKS," AND HAS WORKED, AT KEEPING ITS
BRAND RELEVANT FOR OVER 130 YEARS

I love toy trains and have spent many pleasant hours putting together and sharing Lionel train sets with my kids. Scott Slawson loves toy trains, too. But he took his passion and made a career out of it. He builds real trains—locomotives, that is—for GE in Erie, Pennsylvania. Scott and his equally passionate coworkers are featured in just one of many commercials that GE aired this past year to bring to life its refreshed brand positioning. This one, in particular, captures the exhilaration this Erie-based train team personally experiences at the sight of one of the products they created powering a mile-long BNSK freight train through the panoramic countryside near the Columbia River Gorge in Washington State. GE knows that railroads are the best and most efficient way to transport goods over land. And the designers, mechanical engineers, and other highly skilled

professionals who design and build them are using cutting-edge science and processes to improve this efficiency. It's just one of the many ways in which "GE Works" to make the world a better place, using imagination as its fuel.

I use this anecdote by way of introduction to an incredibly enlightening interview I had with Judy Hu, global executive director, advertising and branding, at GE. In her role, Judy is responsible for taking a complex array of technologies and forging them into a simplified global message for GE that is not just used as the catalyst for groundbreaking advertising, but is the driver of employee culture and the motivation for the work it does around the world. Before I get to this interview, however, it's important to rewind the tape to set some context for our discussion. It was over ten years ago that GE began using "Imagination at Work" as its tag line and as a statement of inspiration for everyone in the company. To get to this message, GE went back to its genesis, its heritage: the imagination of Thomas Edison. From day one, GE has been able to imagine things that other companies couldn't and make them real. Imagination was a big thing, and they could own it. It was simple and it was authentic. It is at the core of everything GE has done and still does. What's more, *being* the innovative people they are, they took this phrase and found an imaginative and intuitive way to tell their story in a format that everyone in every GE business unit in every country worldwide could connect to. They took the new GE equation, as they called it, and drew it on a chalkboard to creatively telegraph its meaning. I called Judy when I learned that the company had undertaken an initiative to review its statement of purpose and determine its relevance. The world, as GE and everyone else knows, has changed a lot over the past ten years.

> **ALLEN ADAMSON:** So, this is all about "Imagination at Work," the next chapter. Your tag line is coming up on its tenth anniversary, which is really a long time in the world of brands. What prompted the decision to look with fresh eyes at what is often referred to as the GE "brand driver"?
>
> **JUDY HU:** What we started out doing a year ago, what with all the changes in the world, the economic crisis, a series of natural disasters from hurricanes to a tsunami, was to take a deep dive and see if "Imagination at Work" was still relevant, both internally and externally. Part of the issue at GE is that we're so complex. It's so hard to get to know us. In the United States some people think of us as just appliances and lighting.

In the rest of the world, the challenge is just getting people to know us at all. The overall objective of our initiative was to see if we needed to evolve the positioning of the GE brand by assessing its current state and future associations. We started by talking to our employees. We interviewed over 100 people from different countries who represented an array of functions and came from different levels. I was amazed at how consistent the answers were. In essence, our employees see GE as a "we" company, not a "me" company.

AA: It's the best of inside-out branding. You can't build a corporate brand without building a corporate culture. The two are inextricably linked. Everything stems from the employees. Every employee has to be a brand ambassador.

JH: Right. When GE focuses on something, as one of our employees said, "It's all hands on deck with everyone rowing in the same direction." It plays out in everything we do. There was a lot of talk in the research about GE being a "builder," not just of the world's technology, but of its people. We found that our employees believe that GE is making a real difference in the world—there's a sense of pride and optimism because there's a higher purpose to our work. They see that what we do every day really changes people's lives. And then, importantly, we found that "Imagination at Work" still resonates with our employee base. In fact, one person in the survey summed it up this way: "We *are* imagination at work. We live it."

AA: They don't see GE as a think tank, but a place where innovation is applied in practical ways. If innovation doesn't lead to utility, what's the value? So what conclusion did this lead you to?

JH: We decided after studying the data that we didn't want to lose "Imagination at Work," but we wanted to shift the balance from "imagination" to "work." We wanted to put more of the emphasis on the work we do, so we use the words "GE Works" just prior to "Imagination at Work" in our branding initiatives, internally and externally.

AA: It's a simple and subtle evolution, but it's powerful. Any company can promise that it thinks great thoughts, but you realized that it's getting things done that really resonates in today's market. It's making things happen as opposed to just talking that hits home, especially given all that's gone on; the "actions speak louder than words" or "a brand is as a brand does" philosophy.

JH: Yes, and to make sure that this evolution in our thinking connected with our employees, we went back to that chalkboard, the one that had worked so well in communicating before, and we wrote out a new equation. This one starts with looking at what the world needs and using our employees as the secret sauce—the multiplier in the equation. When combined with a belief in a better way and our relentless drive to invent and build things that matter, it all adds up to a world that works better. It's about creating things of consequence, water purification, giving people power and energy, our green effort, and medical equipment that can diagnose and treat disease.

AA: When your employees saw this purpose, this new spin on the original position articulated in such a clear-cut way, they were able to understand it and internalize it.

JH: It turned into a template for them, something against which to measure their own stories and contributions. I had one engineer who told me, "I love working in lighting, especially in LED. I've been excited about lighting since my first physics class. Here at GE, I'm constantly inspired to look for the next best thing." This position is like a mantra, it's a way for people to explain who they are and express what they do.

AA: Was there anything about the process of refreshing the GE positioning that surprised you? You certainly did all the right things, from research to testing, before you pulled the trigger.

JH: We were fully ready to walk away from "Imagination at Work." In today's world, people don't want pipe dreams. But it's still working for us. I am continuously amazed at how consistent the culture is here, wherever I go. It's a very GE thing. Let the employees tell the story. Link them back to the culture and make it a proof point.

GREAT BRANDS MAKE GREAT INVESTMENTS

Every year another marketing research company comes out with a study that shows a formulation for assigning a dollar value to brands. Now, every smart marketer knows a brand is an asset to a company. Brands are worth lots of money, which is why marketing firms keep coming out with studies to make sure Wall Street is aware of this fact. The question Wall Street asks, however, is can marketing firms provide an objective analysis? After all, it is only to the marketing firms' advantage that they measure the financial value of a brand. It is proof that their marketing efforts are paying off.

So, it was to my surprise and delight when Credit Suisse, a solid financial institution, came out with a study based on solid facts and figures that established that brand value gives a company a genuine competitive edge. For the investment community, this was a new way of thinking. And if they want to take ownership of the idea, that's fine by me. As long as someone out there raises awareness that, in addition to factors like scalability and proprietary technologies, brand-as-asset is a credible reason to consider a company, well, a solid opportunity. Better yet, for those looking at our industry from a financial point of view, the demonstration that great brands make great investments should finally get the traction it deserves.

There are a couple of reasons that "brand" as an indicator of investment value is often disregarded by financial markets. First, brands are frequently considered intangible in nature. CFOs have always had trouble getting their calculators around them. This is due in part to the second reason: data on brand performance are usually measured on a quarter-by-quarter basis. It goes back to the old saw that you know part of your advertising is working, but you just don't know which part. This doesn't have to be.

Smart branding is a long-term play, like investing. Sure, a nifty one-off promotion will give your brand a boost in the ratings, but this doesn't mean the fundamentals are solid. It just means consumers like a good deal without any regard for loyalty. Companies that take a long-term view of the market and invest in their brand building accordingly will more likely than not become strong contenders for investment portfolio material. Or, as Credit Suisse says in its report, "Companies that focus on brand building consistently generate outsize, long-term growth, profitability and return."

So what brands did the report include and why? Yes, there were the usual suspects for all the right Branding 101 reasons. Apple, Facebook, Ralph Lauren, and Amazon were there because each continues to offer best-in-class products and services that consumers consider relevant and better than others in the companies' respective categories. In addition, there were overseas brands including the Sonova Group, the high-end European hearing aid company; Li-Ning, the expanding Chinese footwear brand; and Mahindra & Mahindra, the Indian truck and trailer manufacturer.

To those of us in the United States, there was ample evidence of how more familiar companies that follow the basic rules of branding got onto the list. For example, Tiffany and Company, the world's premier jeweler since 1837,

continues to design and produce unique pieces that appeal to a growing global audience of Tiffany Blue Box aficionados. Hyundai, the automotive brand whose Genesis, Elantra, Sonata, and Equus models continue to top the charts for most popular cars, has gained incredible market share as a result of meeting the wants and needs of consumers looking for "affordable luxury." The fact that it has taken advantage of Toyota's strategic missteps also factors into its success. Trader Joe's, "your neighborhood grocery store," also made the list for its ongoing ability to find and offer high-end products at great prices. What's more, that the company is poised for international expansion is not going unnoticed.

Before investors sink their hard-earned dollars into brand-name products, let me make one thing very clear. There are specific reasons some brands make for stronger investment material than others. A brand becomes a worthwhile investment only when it is built and managed according to the long-standing rules of branding: Stand for something that consumers find different and that they care about, something that will make their lives better in some discernible way. Stay ahead of the pack by identifying ways to stay relevantly different. Easier said than done, of course, and this is why the Credit Suisse list was limited to "27 great brands," not hundreds.

There will probably always be tension between Wall Street and Madison Avenue professionals who tout the benefits of a strong brand name to investors. That said, there is solid evidence that Wall Street is starting to see the light. Great brands make great investments.

VERIZON'S EDGE? IT NEVER STOPS WORKING ON
WHAT ITS CUSTOMERS FIND RELEVANT

Although you have probably never met Paul Marcarelli, you no doubt know him. He's the iconic Verizon "Test Man" who used to roam the country through wheat fields, across snowy mountains, through airports, along highways, and even into a bowling alley to ask, "Can you hear me now?" This simple question, all too familiar to cell phone users, helped move network reliability to the top of the list as a key purchase consideration for users of wireless telephones at a time (lo, those many years ago) when other companies wanted to make the competition about price and minutes. And, it helped move Verizon to the top of the list as a wireless provider as a result of its changing the playing field in such a meaningful way. In actuality, the "Test Man" was the personification of legions of Verizon employees who would travel around the country testing the reliability of the network to ensure that, yes, we could all literally hear whoever it was on the other end of the line.

While the conversation about wireless has moved beyond just reliability, Verizon has not stopped in its quest to identify what's next on consumers' lists of what they need from a network provider. It's a fast-changing category with a list of fast-changing criteria, and it was with this idea in mind that I put in a call to John Harrobin, vice president of marketing communications for Verizon Wireless. I wanted to get his insight relative to what it takes to keep a brand relevant in a marketplace in which hearing people now, listening to what's important to them, is imperative to keeping an edge.

> **ALLEN ADAMSON:** Verizon is definitely a brand that has kept its edge, even as the category has experienced seismic shifts in its products and its services. But let's go back before we go forward. Tell me about "Test Man" and how clarity became such a hot topic.
>
> **JOHN HARROBIN:** To put it simply, our customers told us they wanted more reliable service. So, one of the things we did at the outset of Verizon Wireless is that we made reliability matter to the marketplace. We did it, first of all, because we had a magic formula that allowed us to deliver a more reliable service experience than our competitors.

But it was three critical things that came together that enabled us to differentiate the brand so significantly in the minds of consumers from the get-go: We knew reliability mattered. We messaged it with our advertising. And we delivered it. To keep an edge you have to evolve your offering and your brand to give customers what they tell you they want. When we saw that our brand, that "Test Man," was starting to get a little stale—you know, any spokesperson is eventually going to have a wear-out effect, especially a large advertiser like Verizon that does a ton of advertising—we refreshed him and the message by putting the network around him. We had him travel with a bunch of support people, all the people who make our service what it is.

AA: So you broadened the story a bit. It became not just him, but a personification of the whole Verizon infrastructure. You brought it to life.

JH: That's right. It allowed us to expand beyond just voice reliability to make the message about smartphones, and text messaging, e-mail, data transfer, and Internet surfing on your phone. Our customers told us they wanted to do more with content and applications, which is why we were among the first to message and deliver content applications—we had exclusive content deals. We launched a phone that was an MP3 player, called Chocolate, and we were the first provider to invest in 4G LTE technology and roll it out nationwide.

AA: This being, in your industry, the next generation of mobile communications standards. So to recap, part of keeping the edge in your world is anticipating network capability requirements, aligning with customer interest, and ensuring you've got your messaging set to go in advance. If we go back to "Test Man," which gave the brand amazing traction, it was based on a simple benefit—reliability—which you hit squarely on the head, and you stayed focused on this as long as it remained critical to consumers.

JH: Exactly. We knew when it was time to go beyond voice. We had to transition to performance because customers wanted different things with regard to their phones—they wanted speed and coverage, applications and experiences. We broadened the message by listening, in a methodical way, to what was on consumers' minds. If you don't listen, you get stuck on last year.

AA: I remember when you moved from the tag line "Can you hear me now?" to "It's the network," and that entire cast of characters—the network support people.

JH: "It's the network" became the unifying campaign theme across our many expanding lines of business, not only wireless, but FIOS and the Verizon global IP network. It gave people a compelling visual and verbal reason to believe in Verizon beyond just reliability.

AA: If you could sum up the lessons learned after all these years as steward of the Verizon brand, what would you say it takes for a brand to keep its edge?

JH: Three things. First of all, the best advertising is based on the truth. Do not put advertising muscle behind anything that will dilute your brand. For example, we put lots of money behind our "push-to-talk" effort, and the product wasn't as good as it should have been. It backfired. Great lesson learned. Second, continue to reinvent yourself, but start from a foundation of strength and one that enables you to springboard. The "Test Man" was a bridge to the network. He allowed us to recast our story in a different context in a believable and authentic way. And third, in order to build a strong brand you have to win the hearts and minds, not only of your customers, but of your employees. Brands clarify ownership. Strong brands are icons based on a belief system. The strongest brands are those whose beliefs are embraced by the employees and whose employees can communicate what makes their brand the best. They need to feel pride. Our employees are our advocates. This is not a hobby to them. They have an incredible amount of passion for, and belief in, what they do. Our culture is one of our competitive advantages.

CHAPTER SIX

To Have an Edge, a Brand Must Know Where It Can Play and Win

It's been a long time since I was in business school, years during which I had the time and privilege to sit in the classrooms of some incredibly smart professors who could bring clarity to very complex topics. They could present the big picture and get me to think about it deeply and from multiple points of view. I thought about this recently when I had the opportunity to hear two incredibly smart professorial types talk about business and investing and how they became so successful. My son, you see, had been given one share of Berkshire Hathaway stock as a gift. Upon looking it over and reading that all shareholders are invited to attend the annual meeting in Omaha, Nebraska, he suggested we go. "Why not," I thought. First, it would be a valuable eye-opener for a kid from New York City to see Omaha, and, second, it would be valuable for both of us to join the more than 25,000 shareholders who come to listen and learn from Warren Buffett and his friend and colleague Charlie Munger.

The experience was all I'd expected it would be, and more. It gave me lots to think about with regard to the business world and my small piece of it in the brand-building arena. While I could write an entire book on the wit and wisdom of Buffett and Munger, I'll save that for the future. Instead, for the moment, I'd like to borrow some of their thinking relative to the subject of this chapter: with the proliferating ways a company has to signal its brand's message, how do you decide where you can play and actually win? Let me begin with, well, the big picture.

Warren Buffett's philosophy descends from what is known as the Benjamin Graham school of value investing. Value investors look for companies, or securities, with prices that are unjustifiably low based on their intrinsic worth, which is generally based on a company's fundamental strengths. Value investors look for products or services that are beneficial and of high quality but that may be undervalued by the market. Buffett looks at a host of factors during his assessment of whether to buy a company, among them its return on equity, how much debt it has, and its profit margins. But—and here's where my branding sensors chimed in—Buffett also tends to shy away from companies whose products are indistinguishable from those of their competitors. If a company does not offer anything different than another firm within the same industry, he generally doesn't see it as a good long-term bet. What's more, if he can't understand the benefit to the consumer, or even get his head around what the company does, he's less than likely to add it to his portfolio. The benefit of the product or service must be simple to understand by him and by those the company hopes to attract as customers. Perfect segue.

Getting consumers to understand what makes your brand different and why they should care—what benefit it possesses that will make their lives better in some significant way—is critical to gaining an edge in the market. As I've been reiterating since the beginning of this book, for a brand to break through, it must be based on a simple idea that is relevantly different from its competitors. It is almost impossible to do effective branding unless the meaning of your brand and its benefits are absolutely clear. If it is, the signals you create to express the idea will have far greater impact in cementing the associations you want people to have about the brand. As you look at your brand, you should have no doubt as to what you want your branding to communicate.

This said, before you begin the process of determining where to spend money communicating your brand's message, you must have a pretty good sense of where your brand touches people—whether through real experiences in tangible places or in virtual interactions. Once you look at this "map," as it were, one of the factors in achieving success is to identify which of these points of touch can have the greatest potential to influence perception—where and how you can generate the greatest measure of brand-*ness*. You need to have a sense of what will drive home the thing that makes your brand different in a way that will resonate best with the people who matter. Decide which branding initiatives will do the most good in getting your idea across. Then put your money there.

Okay, so where's there? With the proliferation of branding channels, how do marketers make sense of the palette of opportunities? There is no single silver bullet of an answer. The stories you'll read in this chapter will illustrate just some of the ways companies with an edge deal with the question. Before I go there, however, let me offer three guiding principles with the help of a few other professorial types I've had the privilege to meet in my career, including a bona fide professor.

WHAT'S YOUR OBJECTIVE?

Many marketers are of the belief that television as a branding tactic is dead. Sure, it might appear that with the declining ratings for many shows, the increasing use of DVRs and other ad-skipping technology, the fragmentation of audiences, and the growing appeal of digital devices that let us take our many screens with us, television as a way to express a brand message might seem the least likely candidate. The fact is, however, it all depends on your branding objective. It still holds true that, despite all the above challenges, television is the best medium to use when your goal is to generate basic awareness of the differences in your brand's attributes over your competitor's to a whole bunch of people at once. Mass-market television advertising satisfies this objective better than the alternatives. According to Nielsen, television ad revenue in the United States last year was up 5 percent over the previous year, and it's on an upward track this year. Mass marketers, many whose brands have an edge (FedEx, AT&T, American Express, GE, McDonald's, Apple, and IBM, among them), say television works just fine for them when they want to reach mass audiences quickly with a broad message about what makes their promises uniquely different.

The key to success when using television to meet this objective, however, is to make sure your story makes the point you want the masses to take away. Just as millions of people may see your spot, so, too, will they be able to rip it apart on YouTube or Facebook or Twitter. Having a good story to tell and making it memorable is important. Who doesn't want to be the hero as millions of viewers play armchair quarterback after the Super Bowl line-up of ads? But memorable because the ad is humorous, or tugs a heartstring, or is just darn clever, is not enough. Ensuring that the story is credible is equally important, especially when part of the objective is to let millions of people know why yours is *not* a commodity product. It was during a fascinating conversation with Brian Perkins, former vice president of corporate affairs at Johnson & Johnson, that we talked about how this is one aspect of branding that is probably more important now than it ever was. Brian had this to say:

"With so many messages out there, so much information, and so much skepticism, the ability to tell a good story that builds credibility about why your product is a better choice is critical. If it can touch a human chord, that's even better. Today, with so many more places for a story to be shared, you have to make the story worthy of conversation, even in the most mundane categories. I remember many years ago when we launched Tylenol. At first, it had been available solely to and through professionals—doctors, hospitals, pharmacists. It was up to these medical professionals to recommend the product. When Tylenol became an over-the-counter product, we were able to tap into this authenticity. We had deep support from the medical community. Consumers would go to the shelves in the drugstore and ask, 'Why *wouldn't* I want to buy what doctors and hospitals use most?' It was a point of difference that was authentic, and it resonated with consumers."

Now, just as smart marketers know what television *can* do, they also know that it is not a one-stop branding solution. It might be a way to get the conversation started, but if your branding objective is to become an active participant in the conversation, then it makes sense to support this mass channel with another of a more intimate nature. AT&T, for example, has made great use of Facebook by establishing it as a credible customer-service channel. It's got a whole team of people ready and able to respond to questions or deal with customer issues quickly. In this case, AT&T is using Facebook exactly the way it should be used—to make connections the moment something happens, whether it's a good something or a bad something. Rather than let comments go into the ozone, AT&T gets what social media is all about and is using this branding touch to listen and learn from its customers about how to make the AT&T brand experience better. They're taking care of business in a place that feels friendly and open and familiar to its users. Whether it's online or off, no matter where you choose to play, it's essential to start with a clear understanding of the objective of the initiative.

WHAT DO YOU OWN?

There's a great difference between the brand assets you own and those you rent. You rent television and radio, for instance. You rent a site on Facebook. It can even be said that you rent space at the end of the aisle in the supermarket. These are worthy branding channels and good places to think about spending your branding dollars. But another significant bang for the branding buck can be derived from taking full advantage of the assets that are proprietary to your brand, the things you own. For example, how about those distinctive white trucks painted with what has become an iconic and very familiar logo? Whether the logos are purple and green, purple and orange, or purple and red, these trucks are unmistakable signals of the FedEx brand and an ongoing reminder of the company's promise to deliver—reliably. Or consider the sight of a coach getting "dunked" by a barrel of Gatorade at the end of a winning game. This couldn't happen with any beverage other than Gatorade. Its placement on the field of play has attained iconic status for very good reason. It's a drink that was created by athletes for athletes, and it's this authentic underpinning that makes this branding signal so powerful. How about the design of the Kit Kat bar and the clever way the company signifies its delicious difference with its "Gimme a break" song and snappy sound effect? This continues to be a very successful branding signal, and the company understands this. As does Apple, relative to the design of almost everything it does, from its logo to its products to its packaging to its retail environments—cool and clean and beautifully functional design is where Apple invests its branding dollars.

Looking for input on the topic of using what your brand already owns as a leverage point for its branding, I decided to call on Kevin Lane Keller, professor of marketing at Dartmouth's Tuck School of Business. As I knew he would, he offered up a terrific example. "Let me tell you about King Arthur Flour," he began. "It's a really neat case. Here's a product that is a commodity product. It's flour. You find it on the bottom shelf in the baking aisle at the supermarket. But, at its core, it's high-performance flour. It has a great reputation among people who love to cook and bake. I'm not an expert on baking, for sure, but this flour is made in a way that makes baking better. Word of mouth, old-fashioned word of mouth, by the way, fueled this brand for years. Cooks and people who are into food love this product, so word got around. Now, at the heart of every great brand is a great product, and while this is necessary, it's not necessarily sufficient. What the folks at King Arthur did was take advantage of the fact that they already had a community of bakers who loved to talk about the product. You get these situations where it's so obvious, and they picked up on it. They picked up on what people were already doing, and through online media they created ways for people to engage even more. More than this, recognizing that the best way for people to understand a brand is to actually interact with it, they found ways to tell their story through real-time experiences, at classes and through contests, and by offering tips and recipes direct from top chefs on their website. They created ways for people to actively engage and experience the brand."

"So here we have this very simple category," Kevin continued, "this commodity, and the folks at King Arthur found a way to differentiate their brand in a meaningful way. You *do* actually bake better with it, and this is what gives them permission to do what they're doing. Their product, by virtue of its proven higher quality, gives them a credible point of entry into both the virtual and real-time worlds of consumer involvement, and they use it as a way to spread the story. Social media is not right for every brand. People who like to cook also love to share. King Arthur is just a natural fit for social media and how it should be used. It legitimately owns the product and is engaging the right people to help tell its story."

YOU'RE EXPERIMENTING, BUT ARE YOU MEASURING?

It's hard to have a conversation with anyone in the marketing business about the topic of where to spend on branding without social media coming up. As I said earlier in the book, while it's always been there, it has become an ex-ponentially powerful force. There's greater opportunity to hit a media home run. But social media as a branding channel have a lot of moving parts. It's not one size fits all (or even *at* all). And it was for expert advice on this topic that I turned to Lee Doyle, who is the president, client development of Mindshare, a company within WPP. "In a pre-web world, we wanted people to talk about our brands," he told me. "This isn't a new dynamic. As much as social media is a buzz, face-to-face is still the most powerful way for one person to recommend a brand to another. Moving across the spectrum, if someone takes the time to write something on a review site, to actively recommend a product or service online, it's still a strong response. But if someone simply clicks 'LIKE,' without any personal commitment, what does this actually mean in terms of measurement? Those who have been active in social media for a while are trying to determine whether 'LIKES' are a real measure of success for a brand. Shouldn't we be measuring something else? Your brand may have a huge number of people who raise their hands to say they're fans, but what does this actually mean? There's a tendency in any sort of media to jump right to execution without giving enough thought to the real strategy. What will my print ad, my television spot, my Facebook page look like?"

"To be effective," Lee said, "you have to step back and take a look at the total branding strategy. Yes, it's fun to think about a viral video. But the success of a video doesn't happen in a vacuum. There's usually a jump in viewership after it's been picked up or supported by a traditional media source. You can't jump right to the solution, but have to think about the problem you're trying to solve. Social media works best when it's part of a holistic program. It also works best when a company is agile and nimble. You have to take some chances. There was a day when we did an annual media plan. Now you still need a media plan, but because there is so much data coming in, you need to be constantly course correcting. Given the organic nature of the market, a company should put multiple programs in the marketplace recognizing that some might fail. The important thing is to have a disciplined measurement plan in place. I'm going to launch half a dozen programs, but I'm going to know within the next 60 days which are getting traction, in which case I'll dial them up, and which aren't, in which case I'll pull the plug. The good news is that with so much data in real time, the means are out there to measure the effectiveness of what you're doing. There was a quote by Peter Drucker in a recent 4A's newsletter that relates to this: 'People who take risks make, on average, two bad decisions a year. People who don't take risks make, on average, two bad decisions a year.' Branding strategy today requires the spirit of course correction. Just make sure every recommendation has a measurement plan."

All of this said, enjoy the following stories, each an example of how others in the business of building brands know what it takes to play and win.

TOP TIPS: KNOW WHERE YOUR BRAND CAN PLAY AND WIN

Pick your battles. Some branding signals have greater potential to drive consumer perception of your brand's idea than others. Not all are created equal in their ability to convey to consumers what your brand stands for and why they should care. As the stories in this chapter illustrate, brands with an edge know where and how to invest their branding dollars. They know where they can play and win. Here are a few tips from their playbook:

- Make sure you are clear about the objective of each branding initiative.
- Know what branding signals you own. Keep them your own.
- Play where others aren't playing. Look for channels that reinforce your brand story in unexpected ways.
- While everyone else is chasing shiny new objects, don't overlook traditional media options. Coupons and end-caps still have their place in the world of branding.
- While it's easier said than done, the medium, the moment, and the message must work in unison. Creativity without focus may be interesting, but it's not motivating.

CHRYSLER AND CLINT EASTWOOD SHARE A CHALLENGE
WITH OLAY, CREST, AND GAIN DETERGENT

First it was Eminem, and then it was Clint Eastwood. In television advertisements for Chrysler, both talked gritty talk against gritty backgrounds about the gritty job of getting the big Detroit automaker, if not the whole US auto business, back on its feet. Both spots, along with the accompanying digital marketing, had a serious and engaging can-do attitude. Or as Chrysler has been saying about itself of late, "This is the Motor City. And this is what we do." I know this is what they want to do, and I hope they can do it, but, from a branding perspective, how does one take all the emotion, the drama, and, most of all, the big brand idea and get car buyers to tune into it in a spotless suburban Chrysler dealership in Peoria or Portland or Poughkeepsie?

I thought about this the other day when I read about a contest sponsored by TED (a conference organizer formerly known as Technology, Entertainment, and Design) that rewards advertisers for creating online marketing videos that people not only want to watch but find compelling enough to share. The idea behind this initiative, to get advertisers to think way outside the television box and its ubiquitous 60-second spots, is right-on from a purely creative point of view. Advertising should be inventive and wonderful and memorable, not to mention worthy of sharing. The trick of our trade, however, is to make sure that the branding we create is impressive enough to carry over to where the rubber meets the road. Or in the case of Eminem and Clint and Chrysler, it must carry over to those spotless suburban showrooms where the goal is to get potential car buyers to make the leap to the driver's seat of the newest Chrysler 300 SRT8.

Anyone in the business of brand building knows how hard it is to come up with an idea that resonates with consumers and clearly defines what makes the brand different in a way people care about. Having come up with the idea, the next challenge is being able to communicate it across a broad array of branding channels, places where consumers experience the brand, the most important of which is the shopping environment. It's one thing to be able to bring a brand idea to life for consumers when they're watching the story unfold online or even in front of the TV. It's quite another to make sure the brand idea is reinforced when they're in the supermarket aisle, their favorite big-box store, or an auto dealership. Looking for more insight on the topic, I decided to call someone whose organization knows a thing or two about ensuring the "shop-ability" of the core brand idea, P&G's global design officer, Phil Duncan. Here are a few key points from our conversation.

ALLEN ADAMSON: Obviously, it's a lot easier to get consumers charged up about a brand through a video or television commercial. It's one thing to appeal to consumers via mass-market media, another to grab them in the supermarket aisle. What do you do at P&G to make sure the big idea transfers to the point of purchase, a generally mundane environment?

PHIL DUNCAN: Obviously, you have to be able to translate an idea to moments when a consumer is in a purchasing mind-set. When they're looking at all the choices on a shelf, what will make them reach for one product over another? This is why we often start our thinking about the marketing from what we call "store-back." We tell our teams that as they develop the idea, they should think first about the most difficult branding arena, which is, of course, the shopping arena.

AA: Meaning that if you can figure out how the brand idea will come to life for consumers in a supermarket aisle, you can get it to come to life anywhere?

PD: Exactly. To do this, we make sure we can translate the big idea, or ideal, into a signature visual or a quick articulation—a telegraphic message or image that will grab shoppers' attention and that will link back to what they may have seen elsewhere relative to the branding. For example, the idea driving the Crest brand is a "healthy, beautiful smile." Our retail branding efforts for the Crest line of products, for instance, be it packaging or product placement, reinforce the benefits of a healthy, beautiful smile. You can't tell the same kind of story you can tell in a television ad or on the website, but you can create visual signals that are shortcuts to the story.

AA: The key to being able to do this effectively is, of course, starting out with a clear, incredibly focused idea about what the brand stands for and what you want consumers to take away. With Crest, it's a higher concept than simply "teeth." It's about all the things that can make your smile healthy and beautiful, which includes everything from Crest Pro-Health Toothpaste to Oral-B toothbrushes to White Strips. It's about getting shoppers to connect to the fact that they can entrust their smiles to Crest.

PD: It's all about continuity of the idea, but knowing exactly how to portray your brands differently in one branding venue versus another so that it all comes together. For example, with our Olay brands, because packaging is essential in retail activation, we use our online efforts to showcase the packaging within a store environment. We pull the primary packaging outside the secondary packaging to help the shopper understand the context and how she will see it on a store shelf. We also use online or television branding to promote how the product is used so that when a woman picks up the packaging, the brand concept is reinforced for her within a store setting.

AA: It's always been a challenge for marketers to help consumers connect the dots on the path to purchase. The key is to think of all the places you can intercept them and remind them of the idea. With so many new media outlets, this becomes even more of a challenge.

PD: Yes, and because you don't have as much control over the store environment as you do over other channels, thinking about the path to purchase in conjunction with the shop-back branding process forces you to go back to the basic idea you're trying to communicate. It forces you to bring a high-level concept down to earth, the objective being to enhance the brand's equity. For instance, the idea behind our newest initiative for Gain detergent is "Love at first sniff." Through our television and video ventures, we encourage people to literally take the cap off the Gain bottle and smell the detergent. Once they actually smell it, they're more apt to buy it. We've essentially shortened the path to purchase. The objective for all marketers is to use the in-store experience to reinforce the brand benefits as communicated in other channels.

FLIPBOARD AND SKYPE FOUNDERS PROVE INNOVATIVE BRAND IDEAS ARE OFTEN RIGHT IN FRONT OF YOUR NOSE

It came as no surprise to me that the iPhone application Flipboard and the VoIP service Skype won top honors in the mobile app category at a recent Webby Awards. The Webby Awards, as if the name doesn't say it all, were created to honor the best stuff on the Internet including websites, interactive advertising, online film and video, and mobile apps. For those who may not know, the free app Flipboard is a social network service that enables users to aggregate and then "flip" through their social network feeds, including Facebook and Twitter, along with content from websites, in much the same way one would flip through a magazine. Skype, which is also free, is a service that enables users to make free calls to other Skype users anywhere in the world, not to mention let

them see each other on their computer screens (a boon to every grandparent I know whose grandkids live on the other side of the country).

Now if you're wondering, after that bit of a ramble, why I was not surprised that these two nifty services won prizes in their respective categories, it's because the founders of each asked one of the most critical questions in the field of brand building: "Ever wonder why?"

Let me explain by going back a few years to a show I used to watch with regularity and that I now watch on reruns whenever I get the chance: *Seinfeld*. I watch it not only because this guy and his incredibly self-absorbed friends make me laugh, but because Jerry has a masterful talent for capturing profound truths about very ordinary things, things people find acceptable without considering how unacceptable they might be, and wondering why they have to be this way. Consider, if you will, "Ever wonder what really happens in the clothes dryer when you leave the laundry room? Why do those socks want to hide? What's with that?" Or, "Did you ever wonder why dogs have no pockets? It's because they have no money, but somehow they manage to get by."

Jerry is often in the back of my mind when I sit down with a client to address a brand challenge. That's because sometimes the right way to come up with an idea on which to differentiate a brand—and win at the game of branding—is to approach the category with the intent of looking for an obvious and universal truth that no one else has seen. Look for some situation that is unacceptable and that people have come to accept without thinking. Sort of like what Target did when it developed easy-to-open prescription bottles for people with arthritis: "Ever wonder why medications for arthritis come in hard-to-open bottles?" Or what Apple does when it designs and develops any one of its products: "Ever wonder why instruction manuals for technology designed to make life more fun are longer than *War and Peace?*"

Get where I'm going? The developers of both Flipboard and Skype asked the equivalent of the same "wonder why" question and came up with products that make you slap your forehead and wonder, "Why didn't I think of that? It's so obvious." In the case of Flipboard, for years marketers have been looking at the Internet and trying to figure out how to come up with an advertising model that makes sense. Flipboard, in contrast to traditional cluttered web pages with distracting banner ads, search boxes, and related links, takes content from the sites you love and puts it together in a "personalized social magazine." It's an app for the iPad (and, I hear, soon for Android devices) that integrates technology and print like nothing else before it. And that's where another "aha!" happens.

When you're at your computer, more likely than not, you're sitting at your desk in a functional, get-something-done mode, be it writing a PowerPoint presentation, putting in a final bid on eBay, or e-mailing a colleague. Any ad-related distraction is a total mood-buster. But, aha!, when you pick up your iPad, a funny paradigm shift happens. You move to the couch, to the bed, to the back porch, and your mood changes. You're relaxed, in browse mode, and looking at content in a magazine format perfectly suits the occasion. More than this, when reading a magazine, people are hard-wired to take in everything on the page, from editorial to advertising. They don't see the ads as intrusive, but as part of the bigger picture. The designers of Flipboard understood this and developed an app that incorporates both editorial and advertising in a totally user-familiar, user-friendly context. The inventive founders, Mike McCue and Evan Doll, wondered why a website couldn't have a graphical magazine-like format with a user interface designed for intuitive flipping, and they created what innovation guru Steve Jobs called a "killer app."

Likewise, the founders of Skype, Niklas Zennstrom and Janus Friis, wondered why, given everything else it could do, the Internet couldn't be used to enable people to communicate with peers by voice, video, and instant messaging. (Microsoft also wondered why and bought the company in 2011.) In its current iteration (and who knows what will have happened by the time this book is published?), Skype features a streamlined interface Facebook integration and videoconferencing functionality. I've used both Flipboard and Skype, and, being an ordinary guy, I've always wondered about the technology that makes them so simple and intuitive and enjoyable. As a branding guy, however, I've never wondered why they came into being. It was founders who knew enough to ask the questions: "Ever wonder why a web page has to look like a web page?" and "Ever wonder why, with all its capabilities, the Internet can't be used to let grandparents talk to and see their grandkids in real time?" Obvious questions in retrospect. But it's only in the asking—and answering—of seemingly obvious questions that clever new brand ideas come to life.

GENERAL MILLS KNOWS EVERY PACKAGE TELLS A STORY, AND IT HAD BETTER BE THE RIGHT ONE

Standing out in the crowd, trying to get consumers to choose your particular brand of whatever from the millions of others on the supermarket shelves has always been among the toughest jobs in marketing. And, though it may be hard to believe, it's getting tougher. It's not just that the number of products has increased, but that supermarkets have become far more experiential. There are lots of diversions and opportunities to interact. It's no longer a matter of just cruising down the aisles leisurely tossing things into your basket. Companies like Trader Joe's, Whole Foods, and trendy local markets have upped the ante for every purveyor of groceries. With more displays, cornucopias of fresh and artisanal foods to sample, and a literal and virtual layering of encounters (including those funky little gadgets that shoot out coupons as you walk by), the supermarket environment has become less static and more active. Add to this the fact that shoppers are just more distracted in general, what with answering e-mails on their smartphones or checking out instant bargains on couponing sites, and it makes the job of getting your box or bag or carton noticed an incredible challenge. For the packaging to break through and tell a compelling brand story, for a marketer to use packaging to take someone from consideration through actual purchase, is simply more difficult than ever.

It was with this challenge in mind that I went to one of the experts in this arena, Elizabeth Nientimp, director of brand design at General Mills. With a few (a gazillion?) consumer packaged goods in her line of sight—Cheerios, Green Giant, Betty Crocker, Yoplait, and Pillsbury among them—I knew that if anyone had a few words of wisdom about what it takes to, well, package a brand's promise, she would. And I was right. Here is a bit of our very interesting conversation.

> **ALLEN ADAMSON:** Anyone who walks through a supermarket can see that the choices consumers have in all brand categories are growing exponentially. And, as marketers, we know that consumers have the ways and means to share their experiences about all these brands. The marketplace has become both more competitive and virtually

transparent. How are you, at General Mills, dealing with this evolving state of marketing, specifically in terms of telling a brand story through its packaging?

ELIZABETH NIENTIMP: Consumers make the choice of which brand to pull off the supermarket shelf in mere seconds. About 90 percent of this decision-making process is simply looking at things and the other 10 percent is reading. That means that the design has to immediately convey what we want consumers to think about the brand. Or, said another way, what the brands stands for, how it will fit into the customer's life, must be communicated in an instant.

AA: It's the tangible substantiation that a picture is worth a thousand words. Your team has to be very clear about the brand's core identity and what it means to the customer before they can even begin to think about the design of the package.

EN: Exactly. We used to think about package design as the "decoration station." It was the last step in the marketing process before the goods went out the door. Not anymore. Package design is a business decision at General Mills, seen not only as the number-one ownable asset, but an investment in the brand. If you haven't figured out the true identity of your brand, your packaging won't be authentic. The box has to reflect the brand's values in order to connect with consumers. The packaging is what you do to get consumers to feel a certain way about your brand.

AA: Focusing on the brand's meaning is critical to setting yourself up for success. Making it clear, through packaging, that your brand meets an essential consumer need drives brand advantage.

EN: Right. Our objective is to demonstrate to consumers that we believe in things that are important to them beyond what's in the package. It's a shared-value proposition. For example, our Box Tops for Education program continues to exceed our expectations because it taps into something incredibly important to parents, specifically moms, who we consider the family "gatekeepers" for our brands. The program is a powerful demonstration of our belief that nourishing children's lives is as much about education as it is about nutrition.

AA: So back to that word "authentic." With everything so visible in today's marketplace, it is becoming more and more evident to consumers that a brand is as a brand does. The Box Tops program is authentic to the General Mills brand. It's believable and successful because it's in sync with your values.

EN: It also gives us the opportunity to have conversations with our customers, to create an ongoing dialog and learn more about what's important to them. It's gaining a better understanding of your customers that leads to success. It's in packaging that we can channel this understanding. Packaging is an opportunity to champion the brand and what it stands for.

A SMALL CANADIAN NEWSPAPER TAKES A PAGE OUT OF WARREN BUFFET'S STRATEGY FOR PICKING BRAND WINNERS

I'm not sure if Warren Buffet knows anything about the *Winnipeg Free Press,* but if he did, he'd be pretty impressed. I was at one of Buffet's shareholders' meetings when, during the Q&A segment, an audience member asked why, when everyone else was running away from newspapers, Warren Buffet was buying them up. It was a legitimate question given that much of what newspapers offer can be had for free, and gotten faster and more easily, from bloggers, tweeters, YouTube, Facebook, not to mention the websites of major news sources. The answer given confirmed for me that, along with his other business expertise, Buffet knows branding. More specifically, he knows that if you can differentiate a product or service in a way that matters to people, you can build a strong brand.

There are two factors that fundamentally differentiate a newspaper from the myriad other sources of news. First is the ability to provide a considered interpretation and analysis of the facts from a specific point of view for readers who are looking for more than just the facts. The second is the ability to cover local news—what's going on in area arts, education, and government, the road conditions, the weddings and Little League games, and all the other small but consequential stuff of daily community living. A newspaper can provide a rich and rewarding experience when it comes to reporting on hometown doings.

Well, it seems the folks at the *Winnipeg Free Press* understand this. And when I read about how they'd opened a News Café as a way to change their business model of news reporting—a way to really bring the news home to the citizens in Winnipeg—I thought about Mr. Buffet. But I also thought about another person brilliant in the ways of business: Theodore Levitt. For those of you who skipped his marketing class at Harvard Business School in 1959 (or who, like me, have the excuse of having been too young at the time to have attended his class), Theodore Levitt was a highly esteemed professor and editor of the *Harvard Business Review* who coined the term "marketing myopia." Simply defined, marketing myopia is when a company focuses its efforts on what it does, makes, or sells instead of on what its customers need, thereby limiting its

growth potential. Much as Professor Levitt made clear that railroads couldn't consider themselves to be in the railroad business but, rather, in the transportation business if they wanted to grow, he'd likely counsel that the traditional model for brands in the news publishing business is also too narrow to portend future success. More than that, he'd counsel that, given the change in how news is told and sold, those in the business ask themselves his seminal question if they want to continue as successful brands: *What business are we really in?*

Well, it seems that in addition to understanding what makes a great brand, the folks at the *Winnipeg Free Press* also know what makes a great business model in this new news age. By opening up a News Café where reporters can interact with readers, where everyday people can offer up their views and opinions, can hear and be heard, the *Winnipeg Free Press* made clear that they're not in the business of news delivery, but in the business of shaping and sharing ideas relative to current events. Building a brick-and-mortar space, they created an immersive and inclusionary experience for their customers—a physical link with the community they serve—enhancing and enriching the overall brand experience.

For all news organizations, this is a great lesson-learned example. As the digital world turns, news organizations must turn their focus away from themselves and look to the needs of the news buyers, adopt a wider view, and take advantage of all channels relevant to their customers. CNN took a page out of Levitt's thesis when it opened a CNN Grill in Denver during the 2008 presidential election, a pop-up place where journalists mingled and conferred with voters before delivering their stories. Other "news common" initiatives have also been undertaken by the *Register Citizen* in Connecticut and the *Texas Tribune*. But none has gone to the extent that the *Winnipeg Free Press* has: to intrinsically change the business model in order to address the needs of its readership. By doing so the company has increased reader engagement, boosted its social media efforts, and generally boosted its ratings as a reliable source of news.

Companies that define their brands too narrowly do so at their own peril, especially as the digital arena expands and evolves. For news publications to be only in print or only online is too one-dimensional. All companies, no matter the category, must be active in any channel that is relevant to their customers. It's time to take off the blinders, to experiment, and to be open to new ideas. If this means opening a café where people can chew the fat with a reporter and chew on a scone at the same time, well, I think Professor Levitt would think it's a fine idea. And I think Warren Buffet might feel it's an investment worth consideration.

Companies that define their brands too narrowly do so at their own peril.

NO CONTEST: TWITTER AND FACEBOOK CAN
BOTH PLAY A ROLE IN BRANDING

Who knows what will have happened in the wake of the Facebook IPO by the time this book gets published? As I write this in the spring of 2012, this social media giant is set to raise billions. The eight-year-old brand has more than 900 million members, and it's reported that nearly half a billion people around the world log onto Facebook every day. It's also reported (by Facebook, I should add) that more Fortune 500 companies have corporate Facebook pages than Twitter aliases. Suffice it to say that the number of articles in the news this week relating to Facebook is not inconsiderable, some waxing poetically positive about the event and others not so much. In any case, it has drawn increasing attention to the fact that Facebook, along with other big social media sites including Twitter, play an increasingly huge role in the way people communicate and in the way marketers should leverage this word-of-mouth-on-steroids technology. Twitter, by the way, has over 100 million active users, with the number of users and their 140-character daily (hourly) missives growing at an exponential pace. While I don't know all that much about IPOs and valuation and such, I do know a bit about the business of helping marketers understand how to use media channels, digital and otherwise, to build their brands. Clients often ask me whether they should use Facebook or Twitter, and, in reply, I suggest that Twitter and Facebook can both play a role in a branding strategy, especially as smartphone usage and capability continues to surge. Having said this, I also think that just as users think about Twitter and Facebook differently, so, too, should companies as they go about their branding efforts.

Before I get into the difference between how one digital tool versus another should be used, however, let me begin with the one major role *both* play in building strong brands. Both Twitter and Facebook enable organizations to learn about what people are thinking and saying and doing about their brands and about life in general. And the first step to achieving brand success is getting insight about human thought and behavior. The better the quality of the insights, the better the chance of establishing a brand promise that genuinely meets consumer needs and expectations. Great insight enables a company to meaningfully set its brand apart from others in the minds of consumers and in the marketplace. Monitoring consumer opinion in the high-speed modes now available also gives organizations a better chance of fixing any situations that need fixing before they get out of hand. The closer an organization can get to its customers, the more opportunity it has to enhance brand experiences, and to make them more relevant, and more valuable to those who matter most to them. Organizations that make monitoring and sharing Twitter and Facebook commentary part of their operational infrastructure have a much better chance of responding to customer needs faster and better.

Having said this, what distinguishes these two digital tools from each other as branding devices is a measure of time and depth. I think of it this way. Twitter is more like an early warning system. It lets marketers instantly know what's going on as it happens. It gives them the opportunity for rapid response. For example, when people caught wind of what they thought was an attempt by Amazon to remove books about gays and lesbians from its sales rankings, the immediate and intense tweeting and re-tweeting acted as a warning flare enabling the company to swiftly jump in and address the untrue claim. Another case in point: Sam Decker, chief marketing officer of Bazaarvoice, a firm that helps organizations gain efficiencies by assessing online word of mouth, told me about his experience with the rapid response capabilities enabled by Twitter. Phoning the customer service department for the retail website Zappos, he was placed on hold for what seemed an eternity. He sent a tweet to an acquaintance saying he was surprised that this usually responsive company had him waiting so long. Zappos, with its fine-tuned digital monitoring system, picked up news of this disgruntled customer, sent him an e-mail with an apology, an explanation of the customer service snafu, not to mention a nice coupon toward a future Zappos purchase. More important, it used the information to its—and its customers'—advantage and made the necessary improvements to its customer service operations.

Virgin Airlines, a well-known early adopter of digital technology for marketing efficiencies, uses Twitter to alert passengers of both negative events, like flight delays, and positive events, like special travel promotions. It also recognizes the power of Twitter to get people to self-assemble and become impromptu, impassioned marketing machines. "Virgin Airlines is now serving absinthe in-flight. No Kidding. Great brand move for the demographic," wrote one impressed Virgin Twitterer to thousands of others. Virgin makes regular engagement with Twitter users a part of its branding strategy—in its unusually cool and colloquial voice—and both brand and fans reap the benefits.

Back to time and scope; Facebook is the social media tool companies use when a deeper dive into details is appropriate to a branding strategy. While Twitter is super for defensive branding initiatives, Facebook is a great forum in which to engage consumers in a more significant way, to share more with consumers, and to get them to share more of themselves in the process. A brand's Facebook page is a public profile that's likely to get more thoughtful conversations going between company and consumer, and consumer and consumer, yielding enhanced insight. While some Facebook pages are of a more practical nature, like Southwest Airlines', which literally asks its loyal fans what they would like to see relative to making the Southwest brand experience more comfortable, affordable, and fun, others like Red Bull's and Mountain Dew's are more about entertainment value, befitting their brand personalities and branding strategies.

One of the most significant examples of how companies use in-depth conversations on Facebook to create better brand experiences relates to the introduction of the Ford Fiesta to the American market a couple of years ago. While 2008 was a pretty nasty year for most US auto manufacturers, the Ford Motor Company undertook an initiative with this European award-winning car to launch what CEO Alan Mulally called the "first totally global platform car." In my conversation with Scott Monty, head of social media for Ford, he told me, "As a result of design, technology, safety and fuel efficiency, the Ford Fiesta was the number-one-selling car in Europe beginning in March 2008. We wanted to get feedback from drivers in the United States before our planned US Fiesta launch in 2010. To do this, we took 100 Euro-spec vehicles, made them available to 100 key digital influencers from a variety of places across the web in the United States, and asked for feedback. We got it. It has been a phenomenal case study in listening to customers to drive product improvement and better value into our vehicles before spending money." The copious feedback, shared on its Facebook page, also saved the company money on marketing. Facebook is the petri dish for word of mouth and is a fantastically efficient tool for creating brand advocacy.

From my branding professional's vantage point, it's no contest. Marketers should not be asking Twitter *or* Facebook? They should be asking how each of these digital tools can be used as a part of an overall branding strategy in the appropriate way. There is no question that marketers can expand the reach and depth of their branding by focusing on social media, with app usage for leading sites, including Facebook and Twitter, becoming among the most frequent activities among smartphone owners. Above all, the key to success is being able to understand how each is being used by consumers and to adopt branding behavior accordingly. In fact, as digital tools continue to evolve, marketers should continue to ask how each one, in its own way, can help them become part of something bigger, to connect with the public and help the public connect with each other as a way of bringing greater value to their lives. As has always been the case, organizations need to use whatever means are available to listen and learn as a way of helping them differentiate their brands in ways that matter.

JOHNNIE WALKER CONTINUES TO STRIDE FORWARD THANKS TO DIAGEO'S FORWARD-THINKING BRANDING IDEAS

Cue the bagpipes. Among the best television ads I've ever seen might be a brilliant five-minute-plus (yes!) spot by Bartle Bogle Hegarty, London, in which actor Robert Carlyle, in a single continuous take, narrates the progression of Johnnie Walker whisky from the backroom experimentation of a humble shopkeeper to the internationally powerful brand it is today. With the evocative music, the setting in the renowned gloomy Scottish countryside, the pitch-perfect copy, and the pitch-perfect visual cues, the piece brought to life the history of a brand as no one-dimensional branding application ever could. This spot, titled *The Man Who Walked Around the World,* is spot-on for the brand in many respects.

The brand was originally known as Walker's Kilmarnock Whisky, and a key feature of every bottle of Johnnie Walker is the "Striding Man" logo, created in 1908 by illustrator Tom Browne to be a likeness of John Walker in traditional attire. The folks at Diageo, the company that now owns this well-loved spirit, explain that the man is walking forward to symbolize forward thinking and the pursuit of excellence. That Johnnie Walker is the most widely distributed brand of blended scotch whisky in the world, sold in almost every country with yearly sales of over 130 million bottles, is testament to the fact that Diageo knows what it takes to keep the brand a leader in its category. And it was about one of its newest and most forward-thinking branding initiatives that I had the pleasure of speaking to Jeremy Lindley, Diageo's global design director.

> **ALLEN ADAMSON:** It used to be that all one had to do relative to a spirit or a packaged good was just to talk about its taste. Today, with so many products and so much noise, you've got to elevate your story, create a way for people to engage. The Johnnie Walker House in Shanghai, designed by UK-based agency Love and commissioned by the global whisky category director, David Gates, is an impressive example of looking far outside the normal channels to tell a brand's story. In fact, it's not actually a channel so much as a full-fledged experience. Tell me about how this physical space, created as a way to showcase Johnnie Walker in the Chinese market, came about.

JEREMY LINDLEY: First of all, getting people to engage with your brand *requires you to be innovative* these days. Even with our unique flavor, the skill of the Master Blender, the iconic packaging, we decided that we needed to find exciting ways to engage with consumers, especially in a new market, like China. We looked at what had been done, at all the existing channels, and determined that we wanted to find a way to really connect with consumers in a manner that would feel real and authentic for the brand. In essence, we decided to create a place for them to go and actually experience the brand. Johnnie Walker House is the first whisky embassy anywhere in the world outside of Scotland, and the idea behind it is that it's where people can learn about whisky, the whisky culture, and everything that goes into our remarkable product. What we've done is build the history and heritage of the brand into the building. We invite people into this relaxed, warm, and convivial setting to enable them to experience the complexity, craft, and luxury details that go into constructing the world's finest whisky. It's a multisensory experience.

AA: It's not like walking into a museum or just looking at a display. Everything in the building conveys an integral part of the brand and the actual process of making the whisky, down to the French and American oak floors.

JL: The original premise was that to develop a whisky culture in Asia, we had to grow people's knowledge and appreciation of whisky and its history. And, although it started out as a venue in which to mentor people about the brand and the products, it's actually turned out to be a successful sales outlet. People want to buy the product.

AA: It's like the BMW Performance Driving School. If you don't want to buy a BMW after spending some time there, you'll never buy a BMW.

JL: It was never our intent that Johnnie Walker House would be a significant sales outlet, but it's a happy by-product. People are really interested in buying something that's exclusive, that's only available here. After doing some research, we found that the earliest record of Johnnie Walker being sold in China is from 1910, and we have the blending notes from the master blender of that time, Sir Andrew Walker, who was John Walker's grandson. We can tell with reasonable accuracy what the whisky would have tasted like, and, while that particular blend is no longer part of the Johnnie Walker stable, what we did was re-create the blend along with the packaging that went around it, made a thousand bottles, and used it for the launch of the Johnnie Walker House. It was intrinsically linked to our history.

AA: This initiative had a genuine sense of authenticity and exclusivity. You didn't just take a bottle and create a sticker for it, but created something that related to your heritage and culture. It had to be done right, especially in this era of social media. If the details hadn't been right, it would have done more harm than good.

JL: Prior to the development of the Johnnie Walker House, a lot of work had gone into understanding the brand's history in China. One of the more interesting things we learned while researching and going through the archives is the linkage between John Walker and tea. There is a real emotional connection when you explain how much John learned from tea, especially to consumers in China and India. We talk about John Walker, the son of a farmer who started his own grocery store and over time developed a luxury goods emporium in Kilmarnock, and the fact that John had access to goods from all over the empire, including tea. One of the things he did was become adept at blending tea to create a smooth, consistent taste. You bought John Walker's tea because it tasted great. It was the same skill set that allowed him to blend whisky so successfully.

AA: So the connection with Asia is just naturally there. The skill in growing and blending tea inspired and informed John Walker's knowledge and ability to blend consistently smooth whisky. You were able to go back to your roots, bring it forward, and create an incredible bond. It's such a great connection, and you've been able to bring it to life in such a theatrical, experiential way.

JL: And there are a number of things we do to create this experience, one of which is an artistic re-creation of Sir Alexander Walker's blending room. We've got hundreds of bottles of whisky back-illuminated representing all the different distilleries and ages. As people sit around the tasting table, we're able to tell the story of each whisky, the roots and core components of each, with the entire range right in front of them. We have a 3D model that demonstrates how the whisky is made, and also a 1910 room that describes and shows memorabilia from the over one-hundred-year history of Johnnie Walker in China. And being Walker, of course it is done in an innovative, progressive way.

AA: It's not just a matter of telling someone about a product in a sales mode, but connecting to a philosophy, a core brand idea. If you connect consumers with a brand's core, its history, you can't help but create a longer-term relationship.

JL: Taking the brand heritage and expressing it in a progressive way that connects to consumers today has been incredibly powerful. The power of this physical space will be a real competitive advantage in the category and something we believe will give us an edge in the market. It was a bold piece of thinking, and it has been such a success that we are looking at developing more sites around the world.

WHICH MARKETERS SCORE BIG BY PLAYING AT THE US OPEN?

Every Labor Day, as summer begins its slow fade, I have the opportunity to enjoy one more special event with my son before he's lost to homework and the
other responsibilities of school: we go to the US Open at Flushing Meadows
in New York. In addition to seeing the greatest names in tennis battle for the
ultimate prize, it's fun for me, as a branding enthusiast, to see what the tour-
nament's sponsors have come up with as a way to win the battle of the brands.
What will each one do to try to connect with the relatively upscale crowd of
spectators in the stadium, as well as the millions of tennis aficionados watching
out in TV land?

The companies vying for attention alternate from year to year and have included
such iconic names as IBM, American Express, JPMorgan Chase, Lexus, Mercedes-Benz, Olympus, Heineken, and Grey Goose, among other less well-known
names attempting to become better known. What the best brands at events
such as these understand is that to win loyal fans and influence those who may
become fans, it takes more than just plastering your name or URL on any piece
of available, viewable stadium space, be it a billboard, a canopy, a rooftop, a
concession stand, or even the nets that cross the courts.

Sporting events have always attracted corporate sponsors to the point that
the practice has become rich for parody. What's more, digital technology has
significantly increased the number of places a consumer can pick up branding
cues. Today, the challenge of identifying where a marketer can play to win—get
the message, the moment, the medium, and the money to line up—is one of
the toughest games in town. The US Open is a great vantage point from which
to watch and weigh in on marketers who understand what it means to hit the
sweet spot. Those who do understand know that the medium and the message
and the moment have to be intrinsically aligned with what the brand stands for
in the minds of consumers.

Take Lexus or Mercedes-Benz, for instance. Each has had the opportunity to
own the on-site parking venues and has offered complimentary parking to

those who drive their brand of ride. In addition, as the official vehicles of the US Open, they have made their vehicles available as VIP transportation for players, coaches, and special guests. They've set up tents where the well-heeled crowd can look at the newest lineup of autos and even have their picture taken next to one of the, let's say, sexiest of the (car) models. (My son was particularly delighted by this.) As car brands, these initiatives are totally in keeping with the category and are as simple in execution and relevant in principle as they are brilliant at making the brand's owners feel appreciated.

Olympus, another former US Open sponsor, also created some totally appropriate branding moments with which it was able to bring home its message. One year, it set aside what was called the Photo Pit for press and other professional photographers of the event, emphasizing its status as the camera of choice for those whose careers depend on getting the shots seen around the world. For amateurs like me who are just happy to be able to take great family pictures, the Olympus booth offering the chance to try out the newest equipment was a smart branding app.

Smart, too, have been the many branding initiatives undertaken by IBM at the US Open, each intended to take advantage of the setting and the audience demographics. Building on its "Smart Solutions" campaigns, it has hosted a terrific website that features a section called "Smarter stats for a better Open," where you get comprehensive, real-time statistics and video highlights of the action. At the last US Open I attended, JPMorgan Chase also made smart use of the venue by hosting a hospitality pavilion where anyone with a Chase account could come in out of the heat, sit down, and enjoy a cool drink and some lunch. What was especially pleasing was that nothing was required other than just showing your Chase bank card—no minimum balance, no purchase required, and no sales talk. In a world where experiences that are meant to surprise and delight the customer have become increasingly scarce, this Chase experience was an unexpected treat and a solid way to demonstrate that they appreciated my business.

On the other hand, a brand that seemed out of place in this expensive, cluttered marketing arena was SpongeTech, manufacturer of revolutionary sponges. Don't get me wrong, I'm all for keeping things clean, but handing out sponges at a tennis event struck me as a little off the mark, unless the company was trying to underscore it stood for good, clean fun. (Sorry.) The *New York Times,* esteemed brand that it is, has also appeared on my "What's your point?" sponsors list. To begin with, I'd guess that at least 80 percent of those watching the games are already subscribers to the paper. And then, what does handing out giant tennis balls have to do with reading "All the news that's fit to print"? If the company wants to be part of the action, I suggest it find a more relevant way to get its brand's message across.

I've had lots of fun watching the US Open, from a sporting perspective and a business perspective. Given the evolution of tennis equipment and training techniques, the play and the players get more thrilling every year. Given the evolution of brands and branding channels, the challenge of connecting in a meaningful way with the viewers gets more difficult every year. Playing to win in branding is about more than just plastering your name on anything in sight.

It's about reaching out to people in ways that truly demonstrate what makes your brand different in a way that matters. In a market where a brand is as a brand does, it's critical to ensure that the branding does something to enhance the perception of the product or service you're selling. The players who win will be those who hit the racquet's sweet spot most often. The brands? Those that hit the consumers' sweet spot.

Playing to win in branding is about more than just plastering your name on anything in sight.

TALK ABOUT KILLER APPS: "PRODUCT" IS WHAT ALLOWS GOOGLE TO KEEP SATISFYING THE WORLD'S BOUNDLESS CURIOSITY

It's hard for me to remember a time when Google didn't exist, and yet, believe it or not, this company is only 16 years old. That's how dramatic its effect has been on my life and on the lives of millions of others. For those who may not know (anyone?), Google began in 1996 as a research project by Larry Page and Sergey Brin, two Stanford PhD students whose goal, simply speaking, was to organize the seemingly infinite amount of information available on the World Wide Web (archaic term now) and develop a search engine that would make this information universally accessible and useful. The name Google is a play on the word "googol," a mathematical term for the number represented by the numeral 1 followed by 100 zeros, reflecting, well, the seemingly infinite amount of information in the universe. By 1996 they had come up with a product that *PC Magazine* reported "has an uncanny knack for returning extremely relevant results." My searches on Google, all yielding extremely relevant results, account for an infinitesimally small percentage of the millions of searches its servers handle every day. Working this hard and only 16 years old. Amazing.

It is amazing. And what continues to keep Google such an amazingly powerful brand is that those in charge understand the difference between the words "brand" and "branding." What I mean by this is that they understand that a brand is something that lives in your head, a set of mental associations. And they know that branding is the tangible process of creating and managing the signals that generate these associations. More than this, the smart folks at Google know that to stay *top* of mind, you have to invest your branding dollars in those signals that have the greatest potential to drive and maintain the perception you want consumers to have. Google does just that. Its most critical branding signal, or being more contemporary in my verbiage, its killer app, is the product itself. From Google+ to Gmail, Google Maps to Google Earth, Google Chrome to YouTube to Picasa, Google continues to come up with innovative ways to appease our curiosity and feed our need for answers to our questions. I once likened Google to sitting next to the smartest kid in school. Well, this kid keeps getting smarter. It was with this in mind that I put in a call to Gary Briggs, who runs marketing for Motorola Mobility at Google, to get his perspective. Here is just part of our great conversation.

> **ALLEN ADAMSON:** Google has been such an intimate part of people's lives since its beginning. We trust it for an array of decisions, big and small. From my perspective, this seems a matter of your keeping an eye on the "North Star," always knowing where you're going. Is there any difference between Google "then" and Google "now"?
>
> **GARY BRIGGS:** Let me answer your question this way. Google never wanted to be anyone else other than Google. We've never wanted to be anything but what we already are. Larry and Sergey built a product and its connection to the user, and we continue to keep our focus on the user's experience with this product. Google went for a long time without a marketing department, famously so, and never really thought about the traditional rules. We're going to build a great product and we're going to focus on this product. All of our conversations are about product and the scaling and the user experience.
>
> **AA:** The thinking being that if your product delivers, if you build and continue to have a better mousetrap, the rest will follow.
>
> **GB:** Yes. If you go back to the classic 4 Ps of marketing, there is only one—product—that is really relevant anymore. Everything we do is determined relative to this.
>
> **AA:** You're referring to the traditional definition of marketing, putting the right product in front of the right people in the right place, at the right price. In Google's case, it's the product that satisfies, if not supersedes, all the other Ps. The Google product satisfies customers' needs and wants on multiple dimensions.
>
> **GB:** Yes, and one of the most critical dimensions is speed. When they started out, one of the things Larry and Sergey were most focused on was speed. Anything that slowed down the user's experience was not allowed. Speed is still important, even if it's just a matter of milliseconds. It's a driver of user satisfaction.
>
> **AA:** The gap between "I have a question" and "I want an answer" is only getting narrower. The perception is that time is becoming compressed. When you need to find out something, be it the directions to a restaurant or the name of a doctor, it becomes mission critical. You sense that something is taking too long unless you get it instantly.

GB: Speed in our product is among the factors that make it a killer app. It gets to people's need for information. We talk a lot at Google about the nature of curiosity. We answer people's curiosity. When someone has a moment in time when they want to find out something, from "Where am I in this city?" to "I want to resolve a bar bet in this city," we can provide the answer quickly. For example, there's now a feature on Google Maps for smartphones, a little icon on the city view that, if tapped twice, will let you know what direction you're facing. It's a compass. Knowing what direction you're facing can save you from walking down the street in the wrong direction. It's such a whimsical little feature, but it creates a bond between the user and the product. The product becomes the brand. There's a tremendous focus on our core belief that's never changed—speed, comprehensiveness, and a bit of joy. Who we are informs what we do.

AA: Relative to this, is there anything you can share that, now that you're starting to get into marketing, informs how you're going about it?

GB: One example that seems quite trivial, but is actually a great insight, is the Google "Doodle," which, again, started in a very whimsical way. Larry and Sergey were going to the Burning Man Festival, and they put up a graphic that was essentially an "Out of Office" sign that had a Burning Man behind one of the Os in Google. It was very simple, but people got it and they loved it. The reaction was great. Now, we all know that one of the cardinal rules of marketing is not to screw with the logo. We screw with it all the time. It's a way for people to have a little bit of delight when they get to our home page. One of the most successful graphics we run to ask people to set their default page to Google is the ad "Never miss a doodle." It's successful because it's a big part of who we are. People can relate to it.

AA: So while the routine of search is functional, when you add some emotion, a smile, it connects. It's been my experience that when you look at tech companies, people want to know there's something more than servers out there. They want to know there are people out there. Tech is so functional and cold; when a brand makes it clear that there are people involved, it becomes more approachable, more human.

GB: And the human part is a big part of what Google is about. It's why the brand has the strength it does, and why so much of the marketing we do is not commercial. For example, we put up the Dead Sea Scrolls.

We made it possible for people to tour the great art centers of the world, major art museums, through their browsers. Information comes in all forms. Curiosity compels us to make these things available to our users. We want to spend our time creating information people will find delightful. We want to bring the wonders of the world to life. Everything we do is built *into* our product, not built *on* our product.

KRAFT'S MIO: THE SAVVY TASTE OF WHAT IT TAKES TO LAUNCH A NEW BRAND IN A CROWDED MARKET

In branding, as in life, you rarely get a second chance to make a first impression. Trite as this may sound in concept, when you have millions of dollars on the line relative to the launch of a new product or service, it's about as far from trite as it can be. Once your brand hits the shelves, once it and all the branding associated with it are burned into consumers' brains, it's very difficult to change, well, their first impression. There are very few opportunities, if any, for do-overs. While all branding expressions must work together to get people to feel about your new brand the way you want them to, there is one that is, perhaps, the ultimate conjurer of images and associations: the brand's name. The sweet spot of naming a brand is finding a word that simply and magically signals what it stands for in a meaningful way, something that is both memorable and sustainable.

Selecting a name for a brand begins as a game of numbers. You can come up with 800 names and your legal department will shoot down 794 of them. Selecting a name is also a game of connotations, positive and negative. Consumers make snap decisions, so it's imperative to get the associations with the name right—right out of the gate. A brand name will be accepted in its ultimate context if you control the context. This whole name game notion came up during an interesting conversation I had with Kimberly Bealle, senior director, Consumer Communications, Beverages, at Kraft Foods. Kim and the MiO team came to Landor a year or two ago and asked us to work with them on branding for an innovative new Kraft product called MiO, a liquid water enhancer that lets you change your H_2O, or any other drink, into a delicious, customized beverage. It was the name, the packaging, and many of the other factors that came together to make a great first impression on consumers that we covered in our discussion, which I'm happy to share.

> **ALLEN ADAMSON:** It takes a lot to change the dynamic in a category as broad as beverages. Kraft seemed to have a lot of the market covered, what with Capri Sun and Kool-Aid for the younger set and Crystal Light for those in an older age group, not to mention Maxwell House. What prompted you to develop a totally new brand?

KIMBERLY BEALLE: First of all, we saw a gap in our portfolio. There wasn't really anything for what's referred to as millennials, a market segment for which choice is a key factor. These 20- to 30-somethings want the ability to personalize. One size doesn't fit all for this group. Sure, there are lots of choices in the beverage category, but you have to take what's offered. There's no way to change it up. *We* saw an opportunity to change up the category, to give this group a way to create their own beverage. With MiO, they can put as much as they want into whatever they want, whether it's plain water, sparkling water, iced tea, or any beverage.

AA: So it was the antidote for personalization. It wasn't just creating a line extension, say, from Crystal Light, but a whole new product. You can stretch an existing brand only so far before you injure its meaning, mush it up in consumers' minds.

KB: Right. And, CPG companies rarely create new brands so this was a big deal for us. It takes a lot of money to get a new product off the launchpad, let alone ensure that it keeps flying. And it wasn't just a new product, it offered a new benefit and required a new behavior on the part of the consumer. Everything we did needed to be distinctive. All of the branding had to point out, "Here's who we are, here's what the brand does, and here's how you use it."

AA: Basic rules of good branding. The product had to be genuinely different and relevant to the target. You needed to create branding that was ownable and had inherently differentiating equities.

KB: We knew that to be seen as innovative we had to be distinctive. The product had to be cool enough for millennials, but with a male skew. Having said this, it couldn't be too cool. We couldn't alienate older people because we needed volume from them.

AA: It's a fine line. You have to be focused, but not myopic. Even though the marketing target was millennials, the consumption target was 18- to 44-year-olds.

KB: And, because the bottle was going to be pretty small in scale, the branding had to be mighty. It had to work really hard. When we started looking at the structure of the packaging, for example, we knew it was important for us to create something that was really different looking, but you had to be able to put it into your pocket or a purse without worrying that it would leak. And, to own the category, we had to design something that was protectable. The valve opening from which the liquid comes out, for instance, is patent-pending.

AA: The packaging became a huge branding element for you. In the old "mad men" days, you could pretty much take a can and put a label on it, and people would accept it. Today there are more elements to a brand story that have to hold together for a product to be seen as genuinely innovative. How did you decide on the package design?

KB: We had all these prototypes, but because we were so clear about what we wanted this product to represent, when we picked up the one you see on the shelves, we knew it was right. It felt good and fit perfectly into your hand. It was cool.

AA: My sense is that a lot of Apple's success is driven by design. People just love the look and feel of the products. This is not data-driven design. It just feels right. It's visceral.

KB: And it's the same thing with the name we chose: MiO. When you say it, it feels right for the product. It flows. It's a natural fit. Obviously, the naming was critical to our success. We looked at over two thousand names over the course of a year. Naming is hard on many fronts, strategic, legal, what with trademark issues. Most of all, the name had to be intuitive, much like the package. It had to feel innate to the product. As soon as MiO came up, many of us spontaneously said, "That's it!" MiO sounds like "mine," and it means "mine" in Spanish and Italian.

AA: Branding is like a puzzle. All the pieces have to come together naturally and authentically. It's a case of building the whole egg, so to speak.

KB: Right. And then when it came to the logo design, the "M" with that little drop and the added swirl element, it was magical. It all snapped into place. In terms of the marketing activation, we decided it had to start with a television campaign. That way we could show exactly how the product works. You can see the beautiful colors swirling in the water. It brought the product to life. We put almost all of our launch marketing money into TV, very targeted. Late night and sports. We spent almost $30 million in eight months, and it was the right thing to do. Among people who tried it, 70 percent had seen the ads.

AA: For a product like this, for a beverage, Kraft understood that you needed to let the pictures tell the story. It's easier and more effective to show people what the product does, especially with MiO for which the benefit is personalization. You can add a little flavor or add a lot.

KB: And, in addition, we used all the digital channels. We developed a really good Facebook engagement strategy. We gave away one hundred thousand samples in fifteen days from our Facebook page. We did a lot in-store, leveraging all the elements that reinforce how you use the product. The "Flip it. Tip it. Sip it."

AA: So you played to your strengths. Kraft knows TV. It knows media. It knows in-store. You stick to your knitting if you want a competitive advantage.

KB: We got out there. We got the basics right first, the name, the packaging, and the way the product works by homing in on the consumers we wanted to reach. Then, in year two, we started pushing things out, pushing the proverbial envelope. We've created some YouTube videos in keeping with the brand personality, including one with a character named Thunder Dave, and we have some very cool initiatives in the works. If you're a change agent brand, you have to be constantly changing things out. As a pioneering brand, we have to keep innovating. And when it comes to beverages, they're much like fashion items. People are always looking to change.

A FINAL POINT AND MY OTHER TOP NINE

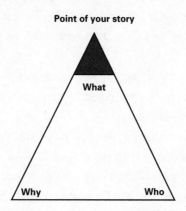

Point of your story

What

Why   Who

Most brand managers can tell you twenty great things about their brand. This is nineteen too many. The most important thing you must do to become and stay a brand with an edge is to be able to express your brand idea as a single, simple, sharply focused point. If you can't do this, you won't be able to, well, get your point across. Your organization won't be able to do the brilliant branding required to bring your idea to life. Your customers won't be able to grasp and tell your story the way you want it told. Your competition will eat you for lunch.

Since the days of Don Draper and mad men and even before, getting to the point, establishing the one essential thing about a brand that sets it apart in its category, has been critical to success. With the intense noise in today's marketplace, with consumers barraged and barraging, this has become an even more important factor in winning and maintaining an edge. Having said this, your point cannot just be based on what or how your brand does something, but on "who" your brand is and "why" you do what you do. In a world where competition is only getting more intense, what and how your brand is different from others can disappear overnight. Who it is and why it exists are differentiating factors that are far more enduring.

Take this point as the first of my ten Top Tips that all brands with an edge know and follow. Here are the remaining nine:

- A brand and branding are different concepts. A brand exists in your mind. Branding is the process of creating signals that generate the perceptions.
- Establish something different about your brand that the consumers you want to reach care about before you start telling the story.
- To find a different and relevant idea, sometimes it's best to look right in front of your nose. It's often the case that the best answers are hiding in plain sight.
- It's not a destination, but a journey. Keep your brand relevant, but never lose sight of where you started. Your brand's heritage holds the clues and cues to moving it forward in a credible way.
- Know who your core customers are—how they think and feel. You need to know who you're talking to in order to have a constructive conversation.
- Get your employees fully on board with what *their* brand stands for. Everyone must have an innate sense of what it means to "be the brand."
- Be real. Consumers have developed a sixth sense. They can tell when branding isn't authentic, and it doesn't make them happy.
- Pick your battles. Not all brand experiences are created equal in getting your point across. Know where you can both play *and* win.
- Most important, deliver beyond your promise, consistently and brilliantly. Nothing else will matter if you don't.

INDEX